DANGEROUS
MEN

ALSO BY MICK LASALLE

Complicated Women

DANGEROUS MEN

PRE-CODE HOLLYWOOD AND THE
BIRTH OF THE MODERN MAN

MICK LaSALLE

THOMAS DUNNE BOOKS
ST. MARTIN'S PRESS ⚐ NEW YORK

THOMAS DUNNE BOOKS.
An imprint of St. Martin's Press.

DANGEROUS MEN. Copyright © 2002 by Mick LaSalle. All rights reserved. Printed in the United States of America. No part of this book may be used or reproduced in any manner whatsoever without written permission except in the case of brief quotations embodied in critical articles or reviews. For information, address St. Martin's Press, 175 Fifth Avenue, New York, N.Y. 10010.

www.stmartins.com

Library of Congress Cataloging-in-Publication Data

LaSalle, Mick.
    Dangerous men : pre-code Hollywood and the birth of the modern man / Mick
LaSalle.—1st ed.
      p. cm.
    ISBN 0-312-28311-3
  1. Men in motion pictures. 2. Motion pictures—United States—History. I. Title.
    PN1995.9.M46 L37 2002
    791.43'652041—dc21

2002005954

First Edition: November 2002

10 9 8 7 6 5 4 3 2 1

FOR MY FATHER,
WHO ONLY LOOKS DANGEROUS,

AND MY MOTHER,
WHO'S MORE DANGEROUS THAN SHE LOOKS

Contents

Introduction   ix

1. Why Are These Men Smiling?   1
(Douglas Fairbanks, Rudolph Valentino, Ramon Novarro, John Gilbert,
and Lon Chaney)

2. "Mammy, Doncha Know Me?"   17
(Al Jolson, John Gilbert, Ramon Novarro, Gary Cooper, and George Arliss)

3. Richard Barthelmess   30

4. Public Enemies—and Heroes   44
(Chester Morris, Lew Ayres, Edward G. Robinson, and James Cagney)

5. A New Kind of Man   60
(James Cagney, Clark Gable, Edward G. Robinson, and Paul Muni)

6. "I'm in Hell"   77
(Lon Chaney, Boris Karloff, Bela Lugosi, Charles Laughton, and Fredric March)

7. "I Got These for Killing Kids"   94
(Richard Barthelmess, David Manners, Richard Dix, Fredric March, the Marx
Brothers, Lionel Barrymore, and George Bancroft)

8. The Smartest Guy at Figuring Angles   112
(*Lee Tracy, Douglas Fairbanks, Jr., Edward G. Robinson, William Powell,*
James Cagney, Warren William, Robert Montgomery, and John Gilbert)

9. "No Longer a Man's World"   129
(*James Cagney, Clark Gable, Rudolph Valentino, Warren William, Cary Grant,*
Gary Cooper, Richard Barthelmess, Ramon Novarro, William Powell, Robert
Montgomery, Maurice Chevalier, and Bing Crosby)

10. Warren William and the Money Changers   148
(*Warren William, George Arliss, Richard Dix, Edward G. Robinson, and Douglas*
Fairbanks, Jr.)

11. Love Hurts   168
(*John Barrymore, Charles Laughton, Edward G. Robinson, Richard Barthelmess,*
Charlie Chaplin, Spencer Tracy, Warren William, Fredric March, Gary Cooper,
and Norman Foster)

12. Remember My Forgotten Man   187
(*James Cagney, Dick Powell, Paul Muni, Douglas Fairbanks, Jr., Walter Huston,*
Frankie Darro, and Richard Barthelmess)

Epilogue   209

Appendix 1: Dangerous Men on Television and Video   217

Appendix 2: A Short History of the Code   227

Acknowledgments   233

Bibliography   237

Index   241

Introduction

M ANHOOD IS NO easy subject. When does it begin? What qualities does it consist of? Girls who are eighteen start calling themselves women as soon as they enter college, while boys the same age tend to think of themselves as . . . guys. The concept of manhood is too imposing, so associated with heroics and domination that it seems like an effrontery to assume automatically the mantle at eighteen—or even at twenty-one.

Anyone writing a book about women would have no trouble identifying examples of women with admirable traits. But in the case of men, there is less common ground. Everyone has an opinion about manhood—good, bad, and ugly—and manhood itself is often under attack.

This book concerns images of manhood in the five years before American cinema went off the tracks and gave up truth telling for propaganda. That five-year period, known today as the pre-Code era, lasted from 1929 to mid-1934. It was an era of lax censorship that finally ended with the imposition of a harsh Production Code that would, for the next thirty-four years, censor much of the life and honesty out of

American movies. If today most people think of old movies as staid and safe, it's because they're only familiar with the classic films made under this Code, which mandated chastity, blind respect for authority, and knee-jerk patriotism. The Code also guaranteed that all crime had to be punished, even if the criminal was really handsome or funny, even if the criminal was right.

The pre-Code era coincided with an interesting time for men, the culmination of a generation-long transformation of the masculine ideal. By the late twenties, the tumult of the new century had made the nineteenth century's notion of the ideal man seem like a rigid buffoon, a repressed stuffed shirt, a deluded optimist, a bull waiting to be made into hamburger. Young men had turned away from an image of manhood as buttoned-down and dour and rejected their father's schizophrenically compartmentalized notions about women and sexuality. Men were finding their way toward a modernity more spontaneous, more jaded, and more instinctive.

In the pre-Code era, conflicts and currents building for decades reached critical mass and found an outlet. The "New Woman" became the subject of a whole genre of films. With equal thoroughness, movies looked at the New Man, taking on subjects such as crime, politics, business, sex, and war. The depiction of these subjects was colored by recent events—the nightmare that was World War I, the widespread disgust with Prohibition, and, later, the economic terror surrounding the Great Depression. Grown men began to look upon government and business with a jaundiced eye. They looked at these institutions and reacted with language once reserved for the carnival barker: Are you trying to make a sucker out of me? Do you think I'm a chump? A sap? Old notions about the glory of battle and the importance of a woman's virtue were tossed overboard, and anything that got in the way of personal freedom was suspect.

In pre-Code movies, men do more than adopt received behavior.

They improvise. They chart a path. It's the common thread that unites the actors who thrived in this era. They epitomized the outsider's understanding of life. From the impish subversion of Cagney, to the tragic grandeur of Lon Chaney, to the loneliness and integrity of Richard Barthelmess, pre-Code heroes acknowledged the world as a jungle and did the best they could.

In the silent days, a screen hero was someone who looked and acted like the audience's traditional conception of a hero. In the pre-Codes, we leave the age of heroic types and enter an age that celebrates individuality. Stories were built around actors who fit no preconceived mold. Rascals and gangsters were allowed vitality and charm. A decade before, Clark Gable, a gruff, big-eared screen villain, might have been tying virgins to railroad tracks. In the early thirties, men and women idolized him, the fellow who bucks the system.

Two assumptions dominated the pre-Code era, one cynical, one romantic. The cynical assumption was that the system was rigged, that if you played by the rules, you'd lose. The romantic assumption was that if you were shrewd and brave enough, you could beat the system at its own game. We find these assumptions everywhere in the pre-Codes, whether in the tragic *Little Caesar* character of Edward G. Robinson, the fast-talking hustlers of Lee Tracy, or in the comic charlatans of the amazing Warren William. At the same time, pre-Code men wrestled with morality as an imperative of manhood. We see that especially in the films of Barthelmess and Fredric March.

It's the profound irony of the Production Code's imposition: Before the censors shoved morality down the public's throat, movies were never more fixated on moral issues. After the Code arrived, American movies were all about, Who will win, the good guy or the bad guy? But before the Code, movies explored the morality of business, the morality of law, the morality of romance. Movies asked, Who *is* the good guy? Who *is* the bad guy? And why? And how can we tell? And who's to decide?

Such questions were threatening to traditionalists, who'd already divined the answers for themselves and everybody else. No wonder they mobilized.

OTHER BOOKS—INCLUDING my own *Complicated Women: Sex and Power in Pre-Code Hollywood*—have dealt, in detail, with how American movies came to be controlled by a backward and draconian Production Code. For our purposes, it will suffice to say that: First, it happened; and second, it was not the result of widespread public reaction against the motion picture industry. (Had it been, we could say that a censored cinema was an expression of the public will.) Rather, it was the result of a well-organized effort by a small cabal of lay Catholics, who, working both within the church and the film industry, threatened the studios with a loss of Catholic business if certain demands weren't met.

Caving in to pressure, the studios appointed publicity man Joseph Breen as the first head of the Production Code Administration, a new organization empowered with the right to approve or deny the release of any studio film. As of July 1, 1934, Breen, a political reactionary and a raging anti-Semite, became the final arbiter of screen content. He kept the job for nearly two decades.

One of the most prosaic things about movies is also what makes them so instructive years later: They're made to please everybody. Even today, in an age of niche markets, few films will ever show a sympathetic character expressing an idea that's repugnant to the vast majority of viewers. Through the pre-Codes, we get to hear the uncensored voice of an era. We see war films in which war produces nothing but men wrecked by war. We see gangsters who are no worse than businessmen, and businessmen who are no better than gangsters. We even encounter a socially responsive cinema that's not afraid to show a country shaken by Depression, whose self-confidence is shattered and whose institutions could easily buckle.

Few would dispute that the absence of censorship makes the pre-Codes of special social and historical significance. But after seventy years, it might be time to admit that the pre-Codes' honest capturing of their day is also part of their artistic value. Keats had it right, after all: Beauty is truth, truth is beauty, and that's all we need to know about the movies.

From all sides and angles, from comic to despairing, the pre-Code men reveal the truth about the difficulty of manhood in the modern age. Many of the actors who emerged in these years remained major names for decades. They include James Cagney, Maurice Chevalier, Gary Cooper, Douglas Fairbanks, Jr., Clark Gable, Cary Grant, Walter Huston, Fredric March, Robert Montgomery, Paul Muni, William Powell, Edward G. Robinson, Lee Tracy, and Spencer Tracy. Yet to see them in their pre-Code incarnations is to see them unfettered, their force not yet diverted into some safe and worthy channel. Coming along at a time when movies could articulate the public's vigorous understanding of the hero's true identity and function, they didn't play upright fellows who restored the status quo, but troublemakers who dented it, sometimes even smashed it.

Watching their films, it's easy to come away with the sense of something lost, not just to the Code but also to the march of history. Nothing against an amiable leading man such as Tom Cruise, but it is rather daunting to consider that, as this book goes to print, he is a full nine years older than Clark Gable was when he made *Red Dust*—and two years older than Gable in *Gone With the Wind*. It's hard to imagine Cruise ever seeming older than Gable.

In the pre-Code era, we find new-fashioned heroes whose manhood was an authoritative force—not pretty boys, not cannon fodder, not pawns of the system, but dangerous men. Together, they represent a vision of manhood more exuberant and contentious, and at the same time more humane, than anything that has followed on the American screen.

Why Are These Men Smiling?

WE CAN DATE the beginning of the pre-Code era to Hollywood's industry-wide acceptance of sound, which took place in stages but took hold completely sometime in 1929. But before we go there, let's burrow a bit further into the past and look in on the silent era, a period that's a mystery to most people, with its distinct artistry and largely unknown roster of stars. If we want to understand the modern men who came along in the pre-Code era, we need first to look here, to sneak up on the heroes who dominated the silent screen. When we do that, we notice something almost immediately that's rather strange about these fellows: They're all smiling.

It's not just that they smile a lot, though they do. It's the way they smile that's striking—big, openhearted, cocksure. If an actor is really flamboyant, sometimes his smiling is accompanied by a toss of the head or a gesture of the arms. It's a way of smiling that seems to have left the planet long ago.

The smiles of the silent heroes suggested a whole attitude toward life, a confidence about the nature of heroism and the ultimate fates of good and evil. Silent heroes not only believed their victories were inevitable but, when they did win, they felt sure enough to gloat a little. They did not go through life expecting the ground to shift beneath their feet. Thus, to our eyes, they look unprepared: *We* know the ground will shift and wonder why they don't guard themselves against it.

In *The Black Pirate* (1926), Douglas Fairbanks, after single-handedly taking possession of a ship, keeps the crew at bay with two cannons. It's at this moment that he feels safe enough to throw back his head and laugh. But shouldn't he be worried? Shouldn't he make sure no one is sneaking up to stab him in the back? No. Such concerns were for a later time—as in 1929. In Fairbanks's *The Iron Mask* (a 1929 silent with synchronized sound), he would indeed get stabbed in the back—and killed. By then, it was the dawn of a new era, and Fairbanks himself, for all his popularity, had an inkling that his style of hero was done for.

The first three decades of the twentieth century saw a dramatic shift in the self-image, the aspirations, and the social and sexual behavior of men in the United States. In the late nineteenth century, men were expected to be sober, disciplined, steady, reliable. To be a man of character was the ideal. As social historians such as Kevin White have pointed out, these were traits ideally suited to the economy in which men then functioned. The late nineteenth century was the era of the self-made man, the small businessman, the farmer—men who worked for themselves and achieved success through sacrifice and self-denial.

Turn-of-the-century men's magazines regularly featured inspirational stories of white-haired businessmen, who came up from nothing through single-minded diligence. These were the heroes, and they were men's men. They inhabited a man's world, struggled with men, formed alliances with men, hired and fired men, and lived lives quite apart from those of their wives, who inhabited the separate sphere of hearth and home.

The ideal model was beginning to change as the new century dawned. Many factors came into play, not the least of which was economic, the shift from an America made up of small proprietorships to one dominated by conglomerates. Men, who a generation before might have started their own businesses, were in the cities, working for large corporations. Or they were salesmen or admen. In this world, personality became central to success—traits such as likability, charm, good looks, snappiness, inventiveness, originality. By 1931, according to a *Variety* survey, the most famous and recognized names in the country would be those of gangsters and film stars.

Youth was no longer considered the age of ignorance, a period of years spent in toil, working to gain a foothold in the world. Consumerism, popular magazines, and movies combined to make youth and dynamism the ideal. Advertising encouraged men to wear clothes and use products that made them look young and smell good. Social critics such as Randolph Bourne in *Youth and Life* (1913) talked of youth as an age of intuitive wisdom. World War I was the final straw. Youth turned on their elders for making a hash of the world. Older men's values had produced a cataclysm, and young men had paid with their lives. "The older generation has certainly pretty well ruined this world before passing it on to us," wrote a young man in the *Atlantic Monthly* of September 1920, expressing the prevailing sentiment. How could the younger generation, the idea went, possibly do any worse?

Much of the rebellion centered around sex. Young men strove to be sexually attractive in a way their fathers could not understand. In the nineteenth century, men didn't need to be sexy. If they wanted sex, they could go to a brothel. For that, all they needed was money, all the more reason to work hard and save for a rainy day. At the same time, men struggled not to give in. It was a sign of manly character to resist fleshly temptation, to make oneself impervious, to master one's energy and channel it into success in work.

Along with everything else, those sexual attitudes changed. The self-denial that the older generation preached was derided by the young as self-destructive and unnatural—and hypocritical. For the first time since the Industrial Revolution, men were once again working with women—not in the home, as their great-great-grandparents had done, but in office buildings. Proximity fostered equality, camaraderie, and the desire for intimacy. In this new climate, looking for sexual gratification was no longer regarded as a weakness, but as a sign of manliness.

The movies of the twenties, lagging slightly behind the times, as movies always do, are fascinating in their presentation of masculinity caught between two time periods. In silent films, we find the nineteenth century's emphasis on character and self-denial, often in combination with the twentieth century's glorification of personality, sex appeal, and youth.

Anyone looking for a good measure of the vast distance American culture would navigate in one brief decade need only look at two film versions of *Dr. Jekyll and Mr. Hyde*—the 1920 silent movie, starring John Barrymore, and the 1931 talkie, starring Fredric March. We'll talk about these films at length in a later chapter. For now, it's enough to note that, though based on the same Robert Louis Stevenson story, the pictures came to completely opposite conclusions as to the story's meaning. In 1920, it was a cautionary tale about the failure of self-denial and self-control. It was about a man's character collapsing in the face of temptation. But in 1932, the story was adapted as a warning about the consequences of needless and harmful sexual repression.

The great silent heroes of the twenties, stars such as Douglas Fairbanks, Rudolph Valentino, Ramon Novarro, and John Gilbert, were hardly sober men of affairs. They projected the modish virtues: youth, confidence, physical beauty, dynamism, and personality. What they, or rather their images, lacked was irony. As historian Paul Fussell has asserted, irony was the great and defining legacy of World War I. That modern sense of irony, seeping into the culture as the twenties progressed, would ultimately make the silent hero and his radiantly unshakable smile seem old-fashioned indeed.

• • •

DOUGLAS FAIRBANKS WAS already thirty-six as the twenties began, mature for a movie star of his day, but with his best years still before him. A Broadway actor, he'd become enormously popular in films of the 1910s, appearing in energetic social comedies with lots of gracefully executed physical stunts. The beginning of the 1920s brought two changes in his life. He married "America's Sweetheart," Mary Pickford, a star of at least equal magnitude; and he made *The Mark of Zorro* (1920), the first of a nearly unbroken series of swashbuckling adventures that would include *The Three Musketeers* (1921), *Robin Hood* (1922), *The Thief of Bagdad* (1924), and *The Gaucho* (1927).

A man in youthful middle age, Fairbanks had his feet in two different worlds. He looked like—as his sound films would prove him to be—a modern-style fast talker. Yet he had a nostalgic streak that connected him with audiences of all ages. Fairbanks's heroes were dazzling, climbing high, leaping and swooping through the air, and they presented a romantic vision of history. Yet what inevitably allowed his heroes to triumph were the same traits that would make a good advertising man—wit, freshness, new ways of seeing old things. It's as if Fairbanks's swashbuckling films were an attempt to show that modern-style cheerfulness and invention would have been legitimate heroic traits in any previous century.

Fairbanks himself did not see his work as polemics on behalf of the new values. Rather, he saw his swashbucklers in idealistic terms. In 1924, he called them "fairy stories" and attempted to explain their universal appeal to the *Brooklyn Daily Eagle*:

I believe that a beautiful fairy story is a story that everyone in the audience will feel is his own. The hero naturally starts off with great obstacles to be overcome. That is practically every man's story. Then the hero falls in love with a princess. This is also every man's dream story. He finds that in order to reach his desires, he must be worthy and do more worthy things. This is what every man's spiritual side has meant at some period of his life. Then the hero goes out and surmounts innumerable barriers. He fights his way through fire; kills monsters of terrifying mien; resists seductive temptations and at the end receives the happiness he has earned, just as every man has thought of doing. We call it fantasy, but it symbolizes the very essence of life itself.

At least it symbolized the very essence of the self-made man. What Fairbanks described might have been a highly romanticized version of a businessman's story. For all his modernity, Fairbanks saw his films as fantasies extolling the importance of sacrifice and hard work, self-reliance and diligence.

Whatever their message, no one did them better. No one put the poetry into this vision the way Fairbanks could. No one exuded such joy. Fairbanks was a delight, and he remains delightful, an appealing figure of fantasy—but he's not *our* fantasy. His films come to us as if from another moral universe. Modern in manner, Fairbanks strove to embody a kind of manhood that would soon be out of style and that today is barely in currency even as an ideal. It's that which makes his much-praised death scene in *The Iron Mask* so poignant. D'Artagnan collapses in a courtyard and is greeted in the sky by the spirits of his friends, the three musketeers, and the four walk merrily off into the clouds. We're saying good-bye not just to Fairbanks or silent film but to a certain kind of guy, a certain kind of dream.

Rudolph Valentino embodied another ideal that was gaining sway in the first decades of the century—that of the primitive or elemental man. He played men who, however smooth they may have been on the surface, were in touch with their animal nature. A culture that had turned away from glorifying repression, that saw modern man as having been civilized out of spontaneity and vitality, saw much to admire in the fantasy of the primitive-type lover.

In movies, the primitive served as the male equivalent of the vamp, a female archetype popular with both male and female viewers. For women, the vamp represented power; for men, guiltless sex—after all, if a woman's allure can't be resisted, he can't be blamed. Likewise, the primitive-man fantasy offered dreams of power and license. He took what he wanted, while the woman, with no choice but to submit, could be absolved of responsibility. Traces of this fantasy would linger on into the pre-Code era, in the films of James Cagney and especially those of Clark Gable.

Valentino on-screen was no vulgar brute. He was suave and Continental. He could also be dangerous. The sexy moments in *The Sheik* (1921) and *The Son of the Sheik* (1926) weren't romantic in the traditional sense, but tense with the threat of rape. Valentino had great success in these roles. He had equal success in *Blood and Sand* (1922), as an innocent bullfighter who succumbs to a vamp. It seems that the only Valentino movies that left audiences cold were ones in which love was not presented as perilous or at least gravely serious.

Valentino is a curious figure. In some moments, he had a rare archness that, today, makes him seem years ahead of his time. Yet he also had his era's mania for smiling. In *The Sheik*, he smiles so much he looks positively loony. He refined his style over time, and his last film, *The Son of the Sheik*, released a month before his death, indicated what might have been a promising direction for Valentino had he lived. The picture combined a faintly tongue-in-cheek tone with some genuinely steamy moments. Though Latin lovers would disappear in the pre-Code era, it's just possible that Valentino, with his sense of humor and capacity for self-mockery, might have held on. At worst, he could have switched to playing urbane heavies or second leads, just as his American look-alike Ricardo Cortez did.

Valentino had started a Latin lover craze in the 1920s. An Italian immigrant from Puglia who came to prominence playing a Spaniard in Rex Ingram's *The Four Horsemen of the Apocalypse* (1921), he could easily have inspired a mania for Italian screen lovers, but audiences and studios were simpler in those days. The public wanted people like the fellow Valentino played in the movie, so Spanish and Hispanic lovers became popular. Of these, the best was Mexican-born Ramon Novarro, who also began his career with Rex Ingram but became a major star at Metro-Goldwyn-Mayer playing the title character in *Ben-Hur* (1926).

Unlike Valentino, there was little suggestion of danger about Novarro. He conveyed a purity and sweetness of spirit, a trait not to be valued in the coming age of Cagney, Robinson, Warren William, and Gable, though Gary Cooper had a touch of that quality. In Ernst Lubitsch's *The Student Prince in Old Heidelberg* (1927), he played a sheltered prince, whose timidity gives way to his longing for connection when he goes away to school. It's moving to watch him blossom.

Novarro's last silent film, *The Pagan* (1929) was a routine studio product. But in terms of Novarro's star image, it was his apotheosis, providing him with a role that capitalized on his physical beauty and sex appeal and made a virtue of his intrinsic air of innocence. He played a native living in an island paradise, on his own land. He falls in love with Tito (Dorothy Janis), a native girl who has been adopted by a white trader, the film's villain, who tells her (in an intertitle), "Tito, you were born half-white. . . . But through my training, you will be all white." But the trader's plan is doomed—she has already seen the pagan.

The Pagan found the thirty-year-old Novarro at his physical pinnacle. Early in the film, there's a close-up in which he looks off at the girl, shakes water out of his hair, and smiles. In those moments, he's as beautiful as any human being who ever stepped in front of a movie camera. Douglas Fairbanks, Jr., once wrote of him, "He might, with equal facility, have had a glorious career either as a priest or roué." That combination, partly wild, partly holy, was nicely exploited in the scene in which he asks why Tito bothers going to church. When she tells him that she goes in order to visit God, he laughs and tells her she could see God everywhere. "Why go see Him in hot church?"

John Gilbert, also at MGM, was an even bigger star than Novarro. Born in Utah in 1899, Gilbert wasn't a Latin, but he shared with Valentino a dangerous quality, a hint of menace that should have put him in a good position when movies switched to sound. Before Valentino's death, Gilbert was known as a great screen lover. After Valentino's death Gilbert was *the* great screen lover. Today, he is most remembered for the silents he made with the young Greta Garbo—*Flesh and the Devil* (1927), *Love* (1927), and *A Woman of Affairs* (1929). But of the three, only *Love*, in which he plays Vronsky in a modern-dress version of Tolstoy's *Anna Karenina*, shows Gilbert at his manly and confident best.

In *Love*, we get a classic Garbo moment that was also a quintessential Gilbert moment. It comes when Anna removes her veil and he sees her face for the first time. Standing in for the audience, he reacts by looking dumbstruck, elated, and mesmerized. And then he does what men in the audience would *not* do but Gilbert would: He leers. He doesn't avert his eyes from the vision of beauty. He isn't afraid.

Gilbert sometimes seemed as if he were struggling against the optimism implied by his screen image. His smile was all white teeth and three dark lasers coming at you, two eyes and a mustache, but with something more going on behind the smile—a complexity, a strangeness, the mystery of a genuine movie star. On-screen, he had the range of a manic-depressive, quick to laugh, but often as if standing on a trapdoor that might open into despair. He conveyed that quality in his interviews, as well. In 1927, loved by millions, at the top of his profession, with every earthly delight at his fingertips, he bemoaned his lot as a twenty-eight-year-old movie star:

> My tragedy is the tragedy of all cinema people, really. We have everything. We have everything—too soon. . . . What can life offer me when I'm forty-nine? What will there be left for me to do? What will there be left for me to want? Nothing that I can imagine. . . . It's so easy . . . to make a mess of life, and if you mess it after you are a certain age, it isn't easy to straighten it out again. After all, four-fifths of life is in the head. If the heart isn't happy, life is all wrong. That's why I want to find the right woman and am afraid that I may never be so fortunate.

What at first sounds like disingenuous complaining gradually sounds like a man who, sooner or later, is going to screw it up. He is going to trash his life, somehow, some way, and inside, he already knows it.

On-screen, Gilbert was a study in contradictions. He could seem flighty and superficial and grave and thoughtful—and that's just in the roles tailored to his star personality. His talent had considerable breadth and scope. In director Monta Bell's *Man, Woman and Sin* (1927), Gilbert played a naïve mama's boy who falls in love with a society woman (the remarkable Jeanne Eagels) and ends up the patsy in a murder case. In King Vidor's *The Big Parade* (1925), he enlists in World War I, falls in love with a French girl (Renée Adorée), and loses a leg on the battlefield. Both films are about a man's journey from innocence to experience. By the end of each, we believe that Gilbert, who started out so callow, has seen the range of life.

The Big Parade ends in bittersweet victory, with Gilbert embracing his experience by returning to his French girlfriend. *Man, Woman and Sin* ends sardonically, with Gilbert running from his experience by returning to his mother. Wise man or stooge, Gilbert had it in him to play it all. Looking back, if any of Hollywood's smiling heroes seemed destined to survive Hollywood's transition from silents to talkies—and America's transition from twenties' optimism to thirties' skepticism—it was Gilbert. He just had more going on than the rest of them.

LON CHANEY WAS the one screen favorite who, at least at first glance, does not at all fit the twenties pattern. Here was a craggy middle-aged man who looked older than his years, who specialized in the grotesque, and whose films were virtual dissections of psychic torment. Yet, in a decade noted for high energy, youthful optimism, and romance, he made some of the most popular films in America.

He was not a horror-movie actor, though even today the name Lon Chaney connotes horror. This may be due, in part, to the fact that his beefy son, Creighton Chaney—known to audiences as Lon Chaney Jr.—starred as the Wolf Man in several films. The main reason is undoubtedly that, whether they qualified as horror or not, his movies spooked his contemporaries to the degree that his name came to be synonymous with *scary*. Chaney may not have been interested in supernatural horror, but he was interested in the horror of it all. He devoted his brilliant artistry to depicting the anguish and torments of life on the edge, yet not quite outside the edge, of existence.

He was unique. At a time when the close-up was new and audiences were worshiping beauty, Chaney made himself ugly. In an era that disdained maturity, he played old men. In an age that valued erotic success, he played men who couldn't get to first base with a map and a compass. Is it any wonder, then, that audiences in the twenties found him frightening? Chaney represented the living essence not of supernatural terror but of *social* terror. He was the picture to the Jazz Age's Dorian Gray. He was what people felt like inside, or feared they were, or dreaded that they might become. And once we realize that, we come to the great truth about Chaney's art—that, far from being out of place in his era, Lon Chaney was one of the deepest expressions of it, the dark alley outside the glittering speakeasy, the embodiment of private terror in an ostentatiously public decade.

His movies were as beauty-obsessed as anything starring Gloria Swanson, Greta Garbo, or Norma Shearer. In film after film, he played tormented (sometimes evil) men who beheld beauty and were profoundly changed—sometimes for the better (they became nicer), sometimes for the worse (they went nuts), but usually to their detriment (they ended up dead). Then again, who would want to go through life ugly in the 1920s?

Chaney was born in 1883 in Colorado Springs. His parents were deaf-mutes, and some of his strength and ease as a pantomime actor was no doubt thanks to having learned from the cradle how to communicate in silence. He appeared onstage while still in his teens and spent most of his twenties struggling along in touring companies throughout the South and West. Starting in 1913, he switched to movies and began appearing in one- and two-reel shorts for Universal.

Interestingly, the second short he did, *The Sea Urchin* (1913), was very much in what would become Chaney's pattern: He played a hunchback fisherman, whom a young woman is about to marry out of gratitude. But he magnanimously steps aside and lets the girl reunite with the young man she really loves. Years later, Chaney would be similarly gracious with his fiancées in *The Unholy Three* (1925) and in *While the City Sleeps* (1928). Whenever Chaney had a fiancée, chances were she had a boyfriend.

Chaney made something of a habit of taking his miserable self out of the way so that others might be happy. In *The Ace of Hearts* (1921), he was part of an anarchist group. Two of the anarchists fall in love and want to marry, prompting Chaney, who loves the woman, to do his part for the happy couple. He goes to a meeting, at which the remaining

anarchists are discussing how to eliminate the two defectors, and deto-
nates a bomb, blowing up himself and all present. Call it a wedding
present. He also committed suicide for the sake of true love in *Laugh
Clown Laugh* (1928). A trapeze artist engaged to marry Loretta Young,
he knows she loves another man. So he deliberately falls to his death
during a performance.

The Hunchback of Notre Dame (1923) made him world famous.
Maybe it struck a chord: As Quasimodo, the deaf, half-blind hunchback bell ringer, he looked the way a lot of men feel inside when they
first approach a beautiful woman. Once again, in this archetypal film,
beauty awakens Chaney. He becomes friends with a young Gypsy, and
through his intervention, he makes it possible for her to marry the man
she loves. In the process, he is stabbed to death by her would-be abduc-
tor; yet he does manage to live long enough to throw his murderer off
the top of the tower and give the bells a few more rings. Chaney dives
into a world of violence so that others can know love.

The villains he played were just as susceptible to beauty. In *The
Phantom of the Opera* (1925), his other signature film, a man's horror at
his own ugliness combines with his passion for a beautiful woman to
create a fatal psychological combustion. The famous unmasking scene
remains striking today—no matter how many times you've seen it,
Chaney always looks just a little more frightening than you remembered. It's not just the makeup that's hair-raising but also the animation
of his face, the naked fear in *his* eyes.

Yet Chaney's most consistently satisfying films are not the ones that
are his most famous today. The best Chaney films were the ones he
made at MGM in the middle and late 1920s, the years of his greatest
popularity. These films, made late in the silent era, were smoother,
slicker, better crafted—and tailored to Chaney's image, his meaning as
a star. Though Chaney continued to be the master of makeup, the
MGM films also tended to show more of Chaney's face. The face these

movies reveal is that of Hollywood's greatest silent actor and one of the most singular talents ever to work in pictures.

It was Chaney who had starred in the first-ever feature made at MGM, Victor Seastrom's *He Who Gets Slapped* (1924), a highly stylized art film about a circus clown whose gimmick is to make idealistic pronouncements and get slapped in the face each time. Love destroys him in this one, too: He falls in love with a pretty bareback rider (Norma Shearer), and to prevent her from having to marry an evil rich man, he turns a circus lion loose on the girl's greedy father and would-be husband. They're killed, and our hero is fatally mauled in the process. It might be significant that MGM's very first movie treated audiences to the spectacle of a lion, its corporate symbol, tearing actors to pieces.

See enough Chaney films and it becomes startling how cruel and vicious he could be, while always retaining access to his humanity. It's what kept him sympathetic. In Universal's *The Penalty* (1920), he'd played a legless mobster, a sadistic maniac who makes people tremble. In *West of Zanzibar* (1928), he sets out to ruin a young woman's life, forcing her to live in a brothel from girlhood. Why should we care about such guys? Perhaps we sympathize because Chaney himself sympathizes, not in the narcissistic way of some actors, who, by seeing every monster as a version of themselves, offer blind self-pity in place of compassion and discernment. With Chaney, a character's humanity is the by-product of the actor's deep and humane understanding. The illusion of Chaney's art is that he's not showing us anything deliberately; we just happen to be privy to a picture of anguish we were never meant to see. But there's nothing more willfully naked than Chaney in close-up.

"The parts I play point [out] a moral," Chaney once said. "They show individuals who might have been different if they had been given a different chance." Chaney's belief in love as a matter of life-and-death consequence was very much in the romantic spirit of the twenties. But his moral concern and his devotion to the plight of the outsider also hinted at the era to come. Chaney's villains could always go either way—only some of his films were tales of redemption—but until they made their choice, there was hope. "I have my own faith," Chaney said. "I believe we desert God, but God never deserts us."

As if to test this faith, Chaney teamed with director Tod Browning, who, often in collaboration with scenarist Waldemar Young, placed Chaney in situations of unimaginable and catastrophic desolation. In *West of Zanzibar,* Chaney finds out that the young woman whom he has deliberately made into a drunk and a prostitute is not the daughter of the man who stole his wife away. She's his own daughter. He goes from evil gloating to utter disintegration in the course of a few close-ups. He makes us believe the moment and also makes us believe that from this disintegration, he can begin to rebuild his moral nature.

Chaney's insistence on the moral dimension of his work was not misplaced grandiosity. At his best, his films implied a larger context, the sense of the divine working its mysterious way through the lives of individuals. In this way, Chaney was very much like Greta Garbo. His movies were fantasies of unworthiness, dress rehearsals for the Last Judgment, in which his sinful protagonists encountered virtue, invariably embodied in the beauty of a young woman. (With Garbo, it was usually an innocent man.) Both Chaney and Garbo were glorious masochists, who gave so much in their art that they cultivated a stony reserve in public. And both had enormous influence on the era to come.

Indeed, to contemplate the magnitude of Chaney's contribution is like trying to hold entire worlds inside one's head. He was a gangster actor, a master of the macabre, a tortured lover, and the inventor of his own genre. As an emotional actor, he not only had versatility, truthfulness, and proficiency; he practically discovered emotions. He went to places few people have ever visited on-screen or in life.

The most profound Chaney film is also the most extreme and notorious of the Chaney-Browning collaborations: *The Unknown* (1927). "In my pictures, I've tried to show that the lowliest people frequently have the highest ideals," Chaney said in 1928. "The hunchback was an example of it. So was *The Unknown*." Chaney played a murderer hiding out in a carnival, disguised as an armless knife-thrower. There, he falls in love with Nanon (a prestardom Joan Crawford), who has, of all things, a phobia about men's arms. For a number of reasons, but mainly in hope of a life with her, he has his arms surgically amputated. But when he gets out of the hospital, the oblivious girl can't wait to give him the good news: She is over her phobia. She likes arms, hands, fingers; she likes them all now. And guess what? She is marrying the circus strongman.

It's at this point that Chaney lets go with a protracted silent-screen laugh, made all the more chilling by the stillness of everything but his face. (He can't slap his knees.) The raw agony of the moment is awful to witness, but beyond that, there's the sense of a terrible violence being set loose, as though something desperate and deadly were welling up from hell, vibrating and convulsing through this man. Chaney stands at the source of pain, a place of utter negation and destruction. And all he can do is laugh.

It's the antithesis of the Fairbanks laugh, not the laugh of someone who has just imposed his reality, but of someone who has just had reality imposed on him. It's the sound of irony, dead silent but echoing in our skulls, alive with dark promises for an unknown and unknowable century.

On a more cheerful note, it's also a strong hint of a sensibility to come—the one which, years later, we can identify as "pre-Code."

2

"Mammy, Doncha Know Me?"

SOUND BROUGHT ABOUT a changing of the guard. Old heroic types were funneled through the new technology of talkies and came out transformed, some for better, some for worse. New heroic types arrived, too, though not overnight. Sound brought a new aesthetics for a new medium and then, as the twenties gave way to the thirties, new heroes for a new era.

The Jazz Singer (1927), a silent with music and some talking sequences, kicked off the revolution. In doing so, it ushered in an awkward period of almost two years, in which nothing was certain. Were talkies a fad or were silent movies doomed? Artistically, the most sensible thing would have been for silent and sound films to coexist indefinitely—for filmmakers to decide, on the basis of a film's subject matter (or its stars) which aesthetic to employ. As late as 1931, producer Joseph Schenck was hoping to make the occasional silent film—he wanted, he said, to make one with Greta Garbo. Nothing ever came of it.

The Jazz Singer not only brought technical innovation to movies; it also introduced a new kind of monster, one beyond the imaginings of even a Lon Chaney—the showbiz monster. Arriving in the form of Al

Jolson, a forty-one-year-old recording and vaudeville sensation, it was a monster as masochistic as those of Chaney, but needier, more self-pitying, and, of course, louder. Jolson took sound and, giving it everything he had, belted it home.

He made a believer overnight of Robert E. Sherwood, the critic for the old *Life* magazine and future Pulitzer Prize–winning playwright. Unlike many in and around the picture business, Sherwood read the handwriting on the wall and said so in his review of *The Jazz Singer*. For Sherwood, the key moment came when Jolson, as the jazz-singing Jack Robin, is doodling at the piano and bantering with his mother. The scene is fresh and spontaneous. Then his disapproving rabbi father enters, and the picture reverts back to silence.

Sherwood, like audiences ever since, felt the jolt as sound shifted back to silence. In a matter of seconds, reality disintegrates and reforms as a dream. The effect is strange, bordering on spooky. The actors become zombies. They leave our immediate presence and get sucked into the vortex of the past. The effect must have been almost as jarring in 1927, because it was the instant when, wrote Sherwood, he knew that silents were finished.

As the first beneficiary of the transition to sound, Al Jolson had appropriate qualities for a man on the cusp of two eras. He was a smiling romantic, like the great male stars of the twenties. But he had an air of insecurity, too, wholly foreign to previous screen idols. While silent heroes strove to prove themselves according to abstract standards of honor, Jolson had but one standard with which to measure his worth: Do you like me? And how much? He needed to know. Accordingly, in film after film, Jolson not only watches himself; he watches you watch him—and watches himself watch you watch him—on and on, in a narcissistic spiral, to infinity.

The spectacle was grotesque. Jolson minces, rolls his eyes, claps his hands, swivels his knees, and does bird whistles until you scream for

Mammy. He is unbearable. He beats you with a stick until you like him, and then the unspeakable, dreadful moment comes when you have to admit you do, sort of.

In *The Jazz Singer,* he cries out, "Mammy, doncha know me, it's your lil' baby!" singing onstage in blackface. What a baby. What a time capsule. In *The Singing Fool* (1928), which became an even bigger box-office smash, he sings the sappy "Sonny Boy" to his son. When the kid dies, he sings it again. Al keeps singing.

Jolson usually played entertainers. It gave him not only an excuse to sing but an excuse for that personality. In his onstage scenes, Jolson was manic and pushy. Offscreen, he could be intermittently snappy and jazzy, but it never lasted. Most often, he was sad, a borscht belt Pagliacci. He was a decent actor. That is, his self-pity was convincing because it was real. In *Say It with Songs* (1929), he's the father of a little boy. In a variation on *The Singing Fool,* the boy gets hit by a truck, causing Jolson to serenade him in the hospital with "Little Pal." Miraculously, the singing does not kill the child. Instead, he recovers. Yet the casualty rate among Jolson's movie progeny does leave us wondering if these illnesses and accidents were not in fact suicide attempts.

Jolson's screen career started out maudlin and got more maudlin, as the men he played mooned after wives that left him, had girlfriends who didn't care, and loved ones who never bothered to notice him. The comparison between Chaney and Jolson is not quite as flip as it appears. If Chaney was laugh-clown-laugh, Jolson was sing-clown-sing—only Jolson's characters never caught on to their monstrousness. They were too much in love with their sensitivity.

In *Mammy* (1930), made when he was slipping and had to have known it, he gets downright grotesque. A traveling singer who becomes a hobo, Jolson goes home to Mammy and serenades her at the piano. It's a scene everyone should see. It should be anthologized in documentaries: Jolson sits there looking forty-five if he's a day, singing to

Mammy (Louise Dresser), who looks fifty. Mammy also looks like she's been drinking. It's supposed to be heartwarming. Instead, it looks like a forty-five-year-old lunatic has become convinced a fifty-year-old drunk is his mother.

Jolson's popularity flared up and receded like an abscess, a weird anomaly of the transition period. But in three ways he anticipated many of the pre-Code heroes to come, particularly the ones who'd emerge at his studio, Warner Bros.: He was ethnic (Russian-Jewish), he was urban, and he was from the stage.

IF JOLSON BENEFITED most from the shift to sound, the biggest casualty was John Gilbert. But to say that isn't enough. Gilbert's misfortune was too epic to define in terms of an era. In the nearly one hundred years in which there has been such a thing as movie stardom, no actor of Gilbert's stature has ever endured such a reversal, such a humiliating turn in his public's affections. He was the best-paid and most popular actor on the planet, an artist respected by critics and a great screen lover adored by the multitude. It was a sunny day; the birds were singing; then a meteor hit him.

The wreck of Gilbert's career constitutes one of the most irresistible and endlessly intriguing stories in film history. It raises questions. It haunts the mind. The garden scene in *His Glorious Night* (1929)—in which Gilbert utters the fatal words "I love you, I love you" over and over—is classic Hollywood's Zapruder film. One watches with the same unwholesome giddiness one experiences watching the *Hindenburg* drop down for a landing. Gilbert, burying himself with each syllable, pours out his heart to a stiff-as-a-plank Catherine Dale Owen. When audiences saw this—or, rather, saw and for the first time heard their great romantic idol—they laughed. From that point on, they never felt the same way about Gilbert, ever again.

Reasons for Gilbert's failure have been discussed ever since. For about forty years after his career ended, film historians just assumed his voice was too high. Most of them were getting their information from legend, from secondhand sources, or by relying on a distant memory, since Gilbert's talkies were rarely shown anywhere.

Then came the revisionists, circa 1980, who insisted that there was nothing wrong with Gilbert's voice, that it was just great. They argued that Gilbert's failure was attributable to other factors—either a campaign by MGM mogul Louis B. Mayer to mire Gilbert in mediocre films or a plot by Mayer to adjust the bass and treble levels in the recording process so that Gilbert's voice sounded tinny. This second argument is the most peculiar, since it usually comes from people who also insist that Gilbert's voice sounds fine in his MGM movies. Another suggestion is that Gilbert was done in by the elocutionists, who encouraged him to adopt an effete Mid-Atlantic accent that was unnatural to him.

In assessing the Gilbert debacle two facts, slightly though not wholly at odds, have to be reconciled: First, the voice wasn't bad (it was a light baritone, sometimes more light than baritone, sometimes more baritone than light, not a great voice, but certainly not something that should have called attention to itself in any negative way); and second, when his fans heard him, they were disappointed. Scott Eyman, in his outstanding history of the talkie revolution, *The Speed of Sound* (1997), strikes the sensible balance, attributing the disappointment to the divergence "between what his audience imagined he sounded like and what he actually did sound like."

The conspiracy theory that suggests Gilbert was destroyed by inferior material falls apart, or at least becomes irrelevant, once we realize that no one needed a conspiracy to destroy Gilbert after *His Glorious Night*. After that one film, his career was reeling; the slightest blow, and he'd hit the canvas. The extent of the disaster was apparent to Gilbert himself when he got back from vacation and found himself in a strange land: "The face of the world had changed. There were no pats on the back.

There was nothing but averted faces. I couldn't get . . . [studio] executives on the phone. . . . The bottom had dropped out of everything."

That Gilbert's talkie feature debut should be received as not just a flop but as something threatening his future in pictures says something not only about the extent of the failure but also about the nature of it. Gilbert was being rejected not only for this fiasco. He was being rejected personally. He was being rejected as a type. And he was being rejected retroactively. Witness the nastiness of *Variety*'s review of *His Glorious Night*:

> A few more productions like this and John Gilbert will be able to change places with [comedian] Harry Langdon. His prowess at love-making . . . takes on a comedy aspect. . . . The love lines, about pulsating blood, hearts and dandelions, read far better than they sound from under the dainty Gilbertian mustache.

Words like "prowess" and "dainty" were the tip-off. What Gilbert faced was not a professional setback. It was a public castration.

The titles of Gilbert's first two talkies come soaked in irony—an irony too complete and too perfect to emanate from MGM's production office but rather from some Olympus where the gods devise ways to torture film stars. *His Glorious Night* brought about a humiliating night of the soul, and the spring release, *Redemption* (1930), resulted in nothing like its title. The picture, in fact, had been filmed before *His Glorious Night* and shelved at Gilbert's request. Its release resulted in outright speculation that Gilbert might be washed up.

"It's the kindness that kills a man half dead," Gilbert recalled of the fan magazine articles that ensued. "One story was titled, 'Is John Gilbert Through?' The question was its own answer."

Redemption was based on Tolstoy's *The Living Corpse*, a further irony, not to mention a source that should have given MGM pause. Gilbert played a man who goes through most of the film in a suicidal depression, drinking himself blotto. Finally, he kills himself. It's curious that, in a film originally intended to be Gilbert's talkie debut, the exuberant side of his personality wasn't emphasized, but, rather, his brooding, poetic side. Actually, that may have proved a promising direction, but *Redemption* was too bleak, too static, and too old-fashioned in spirit to capitalize on it.

In the coming months, MGM would try to help Gilbert adjust his image for the talkies. To counter any possible perception that he was too "dainty," he was cast as a two-fisted tough guy in *Way for a Sailor* (1930). It tanked. Early the next year, with gangster movies becoming the rage, MGM imported director Mervyn LeRoy from Warners, hot off his success in *Little Caesar.* He directed Gilbert in *Gentleman's Fate* (1931), which is about mild-mannered Jack Thomas, who finds out that his real name is Giacomo Tomasulo and that he's from a family of racketeers. Family loyalty drags him into the mob, but without enthusiasm—which meant Gilbert went through the movie ambivalent, guilt-ridden, and inactive. How could an actor hope to convey star magnetism when playing the helpless victim of circumstance?

Gilbert was a fascinating man: a reader, a thinker, a scoundrel, a loyal friend, a compulsive self-revealer, the life of the party, and the death of the day. He was also a cynic with a wicked sense of irony, something that didn't get much of a workout in his silent films and might have served him well in the coming age.

Gilbert's challenge, as it was for all silent stars, was to survive the process of literalizing that attended the move into talkies—or, to put it another way, to be himself and stay popular. That popularity, once lost, he'd never regain, but he did ultimately manage to forge a talkies version of John Gilbert that was appealing. (It's a minority opinion, but I actually prefer him as a talkie star.) And he did go on, for all his other woes, to star in two pre-Code masterpieces before he was through.

The great lover image, his millstone, proved to be more than a prob-lem for him as an artist, more than just a matter of an actor's signature role not translating to the talking screen. More to the point, it seems audiences had actually grown hostile and contemptuous of the great lover image and toward all it represented in terms of artifice, baseless confidence, and a simplified view of life.

This hostility explains the suddenness of Gilbert's collapse and the sadistic glee with which it was greeted in the press. But it also suggests, though by no means proves, that more than a change in medium had come to movies. The talkies either precipitated or coincided with a change in consciousness. When in September 1929—a full month before the stock market crash, the traditional marker for the beginning of the 1930s—audiences laughed at *His Glorious Night,* they were rejecting not only Gilbert but also the fantasies that had sustained them, in one medium or another, for decades.

Audiences even rejected Douglas Fairbanks. Here was someone everyone loved and respected, and yet it's as if one day it suddenly dawned on everybody, including Fairbanks himself, that it was over. He hung in for a while. For his first talkie, he made *The Taming of the Shrew* (1929), with his wife, Mary Pickford, and he was perfectly charming and funny in it. His voice is a bit higher than one might expect, but it was a stage voice, flexible and supported. Then he held off making another film for almost two years. One fan magazine reported in March of 1931 that "sound had knocked him for a twister . . . because he doesn't know if his brand of stuff will get over to the accompaniment of dialogue."

Offscreen, Fairbanks was restless and disoriented. According to film historian Richard Schickel, the stock market collapse, which depressed the economy, also depressed Fairbanks, "for it challenged all the verities about pluck, luck and hard work that had formed such underpinnings as had sustained him." It's an appealing thought: Fairbanks no longer had the heart to make Fairbanks movies because he could no longer believe in the optimistic myths that his films implied.

On-screen, he tried to fake it, and he managed well enough, but now there weren't enough fans left to justify the effort. In 1932, *Movie Mirror* reported that when Fairbanks and Pickford showed up at the opening of the Douglas Fairbanks, Jr., movie *Union Depot*, "hardly a ripple of applause greeted them." But when Clark Gable appeared, "there was a resounding roar."

Today, Fairbanks's talkies, such as *Reaching for the Moon* (1931)—in which he plays a businessman who woos Bebe Daniels—are fun for their novelty. As in his silents, Fairbanks goes through his talkies laughing like a jackal, only now we hear him, and hearing makes him sound a little crazy, though still enormously likable. His swan song, *The Private Life of Don Juan* (1934), is his most successful talkie, in that it's the one that acknowledges his revels are ended. He doesn't have to pretend.

The cases of Gilbert and Fairbanks are enlightening. They tell us that before the Depression, before Gable, before Cagney, before the good-guy gangsters, audiences were already turning from the past and toward something new.

SOUND PROVIDED OPPORTUNITIES for some screen actors. Gary Cooper, who'd carved out a respectable niche as a leading man in the silents, eased into success with his first talkie, *The Virginian* (1929). He had the best line—"If you want to call me that, smile," he tells villain Walter Huston—and he had his best chance yet to show how strong and silent he could be. After all, it's hard to get noticed for being strong and silent in a silent movie.

Ramon Novarro saw in the talkies an opportunity to sing. He had a tenor singing voice almost as gorgeous as he was, and at times he'd toyed with the idea of leaving the movies to make a stab at an opera career. Now he could sing *and* make movies. In his first sound films, which were practically musicals, Novarro sang love songs, and in *Call of the Flesh* (1930), his third talkie, he even did a flat-on-the-high-notes rendition of "Questa o Quella" from *Rigoletto*. Yet within a year, it became clear that sound, rather than expanding Novarro's range and appeal, had limited it.

In silents, Novarro could be, as he had been in *The Pagan*, a romantic dream, an abstraction. But the talkies, rendering him literal, revealed him as a specific guy, one with a light, pleasing, but inescapable Mexican accent, which defined him. In the next few years, he'd play a Spaniard, an Italian, an Arab, an American Indian, and, most ridiculous of all, a Chinese—one with a shaved head, a ponytail, and a Mexican accent (in 1932's *The Son-Daughter*). It would have been more merciful for the studio just to kill him.

In *Devil-May-Care* (1929), his first talkie, Novarro was a Napoleonic soldier hiding out in enemy territory by posing as a footman. In this guise, he attempts to romance an aristocratic young lady, who is shocked at the servant's impertinence. Cute stuff, at best. Novarro's charming insolence scandalized more than one innocent young thing in these early talkies. In *Devil-May-Care* and its follow-ups, *In Gay Madrid* and *Call of the Flesh* (both 1930), these young things were played by virginal Dorothy Jordan, and Novarro's method of courtship was consistent: He teased her until she broke down. In *Call of the Flesh*, she was a novitiate who is tempted away from the convent by the sound of Novarro's singing voice.

To see Novarro in these films while knowing what styles of leading men were in the wings is to feel a measure of pity. Handsome and engaging he may have been, but these stories, and these romantic pairings—not to mention a certain sweetness in his aura—were rendering Novarro innocuous. And innocuous was the one thing a leading man could never be, not in the twenties, and certainly not in the thirties. The future did not belong to the innocuous, nor to the fellows who adopted the grand manner, raising their arms magnificently and laughing with thrown-back heads.

MGM would stick with Novarro until 1934, trying different things. Some of those things would work better than others, but nothing ever quite worked completely, and when his contract ended, he was let go. But at least Novarro's public gave him the bad news in easy doses, and at least when he opened his mouth, a whole nation didn't go into convulsive laughter.

Laughter was the great fear. Audiences laughed at love scenes and they laughed at screen lovers. No wonder, then, that for a brief time the competent, reliable, but hardly exciting Conrad Nagel was in extreme demand. He had a warm voice and could act and, most importantly, there was absolutely nothing funny about him. His film career would continue on and off through the 1950s, but between 1929 and 1930, he was ubiquitous, making seventeen movies, sometimes as the lead, sometimes as a second lead.

Hollywood turned to stage-trained actors, who came with a certain imprimatur and had the advantage of being unknown quantities. For a brief time, audiences liked stage actors to sound stagy—people expected their money's worth—and so George Arliss enjoyed a brief vogue. He was born in London in 1868, which means that he was sixty-one when he became a film star in his first talkie, *Disraeli* (1929). It was based on a stage play, in which Arliss had starred as early as 1911. Arliss was a strange-looking actor, slight, with a wide mouth and thin lips. In photos, he looks positively lizardlike, not to mention rather forbidding, which may account for why he has acquired a reputation for being stuffy: For decades, his films were mainly known by their stills, not for themselves. Arliss may have been affected, but he wasn't a stuffed shirt. He was more smirky than smug, and above all arch, as though always half-listening to sardonic music playing in his head.

Arliss films belong to the last gasp of an era in which people still believed the Victorians had wisdom to impart. In *Disraeli*, he spends as much time bringing together a pair of young lovers as he does raising money to build the Suez Canal. The matchmaking motif is repeated in other Arliss films, in which he is usually kindly and benign, though quite shrewd.

Whatever their value as entertainment, Arliss's films document a late-nineteenth- and early-twentieth-century stage tradition. In his performances we see acting in which the technique and the technician are clearly visible, yet there's nothing cold or austere about it. At the end of *Disraeli*, the old prime minister gets a telegram, believing it to be an announcement of his ailing wife's death. Arliss beautifully conveys Disraeli's fear—and then also his grateful relief when his wife, recovered, comes through the door. He also brought hammy fun to his role as a wicked raja in *The Green Goddess* (1930), a part he'd originated on stage in 1921.

In modern-dress films, such as *The Millionaire* (1931) and *The Working Man* (1933), he played older gentlemen asserting old-fashioned values in a new age. But Arliss wasn't averse to modernity, and he wasn't a stick-in-the-mud. For *The Millionaire*, Arliss needed to cast the role of a dynamic young insurance salesman whose encounter with the retired millionaire changes the latter's course. For the salesman, Arliss insisted on—and got—a pre-stardom James Cagney. Cagney appears in only a single scene. He tries to sell the old gent life insurance, but when he finds out the man is retired, he drops his pitch: Retired men are a bad risk.

It speaks well of the British, classically trained Arliss that he was able to recognize the talents of Cagney, who in age, temperament, and style was so different from himself. Of course, it was that contrast Arliss was after, but he couldn't possibly have known how telling and perfect the pairing would seem in retrospect. In *The Millionaire*, the past and future meet at a moment of ideal stasis, just before the past has started to end and with the future about to start. Two actors, two styles, and two eras are there before our eyes—in a union both incongruous and yet surprisingly harmonious, like that old video of Bing Crosby and David Bowie singing the "Little Drummer Boy" duet.

Talent, of course, is what unites Arliss and Cagney, and Arliss's generosity allows him to throw the scene to the younger actor. But what makes the encounter even more vivid is the contrast in the characters they play: Arliss as a self-made industrialist who amassed his fortune through diligence and sacrifice, and Cagney as a salesman getting by on pluck, energy, and personality. On-screen, they represent two values, two kinds of America, just as—on-screen and off—they represented two kinds of manhood, past and future.

In the meantime, there was the present. And the present belonged to Richard Barthelmess.

3

Richard Barthelmess

A S TALKIES FOUND their voice, Richard Barthelmess emerged as one of the most exciting figures of the era.

Exciting might be an unlikely adjective to use in connection with one of the most low-key and unassuming of major stars ever produced by Hollywood. Though other American leading men have built images around their shyness—Henry Fonda, Gary Cooper, and Jimmy Stewart come to mind—Barthelmess may be the only mainstream matinee idol who wasn't shy so much as reserved, and distant. See one Barthelmess movie and you may wonder how he ever became a screen idol.

His appeal is elusive. He had a handsome face—Lillian Gish thought he was the "most beautiful" man ever to work before the camera—but by the time the talkies arrived, he had big circles under his eyes. He was also short and stoop-shouldered, and his voice was on the high side. Yet he conveyed something, a sincerity, a gravity in his essence that the camera discerned and communicated. He was focused, unfussy, and had an essential integrity. He didn't seem like an actor but like a person you might know, and trust.

Barthelmess grasped early the possibilities of the new realism brought about by talkies and used his stardom to examine untraveled avenues of the American soul. From his first sound film, *Weary River* (1929), until the enforcement of the Code in July 1934, he created a body of work unique in its exploration of racism, corruption, the dark side of business, and the effects of war. Topical in its day, Barthelmess's work is all the more compelling from the distance of time. Through him, we can understand the social concerns of an era, and through his films, discover the outer limits of political expression that a Hollywood studio dared venture in the early 1930s.

No single American film star has ever created a talkie legacy anything like Barthelmess's in its relentlessness of conscience or seriousness of purpose. (Robert Redford, whose contribution has been made over a period of more than thirty years, is his nearest competitor, but no one else is close.) Yet few people know this about Barthelmess. To the extent he's remembered at all today, he's remembered as a silent-screen star. His talkies are regarded as a footnote.

A big reason for this neglect may lie with the actor himself. Perhaps Barthelmess's talkies would have more acknowledgment from history if Barthelmess himself, at the time, had talked more about what he was doing and why he was doing it. Usually, actors try to emphasize the social significance of their work, even when there isn't much to emphasize. Usually, actors with strong feelings about political matters eventually break down and share their passions. Here was the star of some of the most committed, trailblazing films of his era. Yet unlike James Cagney or Edward G. Robinson, Barthelmess never said anything about politics, except on a couple of occasions, in 1929 and 1930, in which he mentioned being a Republican.

For a man who lived much of his life in public, Barthelmess remains a mystery. We might be tempted to write him off as a cipher, an actor for hire who made whatever movies his studio, Warner Bros., told him to make. But no. Barthelmess chose his own movies. We might guess that he chose them cynically, for careerist reasons, for the sake of keeping up with popular trends. Again, no. Barthelmess was ahead of most trends, sometimes way ahead. He constantly took chances, and some of them backfired.

In the end, we may just have to accept Barthelmess's mystery. Perhaps he was simply an artist, guided by an intuitive sense of what roles best suited him as an actor. Perhaps he was apolitical, but drawn to the big moral issues of the day. Perhaps he was a Republican turned zealous New Dealer, who expressed his opinions through his movies and kept a tight lip otherwise. I would guess a combination of all three, but it's only a guess. We do know that Barthelmess was bright and literate and that he cared deeply about his movies. It's hard to imagine any intelligent person going out of his way to make a certain kind of film, over and over, while being oblivious of the films' content. Likewise, it's hard to imagine any serious person repeatedly investing—indeed risking—his stardom to express ideals in which he doesn't believe.

It was in Barthelmess's nature to be reticent. For a star of his stature, he gave few interviews. Herbert Swope, Jr., a journalist who knew him socially in the late twenties and early thirties, remembers him as "extremely polite and very quiet, not a wit. [He was] unusually attentive for an actor, content to sit and watch and listen to other people be amusing." Douglas Fairbanks, Jr., in a 1932 word portrait of Barthelmess for *Vanity Fair*, also talked about his quietness and diffidence, which caused some people to consider him "smug."

Of course, the main thing we know about Barthelmess is what his movies say to us. Watching his films, we are confronted with a world in which government is often the bad guy. Americans are the bad guys. Society at large is the bad guy. Complacency is the bad guy. And the good guy, meanwhile, is sometimes an outlaw or a criminal of some kind. In these plot elements, Barthelmess was in the advance guard. His movies contained ideas and assumptions that would quickly become staples of pre-Code cinema.

BARTHELMESS WAS BORN in 1895. His father, a successful importer, died a year later, and his mother, an actress, earned her living on the stage. After high school, Barthelmess started getting work as an extra and got his big break in 1916, in a movie called *War Brides*, starring the Russian stage actress Alla Nazimova. Barthelmess got the role through his mother, who'd worked as Nazimova's English coach.

He stepped into history three years later when he starred as the "Yellow Man," opposite Lillian Gish, in D. W. Griffith's *Broken Blossoms* (1919). Barthelmess played a gentle Buddhist who shelters a fifteen-year-old girl from her drunken, vicious father. When he kills the father while protecting the girl from a brutal attack, the community converges on him, and he commits suicide. *Broken Blossoms* prefigures aspects that can be found in the films of Barthelmess's maturity: the hero's quiet dignity, his moral uprightness, his courage in the face of brutality, and his helplessness before the mob. The antiracist sentiment, which for Griffith was something of an atonement for *The Birth of a Nation* (1915), fits more comfortably into the filmography of Barthelmess, who, in his talkies, took stands against racism on several occasions.

Barthelmess made his signature silent film two years later, director Henry King's *Tol'able David* (1921). It was a melodrama in which he played a mail delivery boy who single-handedly goes up against a group of outlaws that crippled his brother and hastened his father's death. *Tol'able David* established the Barthelmess pattern: He was always David, and his enemies were always Goliath. In *Tol'able David*, Goliath was easy to spot. He was a gang leader, played by Ernest Torrence, a Scottish actor who'd go on to an active career playing heavies. The villain was large, ugly, and evil, but David's task was straightforward: All

he had to do was conquer this criminal, and the bucolic Virginia coun-
tryside could be restored to peace.

In the talkies, Barthelmess would face adversaries just as strong and
evil, but more insidious—dyspeptic bureaucrats, cruel cops, and heartless bankers and businessmen. He would face situations that were confused, moral choices that were not clear-cut. And he'd achieve victories
that were either ambiguous or altogether empty. As his career went on,
Barthelmess would adjust to the changing times and help push movies
along in the process. He would adapt his underdog image into the
screen's best vehicle for expressing a more adult understanding of the
American reality.

Though a veteran of the early silent era, Barthelmess wasn't nostalgic
in his interests nor deluded in his social vision. He did not see the world
in Fairbanks terms but was a realist, who saw life as often tragic, with
perhaps a slow movement toward the light, but achingly slow. (One role
that he coveted but never got, which would have been ideal for him,
was Clyde Griffiths in Dreiser's *An American Tragedy*.) He once told an
interviewer that he preferred unhappy endings, so long as they were
logical. Unlike other silent idols, he never smiled much on-screen—
what was there to smile about in a Barthelmess movie?—but when he
did, it felt like a gift.

From the beginning, he took movies and their messages seriously. In
1922, with reformers in an uproar over several well-publicized scandals,
Barthelmess spoke on the radio against censorship. "Fanatical agitation
for censorship is unfair," he said, "when people who know nothing of
picture-making would wreck the structure of an artistic screen production by hacking at points necessary to the climax."

Likewise, Barthelmess himself was taken seriously. When the Soviet
director Sergei Eisenstein arrived in the United States, he wanted to
know everything about Barthelmess. "I am deeply interested in him,"
he said. "He has a quiet, beautiful technique of acting. . . . One is

impressed not only by the characters he portrays but by his subtle work with his hands and his gestures. I know of no other actor who can do this."

In the sound era, Barthelmess used his leverage to gain a contractual guarantee that few stars had: He was given his choice of films. He could make any movie he wanted. It's for this reason more than any other that Barthelmess's output was distinct and that it speaks to us today as a consistent body of work. Barthelmess's first talkie—or, rather, part talkie—was *Weary River,* an intelligent film about incarceration and rehabilitation. In its presentation of a gangster protagonist, a man who was no saint, *Weary River* was at least a year ahead of its time.

Barthelmess played Jerry, a dapper bootlegger, who lives with a sexy blond moll (Betty Compson). When his gang is involved in the shooting of an innocent bystander, he is sent to prison, where he joins the prison band and becomes its leader and vocalist. When he sings the song "Weary River" on a broadcast from prison, the station is flooded with calls for an encore, but that's just the beginning of our hero's odyssey. *Weary River* presents a soul redeemed by art, a man finding his truest and best self by looking into a creative, yearning place inside. But here's the thing: He can't live inside—not in his own head, nor, for long, within prison walls. He has to live in the world, and the real challenges come when he leaves prison.

Barthelmess portrays Jerry as a fundamentally decent guy in a shaky balance. When he tries to make it in vaudeville, he has to face a public and rival artists who see him as a criminal. The stress hurts his singing, which undermines his dream of becoming successful. Barthelmess's sensitive performance also suggests another problem—that Jerry's desire to become an artist makes things doubly difficult for him. It's not only the struggle inherent in an arts career that's hard. Yet more painful are the emotions he must open himself to in order to let his creative self breathe. When he finally gives up and goes back to his old life, his relief is manifest. Once again, he can put the shell back on and stop hurting.

Weary River is no Pollyanna piece. Despite the influence of a fatherly warden, Jerry's sincere desire to reform, and his considerable talent, the life of our hero, ten minutes before the finish, is heading straight into the toilet because no respectable person will give him a break. The movie invites us to imagine what an ex-con *without* Barthelmess's looks or brains might have been up against. This was an advanced statement for 1929, made yet more sophisticated by the climax: Jerry is saved from committing a violent crime through the intervention of his moll. In *Weary River,* the gangster is the hero, and the bad girl is the good girl. Over the next two years, this combination would become increasingly familiar.

Barthelmess went on to star in two more talkies in 1929, *Drag* and *Young Nowheres,* both lost films. Considering the consistent quality of Barthelmess's output in this period, any loss hurts. *Drag* was a comedy about a playwright who leaves his wife and takes off with his former sweetheart when he can no longer stand his wife's freeloading relatives. The movie's endorsement of the playwright's dumping of a wholesome wife for the crime of refusing to leave her family and cleave to him might have been interesting. We'll never know. But *Young Nowheres* sounds like the one most worth getting into a time machine to see. Barthelmess played an elevator boy in love with a poor orphan (Marian Nixon).

When *Young Nowheres* was released, the *Variety* critic wrote, "It is remarkable . . . that a star deliberately chooses to impersonate anyone so deficient in glamour as an elevator boy." Exactly. That's what we like about Barthelmess. The movie apparently told a little story about an elevator boy and his girl who fall asleep on the beach at Coney Island. She gets pneumonia, and upon her release from the hospital, he takes her to the luxurious apartment of his boss, who's out of town. When the boss returns unexpectedly on Christmas Eve, he has the couple arrested and hauled into court.

Young Nowheres premiered in New York on October 1, 1929. By the time it opened nationally, on October 20, the stock market had gone into a tailspin. Barthelmess, in his films, had been a friend to elevator boys and sympathetic to crooks during the economy's boom time. Soon, as over the next few years a Depression set in and then deepened, the movies would come to share his point of view.

BARTHELMESS'S SUFFERING, LIKE that of Greta Garbo and Lon Chaney, never seemed his alone but somehow implied the suffering of humanity. It was Barthelmess's great innovation to employ that gift in the depiction of social injustice. At a time when Al Jolson was still singing mammy songs, Barthelmess took on racism in *Son of the Gods*, a story about a romance between a white woman and a Chinese-American man. Some states didn't allow such stories even to be shown in theaters in 1930, and, to be sure, the picture dealt gingerly with the topic—too gingerly for some film critics of the era. Still, it was earnest and made its points.

Barthelmess played Sam Lee, the son of a Chinese department-store magnate, a young man who, for reasons he never bothers to explore, doesn't look Chinese at all—he looks like Barthelmess in any other movie. Although no one can tell he is Chinese by looking at him, whenever the information comes out, we get to see the flamboyant forms racial prejudice took circa 1930. In one scene, Sam drives two buddies and three young women to a posh dance club. When the women find out Sam is Chinese, they insist on leaving. "How dare you bring us out with a Chinaman," one woman berates her boyfriend. "Sam Lee—a Chink—oh, I wouldn't let him touch me."

In *Son of the Gods*, whenever another character abuses or disrespects Barthelmess, viewers experience the unfairness on a gut level—and the outrage extends beyond the movie into the world outside it. "Richard Barthelmess goes by way of the Chinese," wrote the *Paterson Guardian* in its review, "to bring home a picture of un-Christian snobbery and narrowness that is bound to hit some of us right between the eyes." That was the intention. When Sam leaves college, embittered by his encounters with white bigotry, he tells his father, "They are liars and hypocrites. Their religion teaches love and brotherhood and equality. But they worship money and prejudice."

Son of the Gods, released in early 1930, has some of the somnambulant pace of a very early talkie, but the emotional journey of the central character remains an arresting one. After leaving school, Sam goes to Europe, where he meets Allana (Constance Bennett), who becomes immediately attracted to him, but he holds her at arm's length—that is, until she happens to say something to indicate she'd happily marry someone of another race. Barthelmess makes a strong moment of the one in which she finally breaks through his reserve. He doesn't kiss her. Rather, he gets seized by an impulse that's more about emotional longing than physical longing. His face softens, and he hugs her.

She won't let him talk; she just wants to make love. He doesn't get back to his hotel until the next morning—and that same morning she tells her father in flippant flapper fashion, "You'll throw us a lovely wedding, won't you, darling—and give us a nice present?" That she has put everything on the line for Sam is the only explanation for her despicable behavior in the key scene: Having found out that Sam is Asian, she shows up for a lunch date in a rage and whips him with a riding crop: "You cur, you liar, you cheat! You dirty rotten Chinaman!" No one was better at getting whipped than Barthelmess. (In successive films, he'd also show his skill at getting beaten.) He stands there like someone who can't quite take in how quickly disaster has struck.

Criticism of the film at the time focused on the improbable and convenient ending, in which Barthelmess, in the aftermath of his father's death, finds out that he was a Caucasian foundling. That ending is just as disappointing today, but it doesn't negate the film's antiracist message. When Sam finds out he is white, he doesn't consider it good news, and he doesn't tell Allana. On her own, she comes to him, all but begging: "I can't get along without you. . . . I love you, I can't live without you. . . . We'll be married at once, if you wish. But if you don't, I'm still not going to leave you. You're my life, my love. Nothing else matters." Only then does he tell her, and she barely reacts. "You are you," she says, reiterating the message. "You're the one that I love. Nothing else makes any difference." The point is that race doesn't matter, a not-insignificant message for 1930 and as dignified as possible a handling of a plot turn that was deemed necessary at the time. As the critic for the *Brooklyn Standard Union* put it:

> The producers cannot hastily be blamed for their failure to carry through the story to its uncompromising conclusion. . . . Concessions had to be made to a public prejudice as widespread as that against miscegenation. The ending of *Son of the Gods* is weak and unconvincing, but it does not detract from the genuineness of the picture as a whole.

Son of the Gods caused Richard Watts, Jr., of the *New York Herald Tribune*, to notice that "Mr. Barthelmess . . . has a way of using the cinema to discuss important social matters." Barthelmess was different. Eventually, most critics would catch on, but even at that time comments were turning up in the press to indicate the actor was blazing an independent course.

His next film was almost unbearable. Barthelmess was already on record as saying he liked unhappy endings. *The Dawn Patrol*, released in 1930, had an unhappy ending, an unhappy middle, and an unhappy beginning. The most suffocating and harrowing of all pre-Code war films, *The Dawn Patrol*, written by American World War I pilot John Monk Saunders, found Barthelmess as a British squad leader, one of a group of men in a hopeless situation. Every day, about a half dozen of these men go up on bombing patrols, flying over France in cracker box biplanes, and every day, two or three don't come back. Young men arrive to replace them, and they're killed in a matter of days (their names are written in chalk on a blackboard to make them easier to erase). In between missions, the men spend their time drinking and waiting to die.

In *The Dawn Patrol*, director Howard Hawks made a virtue of early-talkie technology, using static setups to emphasize the men's confinement. The effect, gothic and unflinching, is enhanced further by the absence of music underscoring the scenes. When Barthelmess and his friend Scott (Douglas Fairbanks, Jr.) sit and have breakfast before going on a patrol, one can sense the predawn stillness. And one can almost feel the relief of the cool morning air as they leave their cramped quarters. Hawks was wise never to make the morning sky look anything but inviting. The sky doesn't know a war is on. The men go up and risk their lives on days that could be any day. The horror is emphasized by the simplicity of it all.

Barthelmess's gentleness toward younger officers, his lack of self-indulgence, his everyman looks, and his refusal to hate the enemy mark him as the perfect war hero for a pacifist era. In *The Dawn Patrol*, heroism has less to do with patriotism than with maintaining one's dignity, in avoiding the reflexive selfishness that fear naturally inspires. Barthelmess was born to play a concerned flight commander who must, for the sake of his men, keep a tight clamp on his emotions. He lets the mask drop only once, memorably, when his friend, presumed dead, staggers in drunk to his own wake. The look on Barthelmess's face is one of helpless happiness, a hint of who this cheerless officer might have been before the war.

• • •

THE DAWN PATROL was a major critical and box-office success. Thirty-three years later, when Barthelmess died, it was cited as his best talking film, an exaggeration that says something about its enduring reputation. For our purposes, the important thing about its success is that it brought about an adjustment of the actor's contract from two pictures a year to three. That means more Barthelmess films were crammed into the five-year period leading up to the Code, including *The Lash*, which made it to screens in December, as the actor's third release of 1930.

As was typical of Barthelmess, he discovered the story of *The Lash* through his reading. The 1929 novel *Adios*, about the exploitation of the Spanish settlers in California in the aftermath of the Mexican War, seemed to him a good screen story, so he passed it along to Warner Bros. By this point, less than two years into his talkie career, Barthelmess had made films about a criminal's regeneration (*Weary River*), interracial love (*Son of the Gods*), and the horror of war (*The Dawn Patrol*). *The Lash* fit right in. He played El Puma, a landowning Mexican who fights for his people against the incoming Americans.

"The movie doesn't place Americans in a very favorable light after the conquest of California," wrote *Variety*. That was putting it mildly. *The Lash* was next door to a diatribe, presenting the Mexicans as sensitive aristocrats and the Americans as drunken slobs, thieves, and murderers who delight in blood sport—a fight between a bear and a jackass, for one thing—and whose mission is to drive the Mexicans from their land.

For *The Lash*, Barthelmess immersed himself in California history, attended fiestas, studied Spanish, and learned the Spanish dances and songs of the period. "They knew life and lived it as it should be lived," Barthelmess told a reporter. "With love, romance and daring." As a university-educated landowner turned bandit, he robs everybody, kills the loutish land commissioner, and is partly responsible for the death of yet another American, but the movie remains on his side. There is only one virtuous American in the entire picture—the sheriff (James Rennie), who wants to mix his blood with the Mexicans by marrying El Puma's sister. The rest deserve what they get and, in true pre-Code fashion, the movie doesn't punish the hero for giving it to them. The happy ending, which diverted from the book and would have been inconceivable after the Code, saw Barthelmess escaping with his fiancée across the border to Mexico, to safety and the good life.

Today, no one ever thinks of Barthelmess as a prototype for the anti-hero figure we find in Depression melodramas. The integrity of his essence causes us to remember him as a decent and upright everyman. But that everyman had a dark side. He could think and react, get angry, and get even. The notion, played out in *The Lash*, that no citizen owes blind obedience to a morally bereft government would become one of the hallmarks of pre-Code, but it was a fairly new idea for films in 1930.

As 1930 turned into 1931, Barthelmess was exploring a big question in his films: If a culture is corrupt, if the world has gone bad, what is the proper moral stance of the individual? Stoic heroism as in *The Dawn Patrol*? Active subversion as in *The Lash*? *The Finger Points*, which Barthelmess described in an interview as "a story straight off the front pages," continued that investigation. Written by W. R. Burnett, who wrote the novel *Little Caesar*, and John Monk Saunders, it was based on the career of Jake Lingle, a crooked *Chicago Tribune* reporter who'd recently been gunned down by the mob. As Breckinridge Lee, an ambitious and idealistic reporter who comes to the city and finds mob corruption rampant, Barthelmess doesn't opt to keep his head down, ignore it, and just get by. He writes about it and gets beaten up, then finds his newspaper won't pay his medical expenses. That's when he realizes that this is no battle between good and evil, but just some

Hobbesian struggle. He decides to play off the mob and the newspaper against each other for his own profit.

The key thing about *The Finger Points* is that Barthelmess is sympathetic not just because circumstances drive him into corruption. (He needs to pay his medical bills, so he goes on the mob payroll.) Rather, he's sympathetic because the corruption itself seems an act of defiance—against the newspaper but also against the crooks, whom he extorts for greater and greater sums of money. He fights power by learning its rules and meeting it head-on. "Nobody takes care of you in this town," he says. "You've got to watch out for yourself. . . . I'm not going to be a sucker. . . . I tried asking for money. It doesn't work. You have to *make* them pay."

The Finger Points is ten long years from *Tol'able David*. Here again, Barthelmess plays an individual with a spirit too big to cave into evil, but the world had changed. A universe of proven verities had become one big tangle. Watching *The Finger Points* today, it's still unclear if we're to see the plight of the protagonist as the tragic case of a good man gone wrong or as that of a tragic hero. One thing is certain: Barthelmess played the only character who finds the moral scheme of the city unbearable and subjugation to it impossible. "This city is rotten from top to bottom," he says. "The racketeers terrorize the public. . . . And I terrorize the racketeers."

That's either a peculiar moral stance or a moral stance for a peculiar world. Either way, Barthelmess, showed in *The Finger Points* just how adaptable the Barthelmess hero could be in navigating the twisted moral terrain of pre-Code cinema.

4

Public Enemies—and Heroes

IN 1931, NINE days into the New Year, *Little Caesar* opened in New York City. Audiences at the Strand Theater saw a picture of modern life, the likes of which they'd never seen on-screen. They saw a three-o'clock-in-the-morning world of seedy diners, shady speakeasies, and sudden, random violence. They saw flashes of gunfire in an all-night gas station and a story as hot as anything newsboys hawked on street corners.

Audiences also got a good long look at the impossible gargoyle face of an actor named Edward G. Robinson. They decided they liked it. With *Little Caesar*, Robinson, whose vast and varied output would become one of the treasures of the era, was launched. Thereafter, the actor's name became, in the mouths of the public, a slur of syllables ("edwageerobinson") connoting big cigars, a sneering voice, and (oft-misquoted) tough-guy lines like "You can dish it out, but you're getting so you can't take it no more."

The gangster trend would soon become the gangster deluge, as pre-Code cinema found its first ideal vehicle for exploring the moral dilemmas facing men in a changing American society. Gangster movies opened the floodgates for other studies in moral ambiguity, as well. From that point until the ax of censorship fell some three and a half years later, Hollywood would specialize in heroes who were shady, crooked, or outright criminal. Bad guys became the sympathetic focus, but then, why not? They wanted the same things audiences wanted: money, comfort, recognition, and that indefinable thing that movies have and viewers long for—a touch of splendor.

The result was that in the pre-Code era, sooner or later, almost every actor of any stature ended up playing a gangster. It wasn't just Robinson—or, for that matter, James Cagney, who would soon emerge as the other unforgettable gangster actor in *The Public Enemy*. There was also Paul Muni, who'd come to prominence in *Scarface*, as well as a host of other actors in films less known: Robert Armstrong, Lew Ayres, Wallace Beery, Gary Cooper, Ricardo Cortez, Clark Gable, John Gilbert, Cary Grant, Neil Hamilton, Walter Huston, Ben Lyon, Chester Morris, George Raft, Spencer Tracy—even Boris Karloff.

The few prominent actors who, by happenstance, never played one—such as Lee Tracy and William Powell—played fellows who were no better than gangsters. They shared their dubious morality, represented them in court, or rubbed elbows with them in speakeasies. They were men who liked gangsters or who were at least relaxed in their company. Powell, for example, had one of his most acclaimed early roles in *Street of Chance* (1930), playing a famous Chicago gambler who is so mob-connected that he orders a gangland rubout.

Looking back from a distance of decades, we can see plainly that the gangster was to actors what the prostitute was to actresses: the era's mythic, iconic role. Through the gangster, Hollywood found itself able to say everything it really wanted to say about men, the law, and society in general, all the while pretending to be telling cautionary tales from the urban gutter.

Gangsters and prostitutes turned up in pre-Codes at around the same time, and their careers followed the same progression. A sprinkling of gangsters turned into a proliferation in 1930, followed by an explosion in 1931. Then the gangster character tapered off during 1932. Like the prostitute, he didn't disappear. His morals merely went mainstream. By 1932, the movies were able to deal directly with the societal concerns that the gangster movies raised.

Why were gangsters (not to mention prostitutes) so popular? A casual glance at the time line might lead one to suspect it had all to do with the Great Depression: People were down-and-out. Desperate women turned to the streets, while desperate men turned to crime—and Hollywood was there to tell the story. Sounds good, but that's not exactly what happened.

The movie gangster was well on his way before the stock market crashed, and most of the important pre-Code gangster films were in theaters before the fall of 1931, when bank failures brought home the extent of the crisis to average Americans. These pre-Codes were not the result of an economy in flux, though that aspect ended up making its way into the films. Rather, they were the result of morality in flux—a sexual morality, as manifested in the prostitute films, and a social morality, which found its expression in the gangster movies.

Prohibition had created the racketeers, and it gradually created the social climate in which the sympathetic gangster could find a hearing on the American screen. Americans had good reason to sympathize with gangsters. After all, if Prohibition did not, strictly speaking, make a criminal of every citizen who took a drink, it came close. The Eighteenth Amendment, which went into effect in 1920, banned the manufacture, sale, or transportation of "intoxicating liquors," as well as their import and export. That made every person who refused to stop drinking complicit in the commission of crime. It made everyone who drank part of the economic base by which gangsters bought their overcoats and spats, their violin cases and machine guns.

To frequent a speakeasy was to patronize a criminal establishment. To buy a drink was to do business with an outlaw. The Eighteenth Amendment put Americans into contact with lawbreakers, who turned out not to have horns growing out of their heads but to be, in the main, normal people in the community taking a risk to make a few extra bucks. It also put average Americans in the position of sympathizing with the local bootleggers' higher-ups, the gangsters, who were providing a needed product and were, for the most part, only killing one another or those meddlers trying to stop them. By 1930, according to a Gallup poll, 70 percent of the public wanted Prohibition either modified or repealed.

Anti-Prohibitionists had worried from the beginning that the Eighteenth Amendment would backfire. New York senator James Wadsworth believed that Prohibition would "result in widespread contempt of law and the Constitution itself." Now that seemed to be happening. Crime rates climbed, while respect for law was in free fall. Magazines and newspapers told real-life horror stories about federal agents breaking down the doors of American homes or killing innocent people suspected of bootlegging. A growing number of citizens were outraged.

In hindsight, we might tend to think of Prohibition as a law doomed from the minute it hit the books. But people in the twenties and early thirties hardly considered repeal an inevitability. Most thought they were stuck with it, forever—including experts such as the criminal defense lawyer Clarence Darrow, who lamented in several publications about the virtual impossibility of repealing a constitutional amendment.

This is significant, because only by contemplating the seeming endlessness of Prohibition can we appreciate the rage it engendered. In an article in the May 1930 issue of *Vanity Fair*, the humorist Corey Ford wrote a not-very-amused column about his efforts to smuggle three and a half cases of liquor into the country. Referring to himself, for his own protection, as "an entirely imaginary character," he expressed the young cosmopolite's anger at Prohibition and showed how it translated into disgust for American institutions in general:

> In order to be able to offer his guests a highball or a glass of wine . . . our entirely imaginary character disobeyed an Amendment to the Constitution, broke twenty incidental statutes, betrayed the president of his country, spat on the flag, yanked the tail feathers from the American eagle, and trampled Law, Patriotism and Stephen Decatur into the dust. And at least I can say here—at the risk of being censored—that if I had by any possible chance been this entirely imaginary character, it would have been the proudest moment of my civic career.

Calling "every drink I take" a "worthy gesture in a worthy cause," Ford encouraged others to break this "morally obscene" law:

> Break it repeatedly. . . . Urge others to drink. Don't betray the bootleggers who are smuggling liquor to you. . . . Nothing has succeeded in fanning the flame of revolt . . . more violently than the activities of the men entrusted with the task of enforcing the law. The indiscriminate shootings, the killing of innocent citizens by bungling Coast Guardsmen, the unwarranted search of private homes . . . all these things have moved in the younger hearts an utmost shame for their country and their flag.

Ford, who was twenty-eight in 1930, had reached legal age just in time to be unable to buy a legal drink. For Americans of all ages, but particularly those of Ford's, the supposed good guys were no longer the good guys. Perhaps they never had been, but now the secret was out, and that knowledge would make its way into the movies.

IT TOOK SEVERAL years for the gangster to emerge in full, strutting Edward G. Robinson-esque glory. At first, movie gangsters weren't sympathetic. Up through 1929, gangsters were mainly villains, whose usual function was to threaten the happiness of a young couple. Typically, these films ended with the gangster either dead or on the way to jail and with the couple on the way to the altar—satisfied that their love and determination were enough to slay the most scary of modern dragons. Such films found a latter-day parallel in the 1980s and 1990s, when it became a convention of crime films for a man and a woman to meet and fall in love while being menaced by a serial killer. Nothing like a little danger to bring a romance into focus.

Gradually, the presentation of the gangster as purely wicked softened. A turning point came with director Roland West's stylish *Alibi* (1929), in which the ostensible villain (Chester Morris) was handsome and enterprising, a young gang leader and something of a criminal mastermind. Even the camera work encouraged audiences to see things his way: In an early scene, as Chick Williams (Morris) enters a building and heads toward the music and commotion of an underground nightclub, we experience his walk as an extended tracking shot from his perspective.

Without doubt, he's a villain. On a theater date with his fiancée, a policeman's daughter, he slips out during intermission, pulls off a robbery, and kills a cop, then makes it back in time for the second act. The fiancée thinks he just went to the men's room. Yet however awful he may be, the cops are presented as nothing but contemptible. The fiancée says it best when she tells Tommy (Harry Stubbs), a cop who loves her, why, having been a policeman's daughter, she could never stomach life as a policeman's wife. "They're man hunters, and they're cruel and merciless. . . . And they think themselves great heroes. . . . Law? Is third-degreeing, bulldozing people into confessing to crimes they didn't commit, is that law?" The antipolice barrage continues when Chick comes to pick her up at her father's apartment. The old cop thinks he's carrying a gun. "I never carry a gun," Chick answers. "Unless the cops plant one on me, as they did the last time."

In *Alibi* we encounter a profound cynicism about the police and their tactics, in a film made before the Great Depression but right in the heart of an era in which Prohibition had eroded respect for law enforcement. In the end, the filmmakers lose their nerve by abruptly having Chick turn into a brute and a coward. But the more lingering impression is of a police force as sleazy as it is self-righteous. All the things Chick's fiancée says about police tactics turn out to be true. In a pair of interrogation scenes, cops are shown threatening to murder a suspect in order to hasten a confession. It's not a flattering spectacle.

Though *Alibi*, in its outlines, fell into the typical pattern for 1929—a gangster temporarily threatens the happiness of a couple destined to marry (alas, the heroine ends up with Tommy)—the whole feel was different. With its attractive villain and its smug, repellent heroes, *Alibi* was a marker, if not a landmark, suggesting a Hollywood cozying up to the villain as hero. For his performances, Morris was nominated for an Academy Award.

Other films cozied up in less subtle ways, by making gangsters cuddly, or at least softies at heart. In *Thunderbolt* (1929), George Bancroft loses his longtime moll (Fay Wray) to her childhood sweetheart. Though he threatens revenge, the big lug eventually clears her boyfriend of a crime and gallantly goes to the chair. In *Good Intentions* (1930), Edmund Lowe sacrificed himself to save the life of his romantic rival, and in *The Pay Off* (1930), Lowell Sherman did the same. Lon Chaney would have been a natural for such roles. They fit his classic pattern: The monstrous male principle defeated effortlessly, sometimes obliviously, by the beauty and superior rectitude of the female.

Sacrificial gangsters, despite their modern milieu, retained a whiff of a nineteenth-century ethos about them, reflecting the notion of the woman as the keeper of morality, whose virtue could redeem a sinful man. Something more harsh and realistic was on the way. In the fall of 1930, two movies arrived in theaters that almost got it right: *Doorway to Hell* and *The Widow from Chicago*.

The important innovation of *Doorway to Hell* was simple and inevitable. It put the gangster's story squarely at the center of a movie. This made dramatic sense. Gangsters, after all, did the most dramatic things and had the snappiest dialogue. (In 1928, *The Lights of New York*, the first all-talking picture, had contributed the new era's first catch-phrase, and it was a gangster's line: "Take him for a ride.") Even if we ignore the temper of the times, the interests of drama alone would make it inevitable that movies would start focusing on gangsters as principal characters for screen treatment. And not watered-down, heart-of-gold gangsters, either, but real tough guys.

Doorway to Hell did that. It followed a young mobster from Chicago, and when he was dead, the movie was over. Baby-faced Lew Ayres, all of twenty-one, played Louie, a sharpie who brings the rival Chicago factions together by terrifying them, then holds them together with his modern talent for organization. Here was the mobster as businessman, the mobster as gifted young man, the mobster as cheerful, cocky kid. Ayres's clean-cut look garnered sympathy for this fellow taking the speed lane to hell. It also put him in favorable contrast to the tired middle-aged cop (Robert Elliott), who goes through the movie lumbering and sour, with an unbecoming lust to see Louie in a pine box.

The movie had colorful gangster lingo—rivals bumped off were said to have been given "a handful of clouds," referring to the smoke that comes out of a gun. But the movie had a drawback, not significant enough to prevent *Doorway to Hell* from becoming a smash hit, but enough, in retrospect, to consign the film to the historical margins: Ayres wasn't scary. He seemed confident, yes, but too confident, almost complacent. He lacked the rage, the sense of underlying injury, the thirst for some twisted notion of justice—the specific characteristics that might drive a young dynamo to leap into the moral abyss.

Or to put it another way, Ayres was no Edward G. Robinson. A month after *Doorway to Hell*, *The Widow from Chicago* opened, and audiences got a chance to see how a movie gangster should act.

ROBINSON HAD BEEN born Emmanuel Goldenberg thirty-seven years earlier in Bucharest, Romania. Short, stocky, and not handsome— an immigrant from New York's Lower East Side—he had the nerve to think he could become an actor and got a scholarship to the American Academy of Dramatic Arts. Upon graduation, he made the rounds to casting agents, saying, "I'm not much on face value, but when it comes to stage value, I'll deliver." One can almost hear him saying it.

Gradually, Robinson became a successful working actor on Broadway. *New York Times* critic Alexander Woollcott was calling Robinson "an excellent actor" as early as 1920, when Robinson was mainly appearing in supporting roles. He emerged as a star in 1927, with a play called *The Racket*, playing, for the first time, a gangster. Robinson only looked the part. He was a man of sensitivity and refinement, an art collector from his early days, and a pacifist, who, in one presidential election, voted for socialist Norman Thomas. In his youth, Robinson had considered becoming a rabbi.

By 1930, Robinson, a stage success with a few minor films on his résumé, was offered a three-year, $1 million contract to sign with Metro-Goldwyn-Mayer. The money was good. The snag was that MGM production chief Irving Thalberg demanded a full commitment from Robinson, who wanted four months off each year to do theater.

Thalberg wouldn't budge, so Robinson turned down the offer—and upon leaving the building, he went into a savage fit of vomiting that necessitated his being helped to his car. He'd just butted heads with a titan and kissed off a million dollars.

He'd made the right move, though for the wrong reason. Contrary to what Robinson expected, the stage would no longer be important in his life. But refusing MGM left him free to sign with Warner Bros., a move that had ramifications for the studio and for cinema for decades. Robinson would soon become one of the actors who defined and exemplified the Warners style—snappy, urban, and hard-hitting.

In *The Widow from Chicago*, his first film for Warners, Robinson was cast as Dominic, a nightclub-owning racketeer. "What in the name of God was I doing playing a vice baron named Dominic?" Robinson wrote in his autobiography. "What in hell did I know about a vice baron with a passion for nightclubs?" He didn't need to know. He knew in his bones. Though not yet a film star, Robinson as Dominic was utterly in command as a presence and a personality.

Robinson's ability to convey anger, fearlessness, and composure—soon to become required traits for movie gangsters—was in evidence in an early scene. A rival mobster, accompanied by two goons, barges into his office. Robinson acts conciliatory, then pulls a revolver from a cigar box and tells them to get lost. He is the picture of cold-blooded success—well-dressed, impeccably groomed, unsmiling.

Robinson's performance heralded a new breed of screen gangster, one who didn't pretend to be nice and whose very appeal was tied to his competence and brute force. Yet *The Widow from Chicago* was a story in the old pattern. It followed the title character, Alice White, as a woman undercover, trying to find out who killed her brother. Guess who did it?

Though in a supporting role, Robinson made a strong impact. He remains impassive as White tries to get a rise out of him, insulting him for being short ("You can chin yourself on a curbstone"). Later, she changes tactics and flirts with him, but he's just as unmoved. "Now you're not smart," he says with a hint of disgust. "All that hooey you pull on the other guys don't go with me."

As Dominic, Robinson knows all the tricks, all the games, all the manipulations of selfish human nature. This makes him frightening, since the pleasingly daffy White—who really doesn't seem bright—goes through the movie trying to outsmart him. Robinson's authority in *The Widow from Chicago* compels and attracts, and the film never undercuts him. Even when he exits in handcuffs, he remains a man on a grand scale. "Not a few among the audience," wrote the *New York Times* critic, "may have regretted that . . . such inferior opponents should be the instruments for bringing this giant of the underworld to his knees."

Clearly, the public was primed to love the gangster, and the tougher the better.

IN JANUARY 1931, as audiences lined up for blocks to see *Little Caesar*, the *Variety* critic noted the sudden change that had come about in the depiction of racketeers:

> Treatment of crime as picture material has changed radically. Old criminal characters were instilled with a desire for coin and bloody spoils. The modern criminal, in films and public life, thirsts primarily for power. It's bootlegging that gives him momentum, and there doesn't seem to be much objection or there is admiration over bootlegging as a play quest. The wayside killings, bump-offs and rides are just incidental. The chief murderer's power quest is what makes him so interesting.

Mervyn LeRoy, the director of *Little Caesar*, had anticipated the public mood. He'd told Robinson that the title character, Rico, "was a great man, a powerful man who knew what he was doing, but was not always a villain." Robinson himself considered the movie a kind of "Greek tragedy." This wasn't just the story of some freak-of-nature menace.

At the beginning of the film, Rico is like any other great man still unrecognized in his time. We meet him in an all-night diner, which is seen at first in a long shot across the length of a counter. It's another lonely, nowhere place where men pass their hours, as confining as the inside of a submarine. The confinement is a visual metaphor for Rico's state of mind.

Rico sits with his best friend, Joe (Douglas Fairbanks, Jr.), who dreams only of good clothes and women. Joe would rather be a dancer than a crook. But for Rico, crime is a calling. He has just pulled a gas-station job, but it means nothing to him, because he's still just a mug, all his talent going to waste. Like an actor stuck in the provinces, Rico longs to test his metal in "the big town." It's understood that for Rico, with no connections and no education, just brains and a cast-iron nerve, crime is the fastest avenue to the American dream.

Whether playing gangsters, gamblers, or businessmen, Robinson consistently portrayed outsiders who longed for financial comfort and status—and usually achieved it, and enjoyed possessing it, even when they had little or no inner resources to appreciate the fruits of their striving. Robinson himself understood burning ambition. Later, in 1931, he would return to New York, the home of his humble beginnings, and find that he'd become a movie star. Disguised, sitting in the back of a taxicab, he saw his name on a massive marquee, in twelve-foot letters stretching the length of a city block—and cried, realizing that he'd made it.

In *Little Caesar*, Robinson wants success for its own sake, for what it will say to other people about his worth—and also for what it will say to him. He becomes the second-biggest crime boss in the big town, and he's within reach of the top. Yet he blows it all, finding it empty without the companionship of his friend Joe, who has left the rackets to become a ballroom dancer. If Rico is a classical hero with a fatal flaw, the flaw is not his ambition, which never fails him, but his inner motives, of which he is only partly aware.

When *Little Caesar* was released, W. R. Burnett, who wrote the novel upon which it was based, sent a letter complaining to producer Hal Wallis that Warner Bros. had turned Rico into a homosexual. In Burnett's book, Rico and Joe had no history of friendship. In fact, they didn't like each other. In the book, Rico saw Joe as too soft and didn't trust him for a minute. Yet in the movie, Rico's obsession with Joe brings about his downfall.

The homosexual element in *Little Caesar* isn't a matter of reading tea leaves. It's unmistakable. At his peak, Rico lives in splendor in a luxury apartment. His adoring assistant, Otero (George E. Stone), who looks at him with eye-batting admiration, seems to live there, too. Otero has replaced Joe, but how could George E. Stone ever take the place of Douglas Fairbanks, Jr.? So Rico asks to see Joe, who has gone straight and fallen in love with his dance partner.

Rico doesn't approve of the dancing stuff. "You're getting to be a sissy," he says. He wants Joe to drop the girl, give up dancing, and become his right-hand man. "Who else have I got to give a hang about? I need you, Joe." When Joe refuses, Rico explodes. "That Jane of yours can go hang. One of us has gotta lose, and it ain't gonna be me. . . . You go back to that dame, and it's suicide, suicide for both of you." Yet later, when he has a chance to kill Joe, he can't do it, even though now his own survival is at stake. Running through the streets, a wanted man, where just a few hours before he'd been a king, he grumbles, "This is what I get for liking a guy too much."

Observing the homosexual undercurrent in *Little Caesar* is too easy. The real question is, What is it doing there? We might suspect that, in a 1930 film, it would be used to add to the depravity of Rico's nature, but it doesn't function that way. If Rico's sexuality is a form of weakness, it's a humanizing weakness. It keeps him from being an ambition machine. It also provides an extra reason why Rico is presented as a teetotaler. He needs to keep a tight rein on his inner self, even if he doesn't quite know why.

The novel, *Little Caesar*, was about a man who climbed to the top by applying unsparingly the ethos of American capitalism. He was Andrew Carnegie or the young Ben Franklin, but twisted. The film had that element, too, but it ventured into yet more sophisticated territory. Rico's suppressed love for Joe helped make the point dramatically: To succeed, Rico must deny a part of himself. Indeed, that very denial, the energy created as a result of that suppression, fuels his drive. The book was about cruelty at the heart of capitalism. The movie, going one better, was about the tragic incompleteness of a successful capitalist.

Little Caesar was the first film to make an unvarnished bad-guy gangster into a hero. And hero he was. Only heroes get death scenes with curtain lines like, "Mother of Mercy, is this the end of Rico?" To see such a moment, no one but a maniac—or a pre-Code cop—could think, Oh, good, he's dead. Audiences certainly accepted Rico as a hero. Some even considered him a role model. Two years later, a pro-censorship book, *Our Movie-Made Children*, would cite cases of young punks who copied Robinson's style of dress and insisted that their friends call them "Little Caesar" (even though Rico didn't call himself that.) The young men came to a bad end.

But not Robinson, who went from triumph to triumph. From the beginning of his stardom, he never found himself locked into gangster roles. His coarse-featured face was, against all odds, a flexible instrument, capable of rage, gentleness, spiritual loftiness, even beauty—though, surprisingly enough, never cruelty. In retrospect, it's surprising that many of the gangster actors who emerged in the pre-Codes would go on to prove themselves not just vivid types but screen actors of the highest order.

Not the least of these was Spencer Tracy, who scored his first important movie success playing a gangster in *Quick Millions* (1931), Fox Film's answer to *Little Caesar*. Tracy, like Robinson a prominent stage actor who entered movies after the coming of sound, arrived on-screen fully formed, already in possession of that ease and naturalness that would make him the envy of his colleagues for decades. In *Quick Millions*, he was a trucker who achieves power by starting a protection racket but who ultimately meets his downfall when he tries to go straight and his gang won't let him.

For James Cagney, it was *The Public Enemy* (1931) that provided the chance to barge into the public's consciousness. The film was not only a sensation in its time but, like *Little Caesar*, went on to become one of the elite pre-Code films that have never really gone away. It has been revived in theaters, shown frequently on television, and excerpted in documentaries. By now, it's a cultural reference point. Thus, anyone who knows anything about movies has seen James Cagney hitting Mae Clarke in the face with a grapefruit—or has seen him staggering and collapsing in the rain, muttering, "I ain't so tough."

Yet all this familiarity and legendary status, not to mention our memories and affection for Cagney, can make it difficult to view *The Public Enemy* with fresh eyes or conceive of what it was like to see the film in its own time. As Tom Powers, Cagney played nothing less than the impish, smiling, fresh-scrubbed face of evil. To realize this is to be startled at just how far the public had come in its willingness to see the villain as hero.

Compared to Cagney in *The Public Enemy*, Robinson in *Little Caesar* was a prince. Rico never killed anyone out of spitefulness, while Tom kills for pleasure. (He even kills a horse he has a grudge against.) Rico was a thinker, a planner, a manager, while Tom was just a tough guy with a gun. Rico wasn't sadistic, while Tom can't keep the smirk off his face. When he gets his first gun, he gazes at it with rapt admiration. He loves power with the giddy enthusiasm of someone born powerless. That connects him with his audience, not just the audience of the early 1930s, but all kinds of audiences, everywhere and ever since.

Cagney's charm, of course, his ability to make even a sadistic thug just a little bit adorable, can't be underestimated. Playful and impulsive, he exhibits in virtually all his films the freedom of someone who knows he's lovable. He has the confidence of someone whom mother loved best. For all his wise-guy cynicism, Cagney's attitude rarely implied a bitter worldview, but, rather, a buoyant one—as though it were a grand thing to live in a world of pushovers.

Yet no amount of charm could have made *The Public Enemy* acceptable to audiences ten years before (even if there had been talkies). The gangster represented, for pre-Code audiences, a new attitude for a new time. He was a realist equipped for survival in the twentieth century, and he embodied traits moviegoers admired and wanted to emulate—not criminality, but skepticism; not cruelty, but strength, as well as a hostility to fake talk, an imperviousness to platitudes, and the courage to break with the pack.

The gangster was really breaking with the past, from Victorian morality and all it represented—pretense, convention, hypocrisy. Arriving, at first, in the safe disguise of a derby and a tight-fitting over-coat, the gangster was the new American man.

5

A New Kind of Man

THESE WERE EXCITING months in 1931. Hollywood's new wave of actors were refining screen personalities that would define the era and, in some cases, last for decades.

The actors started the year as heavies. But just as prosecutors often become defense attorneys when they become successful, so do bad guys switch to playing good guys when they become popular. This sort of thing had always happened, and continues to happen to this day, but in 1931, the change came in a telling way: When the pre-Code heavies started playing heroes, they didn't graduate into virtue. They stayed crooked, and the movies' concept of virtue kept pace with *them*. Soon America had a new crop of heroes who just a year or two before would have had to have been presented as villains.

A few years earlier, it had been axiomatic that good was good and bad bad. Now, in the thirties, it had become conventional and modish to talk about shades of gray. "All I'm trying to get across is realism," James Cagney would explain late in the decade. "The idea that heroes aren't always perfect gentlemen and villains aren't always stinking blackguards. They can come from the same mold." In a sense, Cagney was echoing Lon Chaney, who'd expressed similar thoughts in the 1920s.

Audiences who discovered James Cagney through *The Public Enemy* could have had no idea they were having a first encounter with a contemplative artist, one who developed new gestures and mannerisms for each character and worked at them with the dedication of a ballet dancer. Cagney was no punk. He gave a lot of thought to his acting. He was also interested in music and talked about social issues to a degree that was, for an actor of his day, unique.

In the months and years that followed *The Public Enemy*, Cagney would speak frankly to anyone holding a pad and pencil. The result is that, when read today, his statements transcend the pabulum of the typical Hollywood interview. As direct and honest in life as he was in art, he was also fearless. By the end of 1931, with only two starring roles behind him, he would strike against Warner Bros. for more wages.

Cagney had been trained on the stage. Yet as much as anyone, he understood the opportunities that the camera presented an actor, and he understood these opportunities before anyone thought to ask him about it. As an established star, he shared his insights about acting with a *Variety* reporter, who paraphrased his remarks in a December 1931 article:

> The screen . . . gives the greatest scope and is the best medium for an actor with intelligence. . . . What makes good acting here is the expression and feeling seen in an actor's face, and which express the thoughts going through his mind. If an actor can't think and has not a mind, he has a dead pan and is actually not capable of acting at all. . . . Today acting is reaching heights it never did before. People can talk of the old days, but the old school was a school of ranters and scenery chewers.

Cagney's actor's intelligence is apparent in the films he made before his stardom. If *Doorway to Hell* is remembered at all today, it is not for Lew Ayres's turn as the baby-faced gangster, but for the appearance of Cagney in the supporting role of Mileaway, Ayres's right-hand man. Cagney comes strutting into the movie as though someone forgot to tell him he wasn't the lead. He takes a throwaway sequence, in which he goes to various mob hangouts and tells everybody about an upcoming meeting, and turns it into a highlight. He accomplishes that by tossing in comic flourishes of a kind that would become his signature: He pulls a cigar from a mug's vest pocket, smells it, makes a face, and puts the cigar back where he found it. He's as beautiful in motion as Chaplin, and funny, too.

Cagney also showed his ability to do the thing he valued: think on-camera. An interrogation scene, in which Mileaway gets the third degree from a room full of cops, marks the turning point of the picture. They have nothing on him, and he knows it. Then the chief reveals that he knows that Mileaway has been having an affair with the mob boss's wife, and a look crosses Cagney's face, a synthesis of emotions too rich for analysis: surprise, anger, aggression, but mostly fear. When the chief further surprises him by demonstrating that he has proof of the affair, Cagney registers surprise, resentment, hopelessness. It's all in his face. The camera, like the cops, stays right on Cagney, all but breathing on him. Mileaway breaks down, while the actor thrives.

Cagney was born on the Lower East Side of Manhattan in 1899. He never forgot his origins, though, in his early years, he often forgot his birthday: Warners publicity for several years claimed he'd been born in 1904. His father was a lovable drunk who had trouble holding down a job and died when Cagney was a boy. His mother, a strong woman, whom Cagney apparently worshiped, held the family together.

Cagney grew up on the streets, where he learned to fight; and he swam in the East River, near where the city sewer opened up and raw sewage floated by. In his later years, his recollections took on a wistful-ness that might be mistaken for nostalgia, but in the thirties, his descriptions were colored more by his anger at poverty and social injustice. Cagney was young, new to success, perhaps marveling at his escape, and clearly wishing some good might come of it. He was a man of the people set loose in the dream factory, and to an extent, he saw himself that way. As early as 1931, *Movie Classic* talked of Cagney's passion for conversation, his habit of staying up late at night "threshing out the problems of economics and philosophy with his friends." His views were, according to the magazine, "extremely liberal."

Cagney's interviews complemented the films he made in the early 1930s, emphasizing their social context and providing a philosophical angle through which to view the tough guys and hustlers he played on-screen. "Sixty percent of the wealth of this country is controlled by one percent of the people," he complained to an interviewer in 1933. He went on to suggest, somewhat naïvely, that all political parties be scrapped "and merged into one, the Humanitarian Party, for the relief of mankind. . . . To forget platforms and remember the crying need for plenty."

He talked about life in the Manhattan slums, the sound of women being beaten by drunken husbands. He recalled the ambulances at night, the CONTAGION signs nailed to doorways, and the familiar sight of hearses riding up to a neighbor's door "to pick up some little body." On a number of occasions, before and during the Code, he returned to the grim memory of looking out his window, as a child, and seeing a school friend rummaging in garbage cans for something to eat. "It was my first contact with the fact that half the world starves while the other half gorges. I tell you, I grew old that minute. I felt sick. I couldn't eat all day. . . . You don't get over things like that. They eat the outer skin away." According to Cagney, that same school friend grew up to become a murderer and die in the electric chair. "Poverty was the exact cause of that old schoolmate of mine going to the chair. *Poverty*. Environment conditioned by the personalities surrounding him."

Another childhood friend, said Cagney, pulled a stickup, shot a cop, and was so kicked and mauled by the police who arrested him that he ended up in a wheelchair. Of these kids gone wrong, Cagney said, "They strike, blindly and bestially, at the blind and bestial forces which have, first, struck . . . blows at them."

While other leading men of the day seemed intent on registering as little impression as possible, Cagney in his public pronouncements had an agenda that went beyond the usual one of presenting a pleasant face. In interview after interview, he did three things: He made the case for the common man, he presented himself as one of their ranks, and then he demonstrated his sensitive and artistic nature. "I hate pain. I can't stand the sight of human suffering, mental or physical," he said in 1933. It's as if Cagney were trying, by his own example, to let the comfortable classes know just what riches of talent—or at least depths of feeling— lay within the ranks of the poor, suppressed by economic hardship. Interviewers consistently noted "his soft, whispering voice, his mild gentle manner" and "his warm and tender heart." He let them know that he took vocal lessons four days a week and owned guitars, a violin, and two pianos. "I play them all," said Cagney, "and all very badly."

In 1933, reporter Gladys Hall asked Cagney if he gave money to children who came up to him panhandling. Cagney said, "No," and left it at that. But she did a little digging and found out, through Cagney's friends, that the actor kept an open account at a Los Angeles restaurant and that whenever hungry kids approached him for a dime, he sent them there for a free meal.

To read such things, then and today, is to get a special angle on Cagney's performances. The actor had sympathy for the criminal because he knew and understood criminals. He had sympathy because he knew that with a different mother and with perhaps a few points

shaved off his IQ, he might have become one. Even monsters like Tom
Powers in *The Public Enemy* had to come from somewhere, and Cagney
knew firsthand they didn't come from hell. They came from his old
neighborhood.

A MONTH AFTER Cagney became anointed by *The Public Enemy*,
another actor blazed into stardom by way of a gangster role. In *A Free Soul*
(1931), Clark Gable—impossibly handsome, composed, and dangerous—
was Ace Wilfong, a San Francisco racket boss and the object of society
girl Norma Shearer's unwholesome lust. It was more than an auspicious
meeting of two charismatic actors. It was a meeting of two mythic
types, the sexualized new American woman and the new American
man—or, as Shearer puts it in the film, "a new kind of man in a new
kind of world."

As Ace, Gable was reasonable and manly early in the film, but it was
his later scenes, as a brute, that held a subversive allure for moviegoers.
Much was made of the moment when he shoves Shearer back onto a
couch saying, "Take it and like it." (One indicator of its impact is that,
years later, just about everyone who saw it incorrectly remembered that
he'd punched her.) Even better is the scene in which he shows up at her
hotel one morning, unshaven, and tries to muscle her into marrying
him immediately.

Director Clarence Brown trained the camera on Gable as the actor
alternated between threatening Shearer and threatening her would-be
fiancé, Leslie Howard. "Take a tip," Gable tells him. "Back out. Right
now. If you don't, you won't live long enough to start the honeymoon."
It was the misfortune of Howard, a genial and dapper lead, to have to
appear, here and in *Gone With the Wind*, as the rival of Gable—an actor
who had a way of making any man in the vicinity look like he should be
wearing a dress. Calm but smoldering, Gable seemed to be drawing from
some bottomless well of rage. The facade is stripped from this gangster,

and we see him for a homicidal fiend. Yet Gable was handsome enough that Ace didn't come across as repellent, but dynamic.

Today, Gable is remembered as an actor with an amiable smile and a mustache, but in 1931, there was no mustache and he didn't do much smiling. He was typed as a bad guy in his first roles. As a villain, he was cold and sly—and good-looking enough not to fall prey to women. His criminals were scarier than Robinson's or Cagney's, perhaps because nothing in his manner suggested a connection to some humble past that made him vulnerable or hungry. If the Gable gangster had a single weakness, it was an inexplicable hint of self-disgust, wholly not present in Cagney's crooks and, at most, only latent in Robinson's.

Robinson and Cagney seemed redeemable, while Gable—in films such as *Dance Fools Dance* (1931), *Night Nurse* (1931), and *A Free Soul*—seemed to understand himself to be a bad guy. He played men who had turned their backs not only on their past but on the capacity for kindness. Gable could do anything and feel nothing—including, as he does in *Dance Fools Dance*, forcing one man to kill another in cold blood.

In these films, Gable is a celebration of cruelty—in a way that's unapologetic and completely male. Often in films, cruelty is associated with androgyny—witness Charles Laughton's decadent, recumbent Nero in the 1932 film *The Sign of the Cross* (not to mention spooky asexual modern villains on the order of John Malkovich and Donald Sutherland). Gable embodied a masculine cruelty, and somehow this, combined with the gorgeousness of his face, became unjustifiably, incorrectly, and inarguably sexy.

The actor himself was a tough customer, the product of a forlorn, hardscrabble background. Born in Cadiz, Ohio, in 1901, he worked on the family farm as a boy. Leaving home as a teenager, he discovered, in Toledo, a fascination for theater. But the journey from initial enthusiasm to stage success had agonizing stops along the way: a two-year stretch cleaning out stills in an Oklahoma oil refinery; later, a stint in a lumber mill. The photos from these years show a Gable barely recognizable. He looks like a big-eared nobody, lost in the American heartland; a skinny fellow with horrible teeth and hair parted in the middle. Yet this youngster must have had some proto-Gable in him, because women consistently came to his rescue.

His first important girlfriend was Franz Dorfler, who, after appearing with him in a small theater production, took him home to Oregon, where her family more or less adopted him. In Oregon, he took private acting classes with a former New York actress, Josephine Dillon, who devoted herself to his career. Gable soon married her, even though she was seventeen years his senior. By 1925, Dillon's training began to pay off. Gable started getting good roles in touring productions starring prominent actresses, such as Jane Cowl (fourteen years his senior) and Pauline Frederick (eighteen years his senior). Gable had affairs with both.

With the exception of Dorfler, Gable's women had two things in common: They were considerably older, and they were in the position to foster his career. They helped get their boy to Broadway, where he met wealthy socialite Ria Langham during his run in the show *Machinal*. Langham got him to Hollywood. She helped provide financial backing for the Los Angeles production of the play *The Last Mile*, which served as a showcase for Gable, who played Killer Mears (the role that had put Spencer Tracy on the map in New York). Screen tests followed. After a couple of rejections due to his protruding ears—and a role as a villain in the Pathé Western *The Painted Desert*—Gable landed a six-month contract at MGM. Langham, forty-six to his twenty-nine, became his second wife.

The Gable that went before the camera in late 1930 to film *Dance Fools Dance* was a man's man, the product of many hard knocks, with a surface both rough and smooth; a man comfortable with women but perhaps nurturing a grudging sense of inner compromise. He hit it off immediately with costar Joan Crawford, and no surprise—both were from the heartland and both had endured hardship and degradation to reach this point in their lives.

Gable had a busy first year. For Warners, he played the heavy, Nick the chauffeur, in *Night Nurse,* in which he plots to starve two little girls to death and collect their insurance. Along the way, he punches out their nurse, Barbara Stanwyck. Also for Warners, he appeared in *The Finger Points,* as the mobster who entices journalist Richard Barthelmess onto the mob payroll.

MGM's answer to the gangster trend, *The Secret Six,* opened in April of 1931, with Gable in a good-guy role as an honest journalist who does what Barthelmess should have done in *The Finger Points*: He turns down mob money. Gable's refusal makes for a memorable, though slightly ambiguous, moment. Wallace Beery, a gang leader, offers him four one-thousand-dollar bills because he's "a pal." This brings on the Gable smile, for the first time on-screen in all its bemused irony. "I'm one of the pals," he says. "Say, that's great, pal."

If *The Secret Six* hinted at Gable's star power, *A Free Soul,* released in June, proved it, and so, in August, he was given star billing in *Sporting Blood.* MGM knew that audiences that thrilled to Gable's shoving Shearer and bullying Leslie Howard did not want to see him play an upstanding citizen. So for his first good-guy starring role, and the first in which he was given star billing, Gable was cast as a gambler. The world of gambling was a convenient halfway house for a bad-guy actor trying to reform.

Considering how huge a star Clark Gable went on to become, it's surprising that *Sporting Blood* isn't better known. It was a milestone in his ascent and presents us with the first full distillation of the Gable hero on-screen. In addition, it's a better-than-average film about an unusual subject, animal abuse, which is used as a launching point to investigate other forms of subjugation.

The central character was a racehorse, Tommy Boy, whose idyllic early years are just a prelude for a series of calamities. As an adult, he is sold to a pair of rich dilettantes, who in turn offer the horse as payment for a gambling debt. This puts Tommy Boy at the mercy of a big-shot gambler, who gets the idea to put the animal on amphetamines and race him into the ground.

Five months earlier, Gable might have been cast as the heartless gambler, but things had changed by mid-1931. Here, Lew Cody played the big shot and Gable plays Rid, a card dealer in the gambler's casino, who also happens to be in love with his boss's desperate, hard-drinking mistress, Ruby (Madge Evans). The movie goes out of its way to make the parallel between Ruby and the horse—both are trapped, miserable, and addicted to stimulants. *Sporting Blood* is a movie about enslavement—women's enslavement to men, men's to other men, animals' to people. Rid and Ruby have nothing but what they get from the gambler, and they are as trapped as the horse.

Gable goes through the film with the knowing cynicism of a man who has spent enough time in the mud to have no illusions. He understands the status quo, knows the soulless idiots who maintain it, and can't be impressed or outraged. That attitude is present in Gable's bearing from the moment he appears on-screen. In a way, it was who he was as an actor. Rid is a prototype for every affable rogue he ever played.

Picture Play called Gable "dangerous as ever" in *Sporting Blood,* but to watch him, it's clear he did everything he could to make sure no one mistook him for a villain this time. Late in the film, Madge Evans gets possession of the horse and takes him to the country, where they can both dry out and regain their strength. Gable comes to visit, and in an unusually lengthy tracking shot, Gable and Evans talk pleasantly as they enjoy the country atmosphere. Gable spends the entire four minutes of the shot grinning and beaming. It almost hurts your face to watch him.

Cagney, Robinson—and pre-Code marvels who'd soon emerge, such as Warren William and Lee Tracy—played megalomaniacs, peacocks, and dynamos: They played men striving to make their mark, who not only believed but assumed without thinking that a mark was something worth making. Not Gable. He had a modesty—not the bashful, blinking modesty of an old-fashioned hero like Gary Cooper, but a cynical modesty. Gable's heroes saw too much to believe *anything* was important, except maybe the moment they were in or the feelings of people they liked. Certainly they didn't think of themselves as important. Imagine Gable playing *Little Caesar* (which Mervyn LeRoy at one point had considered). Imagine Gable asking, "Is this the end of Rico?" It's unthinkable.

Gable's on-screen modesty was emphasized in his publicity, though some of it undoubtedly had an element of calculation about it, a "don't hate me because I'm beautiful" quality. In life, he was a notorious worrier, a brooder, a heavy drinker, who fretted constantly about his roles and his career. In his public statements, he masked his fretfulness with a philosophical air. "Four or five years ago," he said in 1931, "they couldn't even give me a chance as an extra. . . . I suppose styles in actors change just like styles in clothes and plays and things. . . . I just wasn't the type then. Perhaps I am now. . . . But if I wasn't then, and I am now, why, I may not be a year from now."

Sporting Blood was the first film to capture not just Gable's allure but also his mystery. In the end, he saves the horse and gets the girl, but, as is often the case with Gable, one wonders why he does it. We know he feels something, but how much does he feel? We know he cares about the woman, but how much? Are his emotions too strong for him to express? Or is he, at heart, lovably simple, a man running on instinct who's not that deep, not that smart, maybe even a little superficial? Mysteries don't go out of style. The Gable enigma would keep audiences off balance and hovering around his image for the rest of his life.

• • •

EDWARD G. ROBINSON also found in the gambling world his chance
to go straight, sort of. In *Smart Money* (1931), he introduced and per-
fected a type he'd play again and again—the small-town fellow who
makes it in the big city. It would become a familiar scene in Robinson's
pre-Codes, no matter what he played, a criminal, businessman, or combination of both: It was the scene in which the protagonist finally
makes it in his own eyes and, dressed in a slightly too formal suit, he
struts down the street with his spats and cigar, smiling at everyone. And
everyone thinks, "Who's the rube?"

Robinson's heroes gloried in their success and took pride in the money
they made. Dollar figures were prominent in his films. We know that
the fisherman he played in *Tiger Shark* (1932) made $14,000 a year and
the construction worker he played in *Two Seconds* (1932) made $62.50
a week. We know because they tell us. In the comedy *The Little Giant*
(1933), we know how much the former bootlegger (Robinson) spends
per night at the Santa Barbara Biltmore (an outrageous $45 a night),
and how much money he loses in a shady business deal ($300,000). We
know how much he spends to pay off his mistress ($25,000); his secre-
tary's weekly salary ($100 a week); and the amount he pays to rent a
twenty-room mansion in Santa Barbara ($1,450 a month).

A Robinson hero wants his picture in the paper and his name known
by all. "Do you know who I am?" he asks everyone in *Smart Money*. He
played Nick Venezelos, a small-town barber with a knack for gambling.
He comes to the city to get into the "big game" and, after getting
fleeced, turns the tables on the con men and becomes the city's biggest
gambler. Known as Nick the Barber—the film's nod to real-life gamblers Nick the Greek and John the Barber—he uses a barbershop as the
front for a luxurious gambling joint.

In *Smart Money*, Nick may run an illegal empire—with the assistance of strong-arm man James Cagney. Yet he's practically a saint, friendly and generous, while the district attorney (Morgan Wallace) is a party hack who wants to put him in jail. The DA's motive isn't one of principle. He wants to imprison Nick so that "the public and the press will lay off me." When Nick takes in a waif and nurses her back to health, the DA sees his chance. He coerces the girl into betraying Nick by threatening to prosecute her for an earlier offense. It's a pattern seen often in pre-Codes. Bureaucrats are corrupt, law-enforcement officials are malicious, and the supposedly respectable people are the least honest of all.

Two years later, in *The Little Giant*, Robinson would find more treachery in polite Santa Barbara society than he had in the bootlegging racket. "The toughest mug in Chicago comes out here," he complains, "and gets trimmed by a lot of fags with handkerchiefs up their sleeves." In the pre-Code hierarchy of iniquity, the government came first and the rich came second. Crooks were to be guarded against, but beware of the treachery and cruelty of the so-called good guys. They were the worst.

Though his steel inevitably would reveal itself, Robinson liked to show the soft side of his streetwise characters. He played romantics, middle-aged men who were often lovelorn, gregarious, openhearted, and either awkward or overly giving when it came to women. He was the only tough guy to make an air of gullibility an element of his screen personality. The Robinson hero could see through his adversaries, but he was helpless before his friends and loved ones.

In *Smart Money*, Warners cast Robinson together with Cagney for the obvious reason—to cash in on the interest generated by *Little Caesar* and *The Public Enemy*. The idea of the screen's two big gangsters in one big film had its appeal. Yet the universes of Robinson and Cagney were mutually exclusive. In *Smart Money*, Cagney had a minor role, and in retrospect, he could *only* have had a minor role. Had he been in every scene, he'd have been warning Robinson away from all the people he should distrust. He'd have been saving Robinson from his destiny— or he wouldn't have been Cagney. Far from gullible, Cagney's wise guys reacted with an animal delight in watching their lessers try to fool them and fail.

Cagney himself took wing as a star and a personality in the films that followed *The Public Enemy*. Few actors have been as fun to watch. Though Cagney maintained his incandescent spirit throughout his life, just as he maintained his thick head of hair, there is a difference between pre-Code and post-Code Cagney, and it's like the difference between cats and kittens. The rambunctiousness, humor, and mischief that the young Cagney brought to his early stardom is still a delight and a wonder—and never more than in *Blonde Crazy* (1931), which, like *Sporting Blood* for Gable, was Cagney's first starring role as an almost-good guy. To be sure, he was aided by Kubec Glasmon and John Bright's snappy screenplay—"My name is Bert; call me Albert for short"—but the invention and vitality came from the actor.

In *Blonde Crazy*, Cagney played a hotel bellhop—just the sight of him in the uniform is comical—who works every kind of angle to get an edge. He swindles, sells bootleg whiskey, and blackmails, and he does it all with a smart-aleck joy. "The world owes me a living," he tells Joan Blondell, who becomes his partner in crime. "The age of chivalry is dead. This is the age of chiselry."

Cagney often said that one of the secrets of screen acting was "never relax. If you relax, the audience relaxes." Here, his energy is nonstop. As he talks to the middle-aged matron in charge of linens, he plays with the ruffles on her blouse. It's an unconscious form of flirting, or selling—he is constantly dealing, trying to work people, playing an angle. With Blondell, his ideal costar, he is relentlessly on the make. "I was in such a hurry when I bought the [train] tickets," he says, "I just got one compartment." Several times, she slaps him, and he laughs like hell.

Yet for all his boisterousness, Cagney can also bring a naturalism that one doesn't expect in a 1931 film. In a hotel nightclub, he interrupts a maudlin turn in the conversation by saying to Blondell, "But come on, we're getting too serious. Let's dance"—tossing off the line with an ease that feels so real and modern that he could be sitting in your living room.

Blonde Crazy is a testament to the impishness of Cagney and of the era in general. When, in a fight over him, Polly Walters slaps Blondell; whereupon, Blondell slaps Walters and knocks her down; whereupon, Cagney laughs hysterically—well, that's pre-Code. And when Walters picks herself up from the floor and wallops *him*, that's pre-Code, too. It's also anarchy.

There's a point where a movie's wildness tilts into philosophy, a way of viewing reality. We can see that in the pre-Code films of the Marx Brothers, whose point of entry was the mutual understanding, on the part of the filmmakers and their audience, that everything was absurd—not only institutions but the language through which we process that absurdity. In *Blonde Crazy*, the world is mad and "honest men are as scarce as feathers on a frog." Crooks scam innocent suckers and even rob one another. And the supposed heroes aren't. *Blonde Crazy* is another pre-Code in which crooks are seemingly everywhere, and yet the biggest crook—the only despicable character—is the upright, upper-class businessman (Ray Milland) whom Blondell decides to marry instead of Cagney. Milland, a young man from the usual fine family, gets in trouble for embezzling. When Cagney tries to help him by faking a robbery, the fine young man double-crosses him. He calls the police, and Cagney lands in jail for the other guy's theft.

In pre-Codes, the embezzler was the pariah, a child molester among shady types. To be an embezzler, like Milland in *Blonde Crazy*, meant you had a job to begin with, probably a high-paying one, and just got greedy, and sneaky. To be a sneak was only pathetic, and to be a sneak who manages to fool the cops and pin the crime on someone else—it would be hard to imagine anything lower. The all-out street gangster at least put it all on the line—it took guts to go into a bank with a gun and knapsack. So long as a character had courage and steadfastness, pre-Code audiences could overlook a lot.

BY THE END of 1931, the attitude, the lingo, and the larceny that moviegoers had associated with gangsters at the beginning of the year had gone mainstream. Most heroes had a touch of the gangster in them, and gangster elements had found their way into other genres. For example, several women's picture/gangster movies made it to the screen that year, such as *Bad Company*, with Helen Twelvetrees as the wife and sister of gangsters; *The Guilty Generation*, a *Romeo and Juliet* story with a gangster background, starring Constance Cummings; and *The Good Bad Girl*, with Mae Clarke as a former moll who dumps her gangster lover.

With the gangster genre already diffusing into other areas, *Scarface* opened in April 1932. It doesn't feel like a 1932 film, but, rather, like an answer to and an amplification of *Little Caesar* and *The Public Enemy*. In fact, a rough cut of *Scarface* was ready by September 1931; only the complaints by state censor boards kept the movie from reaching the screen before the end of the year.

Arriving in theaters when it did, *Scarface* represented both a throwback and an advance. It was a throwback in that, as was common in the twenties, it presented the gangster as an irredeemable villain. Yet placing such a repellent figure—worse than Cagney's Tom Powers and without Cagney's charm—at the center of a film constituted, in itself, an innovation. Directed by Howard Hawks and played to the hilt by Paul Muni, *Scarface* is the least compromising of the gangster movies. It makes no effort to be warm and fuzzy, and the grimness is unrelieved by humor. With the exception of *Beast of the City* (1932)—which ends in a protracted massacre—*Scarface* was the most violent film of the era.

Gangster movies often came with a disingenuous introduction, which pretended to cast the nasty goings-on in a socially uplifting light. *Scarface* does the same, and yet there's an element of truth to the idea of it as an antigangster gangster movie. The audience isn't invited to root for Tony Camonte (Muni) so much as to observe him as a pathological case. He has courage. He has lusts. He has a ravenous ambition, and he's a little bit crazy. In *Little Caesar*, Rico's implied homosexuality was an undercurrent that, if anything, lent the protagonist humanity. Perhaps taking inspiration from that, the *Scarface* screenwriters gave Tony an incestuous obsession with his sister Cesca (Ann Dvorak)—one not even hinted at in the Armitage Trail novel upon which it was based. In *Scarface*, the forbidden lust, not covert as in *Little Caesar*, is not presented sympathetically but, rather, as the most vivid manifestation of Tony's moral depravity.

The depravity leads to the implosion of what little personal life he has—he kills his best friend (George Raft) when he finds him in Cesca's apartment. He doesn't wait long enough for one of them to tell him they've married. What makes the situation doubly sick is that it's not all that clear the result would have been any different if he had.

Scarface has the feel of being the last of its kind, the ultimate pre-Code expression of the gangster as a type. (This is easy to say, of course, since it *was* the last of its kind, but it's still true.) *Scarface* has more of everything—more violence, more harshness, more perverseness, and yet less appeal. And though the carping of the state censors may have had a lot to do with the cessation of gangster films, to watch *Scarface* is to get the sense that this was not where the art wanted to go.

The appeal of the gangster movies had less to do with gangsters and more to do with what the movies said between the lines. In 1932, Hollywood would find more direct ways of expressing modern-day restlessness and cynicism.

6

'I'm in Hell"

L ON CHANEY'S DEATH in August 1930 robbed the world of the screen's first pre-Code man. At the dawn of an era he had helped create and at the pinnacle of his powers, the forty-seven-year-old Chaney left the scene just as reality was beginning to swing in his fantastic direction.

In the twenties, gangster and horror films had found their most vivid expressions in his work. These silent films anticipated future genres and moods—darker, less sure, more fearful. They also anticipated new kinds of heroes, men who were conflicted, imperfect, even tormented and weak. In hell. The loss of an artist of Chaney's stature, with the pre-Codes about to blossom and horror soon to rule the box office, is beyond calculation. It's as if Greta Garbo were to have died in 1930. There's no telling where he might have taken film had he lived, say, just five more years.

Chaney left behind only one talkie, *The Unholy Three* (1930), a remake of his 1925 silent of the same name. It was a conservative choice of tried-and-true material, but then Chaney had been reluctant to leap into sound, understandably afraid it might rob him of mystery.

The picture, designed to showcase the actor's vocal versatility, cast him as Professor Echo, a carnival ventriloquist who disguises himself as an old lady in order to hide from the authorities. Joined by a circus strongman and a midget disguised as a baby, the trio commits robberies, while using a bird store as a front for their operations.

The film's sentimental side was in keeping with previous Chaney films. Echo is in love with Rosie (Lila Lee), his partner in crime, but she loves an innocent young clerk. The picture ends with Echo's giving the young lovers his blessing, then gallantly waving from a train en route to prison. It was Chaney's last appearance on-screen.

Chaney had never shied from depicting unthinkable and unbearable degrees of mental anguish. "Feast your eyes, glut your soul on my accursed ugliness," the Phantom of the Opera had exclaimed, in what was more a mad expression of misery than an attempt to terrify. Chaney's villains hated themselves, while their awe and love for beauty and innocence left them vulnerable and ultimately doomed. Thus, Chaney's films—however grim and chilling, however much they presaged pre-Code horror—bespoke a universe that at least had an underlying order. Chaney's art, for all its bizarre terrors and unsettling unconscious shadows, was ultimately reassuring.

The pre-Codes changed that, and the change came within months of Chaney's death. In this new world, beauty and innocence could no longer be counted on to defeat evil. The world of pre-Code cinema was much more haphazard and strange—and tragic. We all know the classic example from *Frankenstein* (1931), in which the monster befriends a little girl who is throwing daisies into a lake. The monster, getting into the spirit, throws the little girl into the lake, and she drowns. He is not trying to do evil, and the girl's innocence is no protection against the monster's fluke impulse. The situation is merely senseless and dreadful.

The cycle of pre-Code horror began with *Dracula*, released in February 1931 and directed by Tod Browning, Chaney's best collaborator. Browning had wanted Chaney for the role, and for decades there has been speculation about whether Chaney, who was at MGM, would have been able to star in this Universal film had he lived. Chaney's biographer Michael F. Blake raises strong doubts, but if it had happened, it would have been fascinating. How would Chaney have inhabited a new moral universe, playing a man not just in hell but *from* hell? How would he have played a fiend with power over innocence and beauty—a fiend capable of charming, seducing, and murdering Lucy (Frances Dade) and of luring his friend's daughter, Mina, into the hellish world of vampirism? It would have been a different Dracula, certainly, but it might also have been the beginning of a new Chaney.

Dracula is remembered today for nothing but Bela Lugosi in the title role, but it benefits also from the casting of Helen Chandler as Mina. Chandler, with her cat's eyes and scattered air, seems both dainty and corrupt, fragile and yet potentially demonic. Had the film been made three years earlier, Mina's innocence would have been strong enough to defeat Dracula, but these were more jaundiced days. Here Mina's virtue is too weak to resist his hypnotic power, and the only thing that saves her is practical action: Dr. Van Helsing shows up with a wooden stake and a hammer, and he knows what to do with them.

The very essence of *Dracula* was censorable, with its redolence of bisexuality and sexually transmitted disease. Dracula exchanged fluids with both men and women, leaving just enough of his own essence that his surviving victims became vampires, too. The transference seems in the nature of the act, not necessarily something Dracula does by choice—why create constant competition for a finite supply of nourishment? With *Dracula*, horror took a step beyond Chaney, beyond the notion of horror as being about the interaction of a hellish individual with a routine world. Dracula's existence did more than present the other characters with a practical problem (namely: How do we get rid of Dracula?). His existence presented a challenge to the character's—and to the audience's—conception of a benevolent God and a comprehensible universe.

With *Dracula*, American cinema stumbled upon a way to depict life on the absolute edge, one step from the abyss. The horror genre became a means of addressing ultimate moral concerns and subjects: heaven, hell, redemption, damnation, good, evil—and also blackness, emptiness, a malevolent universe, the existential void. It would be a mistake to regard horror movies as occurring within a bubble, as distinct and outside the mainstream of pre-Code cinema. They were not. They had much more in common with their era than their creators' willingness to test an audience's limits. Like the pre-Codes in general, horror delved into and attempted to define morality in all its modern shadings. The difference is that horror wore its soul on its sleeve.

It was a male genre. The movies were invariably about unhappy men. Women suffered from being in their company, and sometimes suffered at their hands, but the men were the ones in torment. *Frankenstein*, for one, presented audiences with two exceedingly miserable fellows: Dr. Frankenstein and his monster. As played by Colin Clive, Henry Frankenstein is frazzled and racked from the beginning. He thirsts for universal knowledge like a drying-out drunk who can all but see the phantom glass in his hand. He grimaces. He sweats. He suffers and finally succeeds. "It is alive!" He achieves God-like knowledge of creation, but his exultation is followed by a wicked hangover. Dr. Frankenstein hates it, but he can't stop being a scientist.

Frankenstein's monster has his own problems. In a world in which looks matter, he has clearly been sewn together from the parts of hideous individuals, no fun for a sensitive soul. He has also been endowed with the brain of a criminal, which makes him impatient when people recoil in horror at his appearance. It says something about the aesthetic limitation of the entirely scientific mind that Dr. Frankenstein could be so unattuned as to bring a man into existence without first giving him a face that might have made life bearable.

Instead, the monster enters life doomed to friendlessness, knowing not only that he will be destroyed but also—and this is where Karloff's painfully sensitive performance comes in—that he probably *should* be destroyed. The monster seems to intuit this. He cannot be fooled, unlike everyone else who has ever lived, about his own existential unworthiness. He can only be, at best, briefly distracted. Though primitive, he knows enough to have a terrible inkling—that he has no soul.

But does he? That is the metaphysical question every viewer of *Frankenstein* must consider. If the monster has a soul, how did he get it and at what point? When the lightning bolt brought him to life? Conversely, if he has no soul, we are then deep into the land of horror, a land in which science has the power to create life, but not life with any meaning or moral importance. From there, it's just a stone's throw to more disturbing ruminations: Perhaps our belief in life as some kind of divine infusion is merely a fiction to keep us from going crazy—a fiction that the monster, by his existence, threatens to debunk. The mere suggestion of that leaves no surprise as to why a whole town comes out to burn him alive.

This is horror, pre-Code style—not one focused on danger, on fear of a fellow in a ski mask with a knife or a chain saw; not one dedicated to stoking subconscious terrors. It's the horror of metaphysical moral questions.

We see another example of the trend in *Island of Lost Souls* (1932), based on the H. G. Wells story, "The Island of Dr. Moreau." The title change alone indicates the film's emphasis. Charles Laughton was ideally cast as a mad scientist on a jungle island who has devised a way to speed up evolution. By operating on various animals in his "house of pain," as it is called, he transforms these creatures into quasi-men. He keeps these creatures in line by providing them with a rudimentary religion, a code of laws that forbids violence and encourages them to behave like humans. "Are we not men?" the sayer of the law (Bela Lugosi) regularly asks his fellow forlorn hybrids.

"We are men," the sad, hairy fellows reply. They don't sound as if they like it.

Island of Lost Souls was as spiritually unsettling as *Frankenstein*, presenting a subversive parallel between the condition of the creatures and that of humanity in general. On his island, Moreau is a god, bringing humans into existence through a makeshift process of evolution. Only the creatures' faith in the rightness of the law handed to them—and their belief not only in the omnipotence but the righteousness of the doctor—keep them from giving way to savagery. That faith, we know, is misplaced. Their laws are nothing but arbitrary instructions, and their god a sadistic fraud who cares nothing for their welfare. The question is implicit: How sure are we that we're any better off?

For anyone willing to explore the implications of such films, the questions were terrible: Is God dead? Is God malevolent? Is morality nothing more than a self-imposed cage? Is the entire basis of our reality nothing more than a fiction? Horror cannot get more serious.

If *Frankenstein* made Hollywood safe for *Island of Lost Souls*, it also paved the way for Tod Browning's *Freaks* (1932). Unlike the creatures on Moreau's island, the freaks—pinheads, midgets, an armless, legless man, Siamese twins, et cetera—were played by real-life freaks, many of them circus veterans. Just the sight of them frightened audiences. According to one eyewitness, when the film previewed in a Los Angeles suburb, people didn't just walk out of the theater; they ran out. Even today, some find the film difficult to watch. The freaks were created by God, not Dr. Moreau, and their presence raises some of the same questions as the other horror films, less stridently but more vividly. One either shudders at what the freaks' existence might imply or sees the humanity, and the spark of divinity, inside them. Either way, *Freaks* challenges audiences as few movies ever have.

The picture takes a compassionate view of the freaks, who find their friendship and refuge in the circus. The villains are a pair of able-bodied lovers—an aerialist (Olga Baclanova), who marries a midget to steal his money; and her lover, Hercules (Henry Victor), a circus strongman. The two are foiled in their plot to kill the husband; whereupon the freaks close ranks, kill the strongman, and, in a fantastic touch, turn the aerialist into a freakish half-chicken creature.

It's possible that *Freaks*—banned in many cities, flattened by bad word of mouth in its own time—can best be appreciated today. Audiences of the 1930s were rather sqeamish, while decades later audiences are inured to gruesomeness practically from the crib. It's hard to imagine anyone finding much impulse to run screaming from the sight of the freaks today. Indeed, it doesn't take much to perceive their beauty. The balletic grace of the Siamese twins, for example, is a wonder, and the pure-heartedness of the pinheads is unmistakable and touching. Time has only increased the poignancy of the film, which, however much ahead of its time, was right in the pre-Code spirit: Freaks are human, and to be human is to be a freak.

The trend of subversive horror films expended itself by the end of 1932, with *Island of Lost Souls*, which was released in December of that year. The following spring, the return to the more familiar pattern was signaled by *King Kong* (1933), a kind of monster-movie version of a Lon Chaney picture. Kong was the master of his kingdom, and a tear through New York demonstrated his omnipotence, but he was brought down by his obsession for a young woman, played by Fay Wray, who, for his purposes, was too small to do anything but look at. Once again, a sexless awe for beauty is enough to reestablish order and eliminate the bad guy. Kong's epitaph—"It was beauty killed the beast"—might have been used for any number of Chaney heroes.

IT WOULD BE understandable for film lovers to look for descendants of Chaney in the horror genre. Karloff, the most obvious disciple, had the sensitivity, but he was more gentle than Chaney, and he lacked either Chaney's range or filmic opportunities to express it. While Chaney's films often turned on his relationships with women, Karloff remained, though brilliant and distinct in his own way, a rather asexual figure.

In the pre-Code era, Chaney's truest heir was Fredric March. Sixteen months after Chaney's death, *Dr. Jekyll and Mr. Hyde* (1931) saw March come into that legacy. A kind of Chaney for a secular age, March never made another horror film, but he carried on Chaney's tradition through the rest of the era, playing, without compromise, a series of anguished modern men who weren't monsters but who had monsters inside, threatening to drag them to the very bottom.

Dr. Jekyll and Mr. Hyde, which opened in New York on December 31, 1931, represented the apotheosis of the horror cycle. The adaptation of Robert Louis Stevenson's nineteenth-century tale became a receptacle for some of the more popular, enlightened ideas of the pre-Code era— ideas that had nothing to do with either Stevenson's tale or with previous film versions of the story.

Before March, the most well-known Dr. Jekyll had been John Barrymore, who starred in a silent version in 1920. Comparing the 1920 Barrymore version with the March film demonstrates how similar scenarios can be used to make completely different points. It also shows the changes in popular attitudes regarding sex and morality that had taken place in America over the course of barely more than a decade.

The Barrymore version was all about the failure of repression. The opening title reads, "In each of us two natures are at war—the good and the evil. All our lives the fight goes on between them, and one of them must conquer. But in our own hands lies the power to choose—what we want most to be, we *are*." It tells the story of an ostensibly virtuous doctor who is led into temptation by a cynical man of the world, who introduces him to bawdy nightlife and sensual pleasure. Thus weakened, when he drinks the potion, he gives in to a side of his nature he should have suppressed. The Barrymore *Dr. Jekyll* hails from the tail end of an era in which manhood was associated with self-mastery and control over sexual impulse.

The March version also blamed Dr. Jekyll's fall on sex but saw the situation from a different angle. The problem wasn't Jekyll. He was just a normal, healthy fellow. The problem was sexual starvation. Forced to endure an unnaturally protracted engagement to his true love, Muriel (Rose Hobart), he goes through life in a frenzy of bottled-up impulse. It's no surprise then that when he drinks the potion, all the stops are let out, and he becomes a wild beast out on a tear.

Ironically, the original Dr. Jekyll, the character in Stevenson's story, had no romantic problems whatsoever—he had no women in his life at all. In the story, he was an elderly man, whose Hyde persona was able to gain sway simply because the old man's virtue had been compromised by his own ego and ambition. If Hyde, as conceived by Stevenson, functioned as a metaphor, it had to do with drunkenness, not sexual release. Stevenson's Jekyll feels "younger, lighter, happier in body" in his Hyde incarnation. Sounding like a deluded drunk, he assures himself, "The moment I choose, I can be rid of Mr. Hyde."

For Stevenson, Hyde was a release from Jekyll's nonstop rigor and self-denial, his "life of effort, virtue and self-control." It was Stevenson's intuition to understand that the nineteenth-century pillars of masculine virtue—hard work, abstinence, repression—were built on sand. Sooner or later, the edifice had to fall.

The 1931 film, though set in the nineteenth century, presented a

Jekyll who was too much a twentieth-century fellow even to consider self-denial a worthy goal. In an early scene, on a London street, he comes to the rescue of a dance-hall girl, Ivy (Miriam Hopkins), and soon finds himself in her flat. She strips for him (the complete version of this sequence is surprisingly explicit), and moments later she is naked under a bedsheet, and he is kissing her. Only the arrival of Jekyll's straitlaced colleague, Lanyon, interrupts what looks to become a promising situation.

"You ought to control those instincts," Lanyon tells Jekyll as they leave Ivy's flat, to which Jekyll replies, "Are you pretending that you either can or do? We might control our actions but not our impulses."

"Perhaps you've forgotten you're engaged to Muriel," Lanyon says.

"Forgotten it?" Jekyll exclaims. "Can a man dying of thirst forget water? And you know what would happen to that thirst if it were denied water?" Jekyll's remarks verge on admitting he has either been seeing or has considered seeing prostitutes. The conservative Lanyon picks up on this—"You sound almost indecent!"—and the subject is dropped.

Dr. Jekyll and Mr. Hyde is one of a string of stunning works directed by Rouben Mamoulian in the early thirties. When he decided to make the film, he surprised his colleagues at Paramount by insisting on casting Fredric March in the lead role. Mamoulian's reasoning was as intriguing as it was undeniable: He didn't need someone monstrous to play Hyde. Anybody with a makeup job could do that. Mamoulian needed someone who could play Jekyll, who could convey that mix of light and dark, of confidence and desperation, that would allow him to take the potion in the first place.

The casting was inspired. March was not Colin Clive or Karloff or Lugosi in a black cape. He was a leading man and, on the surface, the essence of normality. Yet see March in *My Sin* (1931), which proceeded *Dr. Jekyll* by several months. March played an American lawyer, living in the tropics, who has gone so thoroughly to hell that he *starts* the film as an alcoholic beggar. We never get a flashback to see how he arrived at this state. We just have to accept that he got there. (Later, he begins the process of recovery by defending the village floozy, Tallulah Bankhead, on a murder charge.) *My Sin* revealed March's prime terrain as an actor: the inner depths. Those depths were Jekyll's psychic stomping ground, as well.

The first time Jekyll takes the potion, he does not know what will happen. There is no moral failing involved. He's just a scientist conducting an experiment. The potion transforms Jekyll into a Neanderthal-like menace, violent and threatening. And raving, "You hypocrites—you deniers of life—if you could see me now!" When he comes back to himself, his transformation alarms him, and, recognizing its cause, he goes to his fiancée and begs her to marry him immediately. Having experienced his own demon side, he is desperate, bursting with frustration— but she won't marry him without her father's consent, and that refusal sends Jekyll back for his second dose of the potion.

The sequence of events is worth noting; otherwise, *Dr. Jekyll and Mr. Hyde* could be mistaken for a commentary on scientific arrogance. In fact, the search for scientific truth does not lead Jekyll into trouble. The first time he takes the potion—or "drug," as he calls it—he gets the information he needs and escapes unscathed. It's the second dose, which he takes for recreation, that makes his case hopeless and makes him morally responsible for what follows. From that one reckless but understandable act, he ends up losing body and soul. He becomes unable to resist the return of Hyde. He murders Ivy and becomes a lost man.

The movie ends in Jekyll's defeat—he is killed by Lanyon, the essence of lifeless propriety—which has led some critics to mistake the ending as celebrating the return of the Victorian moral order. On the contrary, the film is a tragedy that places the blame for the hero's troubles on the repressive Victorian scheme within which the story plays out. It's a movie made for a public who'd spent the twenties either reading Freud or hearing enough of his ideas secondhand to come away with one fixed idea: Sexual repression—not good. "I know he's been suffering," Muriel tells her father. "And it's our fault, mine more than yours."

Indeed, the movie almost whitewashes Jekyll too much, threatening to reduce the tragedy to a case of "If only she'd had sex with him . . ." More importantly, it asserts the modern scientific man's understanding of nature over the stodgy Victorian man's assumptions about character. And it presents as the villain not Jekyll or even Hyde, but poor Halliwell Hobbes as Muriel's father, a stuffed shirt whose monumental crime is his stubborn refusal to move up his daughter's wedding day. The movie incites such a dislike of Hobbes—who even disapproves of Jekyll's charity work—that later, when we see Hobbes bludgeoned by Hyde, we don't root for Hyde to get caught, but for Hobbes to get pummeled.

It's March's ability to convey increasing desperation that keeps the audience on his side. Near the end, when Jekyll goes to Muriel to release her from their engagement, his guilt and hopelessness are complete. "What is it?" she asks him, and he answers, "What?"—more a grunt than a word. When she asks why he wants to break their engagement, he sobs, "I want you so I can envy the damned. I *am* damned. . . . I'm beyond help, Muriel." And in case she has any doubt, he gives her his psychological address, a location that March's predecessor Chaney had inhabited on many an occasion: "I'm in hell."

FREDRIC MARCH HAD a happy life for someone so expert at portraying torment. Born Frederick Bickel in Racine, Wisconsin, in 1897, he was the son of a banker and grew up assuming he would follow the same path. He was one of the most popular fellows in high school and also at the University of Wisconsin, where he became active in student government. Following graduation, he got an apprenticeship at a bank in New York City.

Luckily, the job turned out to be a resounding disappointment. Also luckily, though it couldn't have seemed so at the time, he got appendicitis and needed an emergency operation. That brush with mortality pushed the young man in the direction his imagination had already begun to lean. When he woke up, having survived surgery, he resolved to become an actor. He made the rounds, then worked his way up from bit parts over a period of years. He changed his name and, by the time he entered films, was an established Broadway lead, best known for playing a mock John Barrymore in *The Royal Family of Broadway*.

March became such a strong character actor in his middle years that there is a tendency to forget that the young March was as handsome as a matinee idol, almost. His eyes and nose were that of a beauty, but his mouth, long and with a tendency to turn downward, saved him from prettiness. That March had something more going on, something urgent and intense, is apparent from his early films.

Take *Manslaughter* (1930), in which he played an honest district attorney, an ideal pre-Code authority figure, whose stated mission is to administer the law equally, without regard for wealth or privilege. When the woman he loves, a selfish heiress (Claudette Colbert), accidentally kills a motorcycle cop while speeding, he sends her to the slammer; then he quits his job to go on a bender. But it's not a normal bender. He goes on a Fredric March bender. This one doesn't last a weekend or even a week, but becomes a six-month odyssey that takes him from a cushy office to an uncushy park bench.

When he's finally finished drinking his way through a major American city, he cleans up and rebuilds his career—just in time for Colbert, newly released from prison, to use her influence to get him fired. This leads to the film's best moment: She taunts him with the news that she has destroyed his career, and he looks at her with pity and says, "Do you think after all I've been through, loving you, that a job means anything to me?"

It's such moments that fans of March come to expect in his films, ones in which pretense and protection are dropped and the truth is spoken, simply and powerfully. Often these moments come in his scenes with women. March's unvarnished tenderness with women suggested a whole world of feeling underneath his words and gave force to his roles as a romantic lead.

All actors have certain mannerisms and expressions that reappear from film to film. When March played upright men, he tended to stand upright. When he played impetuous or dashing men, he had a tendency to stoop slightly and stand on the balls of his feet, vibrating in place, as if about to jump into action. In an era of personalities, March's traits were idiosyncratic, and employed consistently enough to grant him stardom. Yet, when given the chance, he also brought something new to his characters, located some emotional life for them that was a bit different.

In *Laughter* (1930), he was a classical composer, a compulsive extrovert, impertinent, fun-loving, always going. March found a new walk for him, a kind of strut, lots of elbows and business. He was a buoyant character, in love with a former showgirl (Nancy Carroll), who married for money. Yet, as always with March, he gives the serious moments a special depth: He's riding in a police car with Carroll, minutes after her husband's money has just gotten them out of jail for trespassing. The police, afraid of the husband's power, are sending them home with an escort, sirens blaring, lights flashing, and March looks on with sadness and disgust. "You can't go on with this," he tells her. "With that. With everything that stands for. That's money. That's power. God didn't mean for you to live like this. . . . You're dying for want of nourishment, for laughter. . . . You're dirty rich, and nothing but laughter can make you clean." Like Ann Harding, March could say lines that, in another actor's mouth, might have sounded self-conscious and overly poetic. If there was truth in the poetry, March found it.

Dr. Jekyll and Mr. Hyde, for which March ultimately won the Best Actor Academy Award, made him a star in his own right. His increased stature led to better roles, tailored to a complex screen personality that was all about inner conflict, about a fundamental decency at war with personal weakness or irreconcilable tension. One of his best was direc-tor Dorothy Arzner's *Merrily We Go to Hell*, released in July 1932.

Many actors manage to go an entire career without ever announcing hell as their location. March would say it, in one form or another, in three films that showed in theaters in 1932. *Dr. Jekyll* was the first. *Merrily We Go to Hell* was the second. And *Smilin' Through*, in which he costarred with Norma Shearer, would be the third.

In *Merrily*, he played Jerry, a reporter and would-be playwright who drinks even more than a reporter and a playwright combined. Sitting on a terrace during a party, he meets Joan (Sylvia Sidney), the woman who'll eventually become his wife, in a delicate scene that accom-plishes three things beautifully: First, it establishes the sweetness of Jerry's nature; second, it makes it understandable why Joan falls imme-diately in love with him; and third, it lets us know Jerry is not just drunk but in the grip of a serious alcohol problem. By playing him as if in a gentle haze, March somehow conveys not only that Jerry is bombed but that he's used to it.

It's a sophisticated portrait of an alcoholic. March plays Jerry as a man on the edge of terror, who knows he can't manage his disease. When he stands at the altar, he looks desolate, knowing that the thing bound to drag him down will now also drag down this innocent girl. His best man seems to know it, too, and shakes uncontrollably. It's a strong wedding scene from Arzner. The newlyweds haven't even left the church, and they're finished.

Merrily We Go to Hell takes its title from Jerry's favorite drinking toast. It becomes prophetic, except the part about "merrily." Jerry sobers up long enough to write a play, but on opening night, he's drunk, and soon he's having an affair with his leading lady, an ex-flame. Jerry and Joan agree to an open marriage, living in the same apartment but leading separate lives and taking lovers. Every night is a miserable drinking party—until Joan gets pregnant with Jerry's child and leaves him to rebuild her life.

It's fascinating, over the course of the film, to watch March go from a man of no substance, who is like a hollow tree struck by lightning, to a man of character. The ending doesn't disappoint. Prevented by her family from speaking to her, he finally gets to see her when she is gravely ill, having lost the baby in childbirth. In the hospital, he buries his face in her neck, and she pats the back of his head. "My baby, my baby," she says, referring not to the child she has lost but to him. He has come to terms with it—he needs a mommy. And this is the comfort she has wanted to give all along. *Merrily We Go to Hell* is an unexpected story—one about a weak man who finds the kind of love he needs.

March was on a run of luck. In the fall of 1932, when he won his Oscar, he was costarring in one of the most popular and lauded films of 1932. Today, *Smilin' Through* is remembered only as a Norma Shearer vehicle, and one almost has to stop to remember whether March or someone else was the leading man. Yet, though the film cast Shearer in a double role, both of her roles were saintly, uninteresting, and emotionally identical. March, by contrast, was also double-cast, but ideally: The men were completely different, yet each suffered from the kind of emotional strain that March excelled in portraying.

In period costume, he played Jeremy Wayne, an Englishman who, in 1868, is driven to madness by the decision of his great love, Moonyean (Shearer), to marry another man. At the rehearsal dinner, he shows up and sobs into her lap, "Haven't you any pity for a man in hell?" When that doesn't work, he goes to the wedding and commits the unforgivable faux pas of trying to shoot the groom. He misses and kills the bride.

In modern dress, March played Wayne's son, Kenneth, who grew up in America and arrives in England years later to enlist in the Great War. He falls in love with Kathleen (Moonyean's look-alike niece, also played by Shearer). It's all standard-issue romance until the late scenes, when Kenneth comes back from combat walking on crutches, his legs shot to pieces. A mutual friend suggests he contact Kathleen, and he answers, "Do I look like a man who wants to see a girl?"

In the climactic scene, both Shearer and March are superb, but it's March who wrenches this sentimental picture into the zone of harsh realism. Looking into his eyes, there is no doubt this man has been shot up. His face is haunted. Kathleen doesn't know at first that he's been wounded. His goal is to make sure she never finds out, and as he sits on a couch, he fights to maintain an indifferent front and find the strength to end their relationship. He smokes a cigarette and tries not to look at her. ("Kathleen, I've changed. . . . Four years, you change.") His mouth trembles. His face becomes almost grotesque with misery. When she leaves, convinced he doesn't love her, he is racked. He bends forward, hand on his forehead, and dry sobs.

In pre-Codes, all hell was local. The era's preoccupation with individual over collective concerns, which transformed horror into a vehicle for deep moral questions, also transformed other genres. Even in pre-Code war movies—depicting the most external of all human conflicts—the important battles would take place in the heart and soul. Capturing that bridge or that piece of land was, in the pre-Code scheme, of secondary importance at best. No one watching *Smilin' Through* cared about Fredric March's war record. They cared, as we do now, about him and his inner self, his happiness.

Ten years later, a country in the midst of a world war could not afford such rumination and introspection, but that only makes the pre-Codes all the more precious. This was a rare era in which an individual's involvement with the moral self was assumed to be of prime significance and understood to be of public interest. How does a person live in the world and live with himself, or herself? That's the essential question of these movies and a worthy question for cinema.

7

"I Got These for Killing Kids"

IN PRE-CODE MOVIES, war is a kind of dirty trick, perpetrated by crazy politicians on gullible soldiers and civilians. Characters such as the airmen in *The Dawn Patrol* or Fredric March in *Smilin' Through* are never heard talking about the importance of the cause or the honor of serving one's country. In pre-Codes, such remarks are heard only from characters who are suspect, either fools or hypocrites who stay at home and encourage others to go get killed.

The gung ho Hollywood movies that were to come in the World War II era were products of a completely different mind-set, practically a different world. In the pre-Code era, no sane character ever believed the sacrifice was worth it. No one believed that, in the end, things would turn out for the best. Governments were suspect—our own government, the enemy's government, what's the difference? Governments start the wars in the first place.

In *The Public Enemy* (1931), James Cagney's war-hero brother (Donald Cook) refuses to drink from the keg of bootleg beer Cagney has brought home because there's "blood in it, the blood of men." Cagney replies, "Your hands ain't so clean. You killed and liked it. You didn't get them medals for holding hands with them Germans." This was just not the smart comeback of a gangster trying to score argument points against his hero brother, but a sentiment expressed often in this era. Killing was killing.

All Quiet on the Western Front (1930), which won the Academy Award for Best Picture, was a series of unrelenting horrors. A young German, played by Lew Ayres, is persuaded to enlist in the army by a schoolmaster who uses every tactic of manipulation to make his students sacrifice for the fatherland. The schoolmaster is a gentle-looking old man who, in director Lewis Milestone's close-ups, takes on the look of a ravenous beast—near the end of life, yet on fire with luring able-bodied young specimens toward death.

Death is what they find—and slaughter, hunger, squalor, and terror. ("When we come back, I'll get you all some nice clean underwear," a veteran teases young men who've soiled themselves in fear.) Rats infest their foxholes. Artillery bombardments rattle their nerves all night, and when the bombing stops, they reach for their guns, because they know the enemy is making an advance. There is hand-to-hand combat in the trenches, with bayonets—to watch *All Quiet on the Western Front* is to wonder how anyone on the front lines survived that war. At one point, Paul (Lew Ayres) spends all day in a trench, talking alone to the corpse of a French soldier he has killed.

Throughout, men are screaming and howling in pain. The talkies brought to movies the sound of warfare, and one sound pre-Code war films never shied from was that of grown men giving way to uncontrolled, unvarnished, emasculated shrieking. It's enough to make one understand the derivation of the term *chicken*. The men practically squawk, "My eyes! I can't see!" Or "They cut my leg off! Why didn't they tell me!" These are nightmarish sounds that anyone who returned from the front lines would never forget. Now no moviegoer could forget them, either.

The pre-Code era was one of pacifism. The fact that *All Quiet on the Western Front* could even have been made—much less have become a critical and popular success—is a measure of that fact. Less than a dozen years after the armistice, here was an important American film about the plight of an *enemy* soldier, and it won the Academy Award for Best Picture. Anyone who might take that for granted should keep in mind that with no other twentieth-century war could such a film have been possible, never mind successful. Imagine an American film about a sympathetic German World War II soldier, or a North Korean, or a Vietcong. Imagine a heartfelt exploration of the angst and trauma of the Iraqi Republican Guard.

The Great War (as it was known before the sequel arrived) changed how Americans thought about a lot of things, including war. It marked probably the last time in history in which an American army could be seen parading down Main Street, on the way to combat, and anyone not crazy could think, What a glorious thing. The modern nature of the fighting—aerial bombing, machine guns, hand grenades, and poison gas—made old-fashioned notions of glory obsolete. Killing became impersonal and survival a matter of luck.

Eight and a half million people were killed in the war and another 21 million were wounded. The youth of Europe were decimated. The British saw 36 percent of its military either killed, wounded, MIA, or taken prisoner; the Germans, 65 percent; the French, 73 percent; and the Austrians, 90 percent. The United States, which joined the Allies three years into the action, had it easier, but only in comparison. After less than a year in the thick of fighting, America lost more than 116,000 men. That's two thousand American soldiers killed each week. Slaughter was followed by disillusionment. Americans had entered the war for vague reasons, then fought it for a set of ideals, outlined by President Wilson, that was never implemented. As if that were not enough to create a bitter cynicism, the war ended inconclusively, with the world less stable than it had been before.

With *The Big Parade* (1925), King Vidor's war epic starring John Gilbert—as with other silent films that followed, such as *What Price Glory?* (1926) and *Wings* (1927)—one gets the sense of a national trauma having lifted and of filmmakers finally attempting to relive and process, in personal ways, a terrible event. The films made at this time were antiwar, to be sure, but the war that they depicted feels, in these films, safely past.

Pre-Code films, depicting the same war, became more strident in their pacifism, for reasons that become understandable in retrospect. After all, this was an era haunted not by one ghost but by two—the ghost of world war past and the more terrifying specter, the ghost of world war future. That second ghost threatened to take the worst event in human history and turn it into a prologue. As early as 1930, articles could be found anticipating the next global conflict. Jay Franklin, in the November 1930 *Vanity Fair*, set the date for World War II as beginning somewhere between 1940 and 1950. The first anti–World War II movie, RKO's *Men Must Fight* (1933), had the war beginning in 1940, with an aerial bombardment of New York City by the forces of "Eurasia."

Accordingly, virtually all of the important pre-Code war films were pacifist in spirit, with the possible exception of Howard Hughes's *Hell's Angels* (1930), which was a philosophical muddle. Best known today as the starring debut of Jean Harlow, the picture featured a stunning, extended combat sequence, involving Allied fighter planes and a German zeppelin. Where the movie fell down was in its story of two brothers—a dutiful, old-fashioned, earnest fellow (James Hall) and a charming ne'er-do-well, played by Ben Lyon. Lyon, the romantic lead, was the natural for audience favorite, the exemplar of the new-fashioned man. But the story also presented him as a coward, so there was really no one to root for, though the screenwriters seemed under the delusion that somehow the sanctimonious brother might achieve audience sympathy.

The pacifism in pre-Code war films increased as the era wore on. In the first years of sound, war was depicted as hellish, inhumane, senseless, and altogether to be avoided. Yet films such as *The Dawn Patrol* or the James Whale film *Journey's End* (1930) more or less accepted war as part of the absurdity of the human condition. Certainly the superb adaptation of Hemingway's *A Farewell to Arms* (1932), starring Gary Cooper and Helen Hayes, fell into this category.

Later pre-Codes were more in the pattern of *Broken Lullaby* (1932), a rare drama from the great comic director Ernst Lubitsch. Phillips Holmes played a young French veteran who, a year after the armistice, is still overwhelmed with guilt over taking the life of a German soldier in combat. In such films, war was not just tragic, but morally indefensible. So when a priest, attempting to console the veteran, tells him, "You have done nothing but your duty," the emotionally frazzled young man explodes, "Duty. Duty? Duty to kill? Duty to kill? Is this the only answer I can get in the house of God? . . . Nine million people got slaughtered, and they're already talking about another war. . . . And the world calls that sane? Well, I want to be insane! I killed a man, and I can't escape!"

In the pre-Codes, the public sphere is corrupt, a sham. Governments can't confer or enhance honor, and a clergyman so secularized that he believes a government's lies has no moral authority. The only possible place of purity is the human soul, but maintaining purity is difficult in a world that teaches us more than we want to know.

That's the dilemma of the characters in *The Last Flight* (1931), a remarkable film about an emotionally frail rich girl, Nikki, and four American fliers who go around together in postwar Paris. It's a strange film—indeed, it's unique—and it excites every critic who sees it. But because it hasn't been released on video and is only rarely shown on television, it is barely known.

John Monk Saunders wrote it, introducing Nikki and her fliers in the 1930 novel *Single Lady*. Richard Barthelmess, while making *The Finger*

Points, read one of the chapters in magazine form and decided on the spot that this should be his next film. Producer Daryl Zanuck objected, insisting the movie wouldn't turn a profit, which was where the clause in Barthelmess's contract—his right to choose his own stories—came in handy. "If it weren't for Barthelmess," Saunders told the *Los Angeles Times*, "*The Last Flight* would not have been possible. It was only because he saw in it the newness of ideas and material that it was finally sold."

Barthelmess played Cary, a pilot whose hands were badly burned when he held a steering stick and landed his airplane as it went down in flames. He and his three compatriots—played by David Manners, John Mack Brown, and Elliott Nugent—leave a French military hospital at the start of the film, each one too rattled and damaged to go back to the United States. All the men find a palliative in alcohol, so they stay in Paris and stay drunk. Nikki—played by the fragile and wonderfully strange Helen Chandler (of *Dracula* fame)—is a flighty American who is just as aimless. They meet her, of course, in a bar.

Seen today, *The Last Flight* seems, if not modern, at least thirty years ahead of its time. Precious little happens, and the nonsense banter that makes up much of the film sounds less like 1931 than 1965—like something out of a Richard Lester movie. In one scene, Nikki changes her shoes because, she says, "I can walk faster in red shoes." When she gets up to go to the bathroom, she says she is going to take "a Chinese singing lesson." (Another character, in the same circumstances, announces he is about to "shave a horse.") Behind the nonsense is a philosophy, as if the characters are determined to act playful and innocent in the face of existential absurdity.

In a typical scene, Barthelmess wakes up Manners, then hands him a drink:

MANNERS: What day is this?
BARTHELMESS: It's Wednesday.

MANNERS: Wednesday. Wednesday, what?

BARTHELMESS: The twentieth.

MANNERS: What month, I mean.

BARTHELMESS: You mean to say you don't know what month this is?

MANNERS: I knew once, but I forgot.

BARTHELMESS: It's June, the merry month of June.

MANNERS: June! Say, maybe I better get up. What town are we in?

The flip dialogue doesn't conceal the despair; it's an expression of it. On the night they meet Nikki, the men follow her back to her hotel suite, and she emerges from her bedroom, asking if one of them might scrub her back. The men immediately pile into her bedroom, and while one scrubs her back, the others admire her back, legs, and feet: "Did anyone ever see such a back in their life!" The tone is light, lyrical, and meaningless. These men are past an interest in sex, too smashed up inside for small human things to make much difference. Their playful mooning over legs, feet, and back is ghostly, as if evoking some dim memory when such things were to live and die for.

Unlike Jake Barnes, the hero of Hemingway's *The Sun Also Rises*, a novel with at least a passing resemblance to this story, Cary isn't impotent, but he is impotent in spirit. There is no sex or sexual content in the film, and the one man, an obnoxious journalist, who makes a pass at Nikki is immediately repulsed. Of course, this didn't stop the copywriters. "Nikki—and her incredible boyfriends!" shouted the advertisements. "Richard Barthelmess as the leader of the most amazing group of love-makers you ever saw or read about."

Nikki isn't a woman of the world, but an airy figure with a child's honesty and an adult's sadness, a female version of the men. (Chandler, whose own hopeless alcoholism would lead to tragedy, couldn't help but bring a special truth to the role.) Having seen the worst of life, Nikki and her fliers go through the film attempting to regain their purity, an impossible task. The best they can manage is to pickle in alcohol their knowledge of good and evil. "Isn't he sort of wasting himself?" Nikki asks about Cary, to which his friend replies, "On the contrary, he's trying awfully hard to get hold of himself." The men are trying, and yet they're also trying to obliterate themselves. The struggle between those impulses—life and death—is really the movie's one source of dramatic tension.

The critics recognized the uniqueness of *The Last Flight*. Some considered it an interesting failure, others an idiosyncratic success. The *Brooklyn Times* wrote that the "daring thing" was "the yarn itself. It doesn't fit into any of the accepted files." The *New York Daily News* advised audiences that "to properly enjoy *The Last Flight* you've got to forget completely your every day doings in life and allow yourself to be carried away by the whimsicality." The *New York American* put it best for all time: "A rather baffling and almost magnificent film." But audiences stayed away. Barthelmess may have succeeded in making an art film that would seem fresh and pioneering generations later. But Zanuck had been right about *The Last Flight*'s box-office prospects.

THE WAY WE remember World War I fliers today has a lot to do with John Monk Saunders, who immortalized their ordeals in the most fervent antiwar films of the era. Saunders's stories captured the monotony of barracks life, the dread, the hopelessness, the sadness, the endless parade of young men disappearing into the clouds. His stories are horrific, and could only have been told by someone with firsthand experience, who was there in France, in those barracks, on those missions, with those men—so one might think. In fact, Saunders spent the war in the United States as a flight instructor, and, to his grief, the armistice came before he was called to Europe. Fay Wray, who was married to Saunders in the period of his best work, recalls his telling her that when he heard the war had ended, he went to his plane, leaned against the propeller, and cried.

So these war movies are testaments, not to the depth of Saunders's experience, but to his imagination, empathy, and inside knowledge. He wrote two more films about World War I fliers. Both were released in 1933, and both are strong stuff. *Ace of Aces* starred he-man Richard Dix as a peace-loving artist, a sculptor, who is shamed into enlisting when his patriotic fiancée (Elizabeth Allan) calls him a coward and breaks their engagement. To prove her wrong, he becomes an aviator and, with his first kill, discovers an insatiable blood lust. He eventually gets to the point where he even takes delight in loading his machine-gun belt every night, bullet by bullet, like a miser counting his gold. "This is a great war," he says, "and I'm having a grand time."

The turnaround comes when, recovering from a minor wound, he finds himself in a hospital bed next to a young German whom he has just knocked out of the sky. The German has a stomach wound and is screaming for water—screaming as they only scream in pre-Code films—and the young cadet's hysteria and torment bring home the reality of killing. "Are these worth forty-two dead men?" Dix says, looking at his box of medals. "Are they worth one dead man?" The result is that the next time the seasoned aviator goes up on a mission, he finds himself surrounded by enemy planes but too haunted to fight back.

Ace of Aces resolved itself a happy love-story ending, with Dix and his fiancée back together and the former ace installed as a flying instructor. But another film based on a Saunders script that same year, *The Eagle and the Hawk,* left no space for light or compromise. It was dark through the finish—as vociferous a pacifist document as ever released by a major studio (Paramount). It starred Fredric March as Jerry, an American who, out of a spirit of adventure, becomes a reconnaissance pilot, then experiences a gradual psychological meltdown.

The first time he goes up, he shoots down two enemy planes and arrives back at his base exhilarated. "Why didn't anybody tell me about this man's war!" he exclaims—but it's the last moment of satisfaction he has. Seconds later, he finds out that his gunner has been killed. He is stunned and disoriented. He returns to his barracks and finds an orderly whistling and packing up the dead man's belongings. He lingers at the gunner's desk, where there is a photo of the man's wife and child, and a letter that he never completed.

The credited director of *The Eagle and the Hawk* was Stuart Walker, but in later years, Mitchell Leisen, credited as assistant director, maintained that he had directed the bulk of the film. It's a movie anyone should want to take credit for, and certainly the film itself—with its assured pace, strong performances, and smart camera work—suggests a first-rate directorial hand. In one scene, March shares the frame with two actors, but while they stand in light, March is a silhouette, a dark outline of doom in the middle of the screen. The shot's intent isn't overemphasized, but its effect seeps into the viewer's consciousness. The movie also contains an unusual number of extreme close-ups for 1933, a decided virtue in a movie that's all about what's going on inside a man's head.

Jerry loses five gunners in his first two months, but he keeps surviving and shooting down German planes. He becomes depressed and guilt-ridden and, as in all Saunders war films, he starts hitting the bottle (a weakness that Saunders himself shared). Drinking doesn't help. "When you see a guy falling and burning, and you know he hasn't got a chance—you can't snap a picture like that out of your mind," he says. When a friend jokingly suggests Jerry needs to drink more, he answers, "I can't drink enough." In a grim scene that makes a mockery of medals and honors, he is decorated with the French Croix de Guerre while so blotto he can barely stand.

In *The Eagle and the Hawk*, March faced the challenge of playing a man slowly cracking up. While never indulging himself, he brilliantly scores and modulates Jerry's slide. March makes it clear that Jerry is getting worse and worse, even as we see him trying to keep a handle on himself, trying to remain polite and disguise his distress. In one scene, Jerry, on a short leave, goes to a dinner party and is introduced to a little boy who wants to be a flier when he grows up. The boy wants to know if the enemy planes look like Roman candles when they're hit and if "they explode with a great big bang."

"Yes, with a great big bang," he tells the little monster, looking like he himself might explode any second. He flees the party soon after.

March's art was not just about presenting psychological extremity but about conveying the moral conflicts from which such states originated. As such, *The Eagle and the Hawk* must be regarded as containing one of the supreme and defining performances of a great actor. Two moments stand out in particular. In one, he is called upon to give a pep talk to young cadets who have just joined the front lines. A veteran officer and a "shining example," he is an inspiration to the men, but he can barely make it through his speech. "The first time you shoot down a man," he stammers, "don't let it get to you. Uh, remember . . . you're fighting for humanity, and for the preservation of civilization." Thankfully, the director, whoever he was, filmed the speech in extreme close-up, so that we can see what the cadets somehow fail to perceive. March doesn't believe a word he's saying.

The other great moment comes after Jerry kills Voss, a German ace, and is sick to see that he is "just a kid." Feted by his fellow fliers at a banquet in his honor—"A binge to celebrate the killing of a twenty-year-old kid; gee, it's great, I wouldn't miss it for anything"—he can no longer hold it together:

> I went to the field hospital to see [Voss]. Thought I'd find a man. I
> found a blond kid, like a lot of you. Two bullet holes in him. They
> congratulated me for it, congratulated me all day, told me I'd done

a great thing. They set me up as a shiny tin god, a hero, an ace. . . .
I got these [medals] for killing kids. They're all chunks of torn
flesh and broken bones and blood. And for WHAT?!

He storms off, goes back to his room, and blows his brains out.

Jerry's suicide makes for as hopeless and as pointed a finish as could
be imagined in a pacifist war film. It also, sadly, had its real-life parallel.
Seven years after the film was made, Saunders, age forty-two, hanged
himself.

ONE CONFRONTS THE pacifism of pre-Code war films with a mix of
feelings. The films convey, better than any others, the spiritual lacera-
tions that World War I had inflicted on the American soul. They also
speak with an honesty about war and its consequences that's refreshing,
especially considering the militaristic nature of most American war
films up through the mid-1970s. Yet one doesn't have to be a historian
to have an awareness of the time line. In the same year that *The Eagle
and the Hawk* and *Ace of Aces* debuted, Adolf Hitler came to power in
Germany. Had the United States and its allies found the will that year
to throw a net over Hitler, tens of millions of lives might have been
spared.

Yet as Jay Franklin wrote in 1930, "The world can afford a world-
class war only once a generation. The generation which fights a war
decides . . . that it will never love another country." The American
public was just not in an interventionist mood. Rather, it was in the
mood to see movies like *Heartbreak* (1931), with Charles Farrell as an
American World War I aviator who disobeys orders and flies across
German lines so he can see his German girlfriend (Madge Evans).
Imprisoned and court-martialed, he eventually reunites with her in
Germany—for a happy ending, pre-Code style.

Pre-Code movies were made by a number of different studios, run by moguls with different political affiliations. Yet they were made for the same public and perhaps for that reason tended to express consistent points of view. At first blush, some of these reoccurring ideas might seem in opposition, an uneasy mix of libertarianism and liberalism. But this was a mix distinct for the period, a sensible reaction, part emotional and part rational, to past history and present circumstances.

More than anything else, movies of this time emphasized the primacy of the individual and the importance of individual concerns, treating the government as a malign, or at best neutral, force. Shady characters, sly operators, and fast-talking con men were often heroes, if for no reason but that they were individualists making their way in the world. Meanwhile, anyone representing organized power, such as business or government, was part of the problem. That's why private detectives were almost always good guys, while policemen were usually nuisances.

The popularity of the Marx Brothers, who were at their most anarchic in the early thirties, was a manifestation of the era's love of individuals and its distrust of institutions. In film after film, the Marx Brothers moved into some staid setting and proceeded to demolish it. In their last pre-Code—and best film—*Duck Soup* (1933), Groucho played the leader of a small country who instigates a war with a neighboring nation. The movie's burlesque of war and government, and its subsequent critical and box-office failure, have led some latter-day critics to assume that the film's implicit politics were too strong for 1933 audiences. Not true. *Duck Soup* failed only because it was decades ahead of its time artistically, made for an audience with a limited tolerance for absurdist humor and nonstop irony. If anything, its politics should have endeared it to an audience that was ravenously antiwar and would remain so for years. In a January 1937 Gallup poll, 70 percent of Americans surveyed said the United States should never have entered World War I.

If pre-Codes exalted individuality and expressed a distrust of government, it was for what legitimately could be called liberal reasons. Government not only led people into pointless wars; government was useless because it was unable or unwilling to do anything to end poverty and want. Thus, the era's love of the individual translated not into movies that extolled laissez-faire capitalism, but those that were vocal in favoring government assistance to individuals in need. Human lives were not to be wasted just for lack of money.

That's why, in pre-Codes about politics, good politicians were invariably and identifiably liberal, some of them holding positions that would still be on the outer-left fringe of today's political spectrum. Yet, as suited the temper of the times, they framed their arguments in traditional terms. Take *Washington Masquerade* (1932), in which Lionel Barrymore played Jefferson Keane, a crusading lawyer who is elected to the U.S. Senate. As his first significant act in office, he makes an impassioned speech calling for the abolition of power and light companies and the nationalization of the energy supply:

The almighty hand that made the world . . . that placed all the ingredients for the creation of power and light at the disposal of mankind—nowhere do I find the slightest suggestion that he granted a stranglehold to the few people who might rise from the ranks and no one else. . . . There's nothing communistic in that statement. It's plain American—the very essence and foundation of plain American. This land belongs to its millions of people. If we haven't learned the lesson that every wind has carried these three tragic years, one hundred million people in this country *have* learned it, with the tears streaming down their cheeks and their families famished, in this land where there's more than plenty. It's my solemn belief that one hundred million people are making up their minds that the things they own, the things that belong to them and to nobody else, have been taken out of their hands and are being given back to them again at heartbreaking and impossible prices.

The press and the public respond to his words, but his opponents label him a Communist. From there, corrupt political and business interests collaborate to destroy him.

The movie's parallels with the 1939 Frank Capra film *Mr. Smith Goes to Washington* are obvious. Yet more interesting, the films' divergent emphases illuminate the differences between pre-Code and post-Code attitudes. While both films feature idealists named Jefferson, Lionel Barrymore was clearly playing a man with pronounced political views, while James Stewart's Jefferson Smith was an apolitical nice guy whose only mission was to build a boy's camp. Moreover, Keane is brought down by corruption understood to be pandemic—the whole "Washington masquerade," as it were—while Smith is assailed by one main crook, operating a political machine in a single state.

Mr. Smith Goes to Washington is still the superior picture—it's a delight, while *Washington Masquerade* gets confused and messy halfway through. Yet the pre-Code film's ability to touch on ideology and explore political corruption as something hardly unique marks it as a work meant for adult minds. The parallel endings demonstrate that. In both, the hero, in the midst of an address, passes out from the strain. In *Mr. Smith*, Jefferson has only fainted. In *Washington Masquerade*, Jefferson has dropped dead of a heart attack.

Liberal heroes. To those weaned on movies made during the Code, it's hard to imagine that any such creature existed in American film before the late sixties, but in pre-Codes they were everywhere. Even in *The Dark Horse* (1932), in which Guy Kibbee played a complete idiot running for governor, the protagonist was the "Progressive" party candidate, while the competition—who was even worse (dishonest, crooked)—represented the "Conservative" party.

In the urban drama *Blood Money* (1933), George Bancroft played a shady bail bondsman, a big man about town who knows where all the bodies are buried. Someone praises the conservative mayor's stand against vice, but Bancroft has no use for the mayor's moral posturing:

> As long as you have cities, you're bound to have vice in them. And you can't control human nature. . . . The only difference between a liberal and a conservative man is that the liberal recognizes the existence of vice and tries to control it, while the conservative just turns his back and pretends that it doesn't exist.

Yet another liberal hero turned up in *Washington Merry-Go-Round*, a political film released in anticipation of the 1932 presidential election. Lee Tracy played a freshman congressman who no sooner gets off the train than he's being told by a political boss how to vote. By nature obstreperous—as were all Tracy characters, not to mention Tracy himself—he refuses to take orders. The rest of the film pits Tracy against the political bad guys, who are very bad indeed. They even murder an old senator.

Washington Merry-Go-Round was made in the summer of 1932, the same summer that the Bonus Army set up its camp in Washington. Thousands of unemployed World War I veterans had descended upon the capital, requesting that the government pay off immediately on a bonus that was not, in fact, due them until 1945. They called their camp "Hooverville." At the end of July, President Hoover, fearing an insurrection, called out the U.S. Army to evict the Bonus Army, with Gen. Douglas MacArthur in command. Tear gas and bayonets were used, and one infant living in the encampment died of asphyxiation.

Less than a week later, on August 4, *Washington Merry-Go-Round* began filming. One of the first places the new congressman is seen visiting in the film was the campsite of the Bonus Army. He goes to express solidarity with their cause. By showing a congressman standing with the Bonus Army, the filmmakers were consciously announcing the hero's politics, while presenting their pessimistic story as something hot off the presses, with relevance to America in the present day.

The notion that in a corrupt system citizens can and should take the law into their own hands was present in *The Mayor of Hell* (1933). The film took place in a hellish reform school, in which evil warden Thompson (Dudley Digges) eats bacon and eggs for breakfast in the same hall where the kids—a cross section of urban Jews, Italians, blacks, and Irish—eat food not fit for human consumption. The warden is a typical pre-Code power figure, sanctimonious, sniveling before his superiors, and crooked, lining his pockets with the money allotted for the kids' food.

The Mayor of Hell was a political parable. When the warden is sent away on a forced vacation by the new deputy commissioner, a gangster political appointee (James Cagney), the kids set up their own government, and conditions improve. But when the warden returns, so does tyranny. The food turns into slop again, and a sick child dies as a result of the warden's harsh punishment. The boys rebel, and in the ensuing riot, the warden is killed.

Only in a pre-Code could the death of a public official be tossed off so blithely: "There is no doubt this tragedy was Thompson's own fault," the head of the prison system rules—and that's that. Democracy triumphs over oligarchy; the government is restored to the people. Warner Bros. made it look easy.

Pre-Codes depicted an America in which institutions alone could not protect the weak and unconnected from exploitation. The institutions themselves were subject to corruption, and entrenched power saw every conventional gambit coming. Legal problems required extralegal solutions. Since the bad guys either wrote the laws to suit themselves or cocooned themselves inside the law to protect themselves, good guys had to stretch the law or break it when necessary.

If Americans wanted to survive, these movies seemed to say, they had to cultivate a kind of heroism that had nothing to do with battles and flags—and everything to do with getting wise. To come out ahead, people had to become a little like Lee Tracy.

8

The Smartest Guy at Figuring Angles

H EROES ARE PEOPLE who do good things that others can't, things that enable them to survive where others wouldn't. In the movies, they rescue us from our terrors by triumphing in situations in which we'd feel threatened. They have qualities we wish we had—if we had them, we'd stand a better chance in the world.

Though in real life heroes are most often associated with sacrifice, heroes in movies almost always survive and thrive. During wartime, physical courage and stamina are the qualities most important for survival, and so the brave and strong are heroes. At times when moral courage is called for, the person who remains steady and true in the face of social disapproval captures the imagination.

Even before the Great Depression set in, there was a sense that the old heroes weren't quite cutting it. As early as 1930, business author Merryle Stanley Rukeyser had written, "In the rail-splitting, pioneer days, leadership invariably went to forceful men—men with a powerful will and a sense of mastery. . . . But since America has come of age in a business sense, the older qualities are not enough." When the Depression deepened, old values devalued along with the securities market. In

1934, *American Magazine* published a letter from a young man who complained that everything his parents had taught him was useless in modern America: "So [give me] one good reason, Mr. Editor, why an ambitious young man should be honest. It's got to be a real, practical reason, too. And don't talk to me about great men having been honest. I don't want to be great. I want to be comfortable."

Different fears bring about different fantasies and those fantasies create different heroes. By the early thirties, as people worried about the prospect (or the reality) of financial ruin, audiences took delight in characters who solved their problems not with muscles but with shrewdness, a touch of larceny, a cynicism about the world, and confidence in themselves. Movies centered around fellows who thought fast and cut corners, "fixers" who could get by any which way.

Lee Tracy was the embodiment of this kind of pre-Code star. Had he come along ten years earlier, he would have been an unimportant comic. Actually, he couldn't have had a career in films at all before sound. On-screen, Tracy bombarded people with torrents of bluster, ballyhoo, and lies, talking a mile a minute in his piercing, unmistakable voice. And all the while—and this was a delight about him—he was thinking. Today, with video, we can rewind a Tracy monologue and watch all the wonderful instantaneous transitions he makes and see the pistons firing in his eyes as he launches another display of verbal pyrotechnics. We have that luxury, while in the early thirties, audiences could only hang on and on as ev-er-y syl-la-ble went by in a crazy flash.

Tracy usually played reporters and publicists, media men, fellows who could sell snow to Eskimos and make them like it. He played men who made nothing, who built nothing, whose talents would have gone unrecognized in any other country; men who sold information, precursors of workers in today's information economy.

He played a reporter in his first important film role, in *The Strange Love of Molly Louvain* (1932), opposite Ann Dvorak as the title character. They live in the same boardinghouse, and he keeps coming into her room to use the phone, lifting up the base and flipping the earpiece into the air with one hand. He has no idea that this "tinsel girl," whom he starts romancing but doesn't take seriously, is the fugitive from justice whose story he has been covering. He's a wise guy and know-it-all who thinks he understands women, but he does have redeeming qualities. As the *Daily Mirror* wrote at the time, "The character's fundamental decency is skillfully established by the engaging Mr. Tracy." That was the story with Tracy's characters: Beneath the smoke screen, there was a decent guy in there, someone who had a conscience and was nice to his mother.

Tracy was born in Georgia in 1898. After service in World War I, he went to New York and tried to bluff his way into a stage career, claiming to have all sorts of experience he didn't have. The ploy sounds like something out of a Lee Tracy movie, except it didn't work. Even so, after just a few months of stage training, he did start to get roles, and in 1926, he became a star in a play called *Broadway*. James Cagney was his understudy.

The Ben Hecht–Charles MacArthur play *The Front Page*, in which he originated the role of ace reporter Hildy Johnson, solidified his stage reputation and established the Tracy type. He made four movies over the course of 1929 and 1930, appearing in mostly small or supporting roles, spent a year back on Broadway, and then went back to pictures with *The Strange Love of Molly Louvain*.

Most pre-Code actors were fairly sedate in their real-life incarnations. Cagney was a homebody. Robinson was an intellectual and an art collector. Gable was a worrier. But Lee Tracy was as colorful as the characters he played; if anything, he was wilder. Unfortunately, that very wildless—his drinking, his tendency to shoot off his mouth, and his disdain for authority—hurt his career and is probably why Lee Tracy isn't a household name.

Lon Chaney in a December 1927 portrait for *Laugh, Clown, Laugh*.

Al Jolson almost cross-eyed with piety in *The Jazz Singer* (1927).

The most amazing of Chaney's thousand faces was his own.

Ramon Novarro.

ABOVE: Richard
Barthelmess, as the
scourge of land-
grabbing Americans
in *The Lash* (1930).

BELOW: David
Manners and Richard
Barthelmess as scarred
veterans in *The Last
Flight* (1931).

Richard Barthelmess.

Edward G. Robinson.

★ H. B. WARNER
★ MARIAN MARSH
★ ANTHONY BUSHELL
★ GEORGE E. STONE
★ FRANCES STARR

Ona Munson , Robert Elliott

Directed by
MERVYN LeROY

Frank! Powerful! Realistic! A heart-stirring
cross-section of modern life that fairly hammers
on the emotions . . . . . A sweeping drama of
pathos and passion—betrothal and betrayal
—honor and hypocrisy—with lives and loves
sacrificed to the Juggernaut of newspaper cir-
culation . . . . . Greatest picture of the year—
with the outstanding screen actor of the day,
and a powerful supporting cast. * * *

FIVE STAR FINAL

with the most versatile actor
on the screen today..

Edw.G.ROBINSON

A FIRST NATIONAL & VITAPHONE PICTURE

"Vitaphone" is the registered trademark of The Vitaphone Corporation

ABOVE: Robinson
in *Little Caesar*:
The gangster arrives.

BELOW: A 1931
advertisement for
Five Star Final.

Barthelmess at his zenith, and Gable getting there, in *The Finger Points* (1931).

James Cagney, with Jean Harlow, in *The Public Enemy* (1931).

Clark Gable, with Norma Shearer, in a March 1931 photo for *A Free Soul* (1931).

Clark Gable.

ABOVE: Cagney, with
Loretta Young, in *Taxi*
(1931).

BELOW: Gable, suffering a
rare attack of innocuous-
ness, circa 1931.

Robert Montgomery.

Maurice Chevalier, too busy sizing up Jeanette MacDonald to use his tape measure correctly, in *Love Me Tonight* (1932).

An immortal pairing: John Barrymore with Greta Garbo on the set of *Grand Hotel* (1932).

John Barrymore.

ABOVE: Lionel Barrymore as a crusading politician in *Washington Masquerade* (1932).

BELOW: Charles Laughton as Nero in *The Sign of the Cross* (1932).

Gary Cooper.

Warren William eating bacon and eggs in the Warners commissary.

William in a portrait for
Skyscraper Souls (1932).

Gable in *Red Dust*
(1932).

Gilbert hoped to write his way back to success with *Downstairs* (1932).

Gable, 1932.

The Douglas Fairbankses, Jr. and Sr., after a round of golf in 1932.

ABOVE: Fairbanks, Jr., with first wife Joan Crawford, back from vacation in August, 1932.

BELOW: Fairbanks, Jr., on vacation, pre-Code style, in *The Parachute Jumper*.

ABOVE: Lee Tracy in a portrait for *Blessed Event* (1932).

BELOW: Lee Tracy on the set of *Advice to the Lovelorn* (1933).

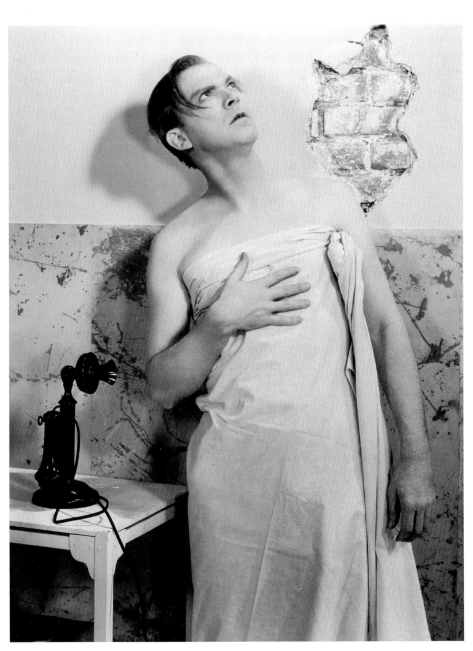

Lee Tracy in *Advice to the Lovelorn* (1933).

Cagney demonstrates his tough love for Alice White in *The Picture Snatcher* (1933).

Cagney with Mary Brian in *Hard to Handle* (1933).

Cagney appreciates Claire Dodd's back (1933).

Paul Muni, with Noel Francis, in *I Am a Fugitive from a Chain Gang* (1932).

Warren William, with Clarence Muse, after a hard night fleecing the public in *The Mind Reader* (1933).

An unretouched portrait of Robert Montgomery.

Fredric March, with Constance Bennett, in *The Affairs of Cellini* (1934).

March's unaffected tenderness with women was one of his most appealing traits.
With Claudette Colbert in *Tonight is Ours* (1933).

Fredric March.

ABOVE: Barthelmess fought the law in *Massacre* (1934).

BELOW: Barthelmess, with Jean Muir, in his last pre-Code, *A Modern Hero* (1934).

He followed *Molly Louvain* with *Love Is a Racket* (1932), as the reporter friend of fellow reporter Douglas Fairbanks, Jr.. It was a supporting role, but in a good movie with a strong director (William Wellman) and an atmosphere, both romantic and hard-boiled, that was ideal for Tracy. The horror movie, *Doctor X*, (1932)—a lead role for Tracy, again as a reporter—was a routine showcase.

Doctor X hit theaters on August 27. Film stardom followed two weeks later (September 10) with the release of *Blessed Event*. In a part originally intended for Cagney, who was on strike, Tracy played a Walter Winchell–type columnist who becomes a sensation by reporting on the pregnancies—the upcoming "blessed events"—of Broadway stars and socialites, some of whom are unmarried.

Though not originally conceived for Tracy, *Blessed Event* contained elements that would be repeated in other Tracy films. He has a sweet old mother. He is fearless and cocky when threatened by the mob over a column. He has an upright fiancée who hates his line of work. And he abuses his power: At one point, he includes a column item about the pregnancy of a showgirl, even though the woman has begged him to keep quiet and he has promised not to report it.

Tracy's movies—at least the ones in which he starred—were usually about monomaniacs who, having taken the temperature of the times, find themselves uniquely suited for success in modern America. The moral tension within such films is invariably between the hero's obsessive drive and his humanity, and the dramatic question turned on which side would win out. Since Tracy was a figure of light, not darkness, and his movies were intended to say positive things about the go-getters he played, his characters would ultimately choose love over ego. What else would you expect from a guy who is so good to his mother? This made for satisfying endings—then as now, audiences love Tracy and don't want to see him double-crossing scared and pregnant women. Yet these endings also defined the limits of the Tracy-movie formula.

With *Blessed Event* in the can, Tracy must have seemed on the way to stardom. Yet Warner Bros., after four pictures with him, decided not to renew his contract. He was too unreliable. So he went to Columbia, where he made two films (including *Washington Merry-Go-Round*). The press, already aware of his reputation, reported that this time Tracy was "being a very good boy." His bad behavior returned while making *The Half-Naked Truth* (1932) for RKO. His latenesses and missed days—allegedly the result of hangovers—caused the studio to sue him for ten thousand dollars. Tracy, through a lawyer, claimed to have been suffering from a nervous breakdown and stomach trouble. The suit was settled out of court.

Most new stars try to present a positive image to the press and say good things about Hollywood. Tracy, in the first bloom of stardom, seemed to say whatever crossed his mind. "I can count on one hand the number of parties I've been to since coming to the coast," he said in 1933. "And I consider those evenings wasted." That was one way to discourage unwanted invitations.

Instead of making nice and talking about settling down someday and raising a family, Tracy portrayed himself as a restless bohemian who didn't even want a home of his own. "God, NO! . . . I always live in hotels or in furnished apartments, and the more transient I feel in 'em the better." He didn't want children: "What for? I should hope to have the good fortune of falling in love with a very modern young lady. A young lady modern enough to believe that she would go on living happily without children."

He wanted nothing like normal life. When he lived in New York, he told reporter Gladys Hall, he'd go to the Long Island station whenever he was depressed "and watch the commuting husbands . . . with that strained and anxious husband look in their eyes." Then he'd feel better.

The Half-Naked Truth cast Tracy as a carnival barker who becomes a successful publicist. The role of publicity man suited him as well as that of reporter. In 1933, he signed with MGM and starred in *The Nuisance*, as an ambulance-chasing lawyer. He is shameless, hiring fake witnesses and fake victims in order to fleece a streetcar company. But as always, Tracy had a reason for his behavior. We're to understand that he once represented a legitimate client but was outmaneuvered by the company's slick lawyers.

MGM had the right idea of how to cast Tracy. They put him in either colorful supporting roles in major productions or in lead roles in small movies tailored to his personality. This made sense, since a steady diet of Tracy formula films, such as *Blessed Event* and *The Nuisance*, would have been too limiting. Tracy was, for all his distinctiveness, a versatile actor, one who could be silly or poignant by turns, and who could kiss the girl at the end of the movie without making an audience laugh or throw up. Perfectly placed at MGM, Tracy made his three best movies in 1933, and he was on the way to making a fourth, when his career derailed.

In *Dinner at Eight*, he played the theatrical agent of a faded Hollywood star, Larry Renault, played by John Barrymore. The most painfully funny moment in the picture comes when Tracy tries to convince his client that a bit part he is being offered, that of a beachcomber, is better than the lead role, "He comes on once—swell scene— he goes off—they keep waiting for him to come back—ha-HAH!—and he never does! What a part!" The clucking "ha-HAH" is priceless, completely absurd, and so funny, the false laugh of someone whose entire professional life is spent pushing and cajoling.

Later, when the drunken actor accuses him of betrayal, of being "in with the managers," Tracy becomes enraged and drops the facade. With a cold eye and relentless focus, he delivers a dressing-down that, in part, results in the actor's suicide, "You're through, Renault. You're through in pictures, in plays, in vaudeville, and radio. . . . Go get yourself buried."

Dinner at Eight showed something of his comic and dramatic range, while *Bombshell* (1933) gave audiences the apotheosis of Tracy as publicist. Jean Harlow played a movie star and Tracy was a studio publicity man almost deranged with energy. In between those two blockbusters came *Turn Back the Clock* (1933), a smaller film that was all Tracy and provided him with his best opportunities as an actor.

Like a lot of Tracy's movies, *Turn Back the Clock* dealt with the question, "What's more important, worldly success or love?" But it approached the question in its own way, with a story outside the pattern not only of Tracy's movies but of the era's in general. Tracy played Joe, a middle-aged guy who owns a cigar store. He makes a decent living but knows that he missed his one chance at wealth when, as a young man, he chose not to marry a rich girl (Peggy Shannon). He chose love (with Mae Clarke) instead.

The gimmick of *Turn Back the Clock* is that Joe gets to go back in time and relive his life. Since he knows where he went wrong, he resists the temptation to marry his sweetheart. He marries the rich girl and becomes rich himself. Advance knowledge of history puts him a step ahead of other businessmen. He gets into the truck-making business right before World War I and makes a fortune on government contracts. In the late 1920s, he knows to get out of the stock market.

Turn Back the Clock called for a mellower Tracy. The huckster/public man aspect of the character was there, but there were also quieter moments calling for subtlety and feeling. Early in the film, he wakes to find that, somehow, he is in his boyhood room of thirty years before. He goes to the mirror, sees a young man staring back at him, and just touches his face with wonder.

He has another fine moment, when making a speech at a rally for soldiers about to enter World War I. He is telling the men what they can expect when they return from the war. "And when you get back—" he says, then realizes some of them won't make it back. He taps his palm against the railing with emotion and adds quietly, "most of you . . ." Tracy's speed as an actor was not just a matter of machine-gun patter. His transitions were fast and his emotions were genuine.

He was at the pinnacle in late 1933 and should have been able to stay there for a while. In the fall, after starring in a poor man's *Blessed Event* while on loan to Fox (*Advice to the Lovelorn*), Tracy was cast in another future classic—as a reporter in *Viva Villa*, starring Wallace Beery. The picture was to be shot in Mexico.

Hollywood history is filled with tales of performers who could be said to have "pissed away" their stardom. Tracy is the only one ever to have done it literally. In Mexico City, having just completed filming *Viva Villa*, Tracy went on a drunken tear. Nothing original there. The pivotal event came the following morning. Tracy woke to the sound of a parade, walked over to the window, and—perhaps feeling festive, perhaps mistaking the window grate for a urinal—urinated on the aptly named Chapultepee cadets.

The Mexicans, understandably, took offense, and they arrested Tracy, which resulted in an international incident. In response, MGM invoked the "morality clause" in Tracy's contract. The studio fired him and reshot all his scenes in *Viva Villa*, using Stu Erwin, a comic actor whose slow delivery was the antithesis of Tracy's.

The Mexico City incident was in every newspaper of the day, and yet the story was so suppressed and disputed in all its details that it's impossible to know exactly what happened. At the time, no one said anything about Tracy's confusing a military procession for a toilet. MGM claimed Tracy was naked and that he had done something lewd from a balcony. Tracy claimed that there'd been no balcony, and that he'd been dressed in pajama bottoms but no shirt.

According to Tracy, all he did was shout and wave at the cadets, who were supposedly amused by his "hilarious conduct." Yet the authorities couldn't have been too amused. According to contemporary news accounts, Tracy only escaped prosecution by chartering a private plane to fly him across the border, after being released on his own recognizance.

Arriving in Los Angeles by train, he was met by his girlfriend, actress Isabel Jewell, and by reporters, who overheard him as he called to her: "Holy cats, honey, but it's been a dizzy week." Fans couldn't have hoped for a better Lee Tracy–type line.

Tracy's career, unlike that of Larry Renault, was hardly through. He continued to work for the rest of his life, occasionally in Hollywood, often on Broadway, and, in later years, on television. The public didn't turn on him—in fact, people in 1933 seemed to find the story amusing. Soon after the Mexico incident, columnist Louella Parsons reported that audiences were cheering whenever a trailer for a Tracy picture was shown. And the following April, *Modern Screen* declared that "the jury of public opinion has acquitted Lee Tracy."

Tracy himself never saw the need to pretend at contrition. "I have no apology to make to anyone," he said—and he went out of his way to assure one interviewer that his quiet demeanor didn't mean he'd reformed. "This is just exactly the way I lived and acted before," he said. "I don't think even my most hectic critics have ever accused me of being drunk *all* the time." Had it been up to the public, Mexico would have been a speed bump in Tracy's career. But studios, not audiences, take the financial risk in making films, and studios became reluctant to invest in Tracy's stardom.

The actor's continued flair for making newspaper headlines in the years that followed could only have reinforced the studios' concerns. The record is of one absurd incident after another. In March 1935, he was arrested for getting drunk and firing five shots through the floor of his apartment into his downstairs neighbor's kitchen. Following a hearing in court, Tracy explained his behavior to reporters, "When I got home last night and sat down in a chair, I saw, across the room on another chair, a certain ashtray. Now I didn't like that ashtray and never did. . . ."

He was back in the news less than a year later, this time for a peculiar incident in which he called the police about a threatening note he said he'd received. Tracy claimed the note had instructed him to make a phone call and set up a meeting. When the police arrived at Tracy's home, they found him in his bathrobe and slippers, drunk and incoherent. They called the number. It was for a grocery store.

The following year, Tracy took "the cure" on his yacht. Perhaps that's what enabled him to stay out of the newspapers up until 1938, when some items on his tax return made the news: $161 in tips to studio employees; $2,600 for food and lodging while working in Hollywood, "away" from home. Home, he claimed, was "Truckville, Pennsylvania."

Before she died, Tracy's mother asked him to promise to give up drinking. He wouldn't, because he didn't want to make a promise he couldn't keep. In 1946, Tracy apparently fell off the wagon again, when he was arrested on an intoxication charge after a run-in with a pushy autograph hound.

That Tracy, in his heyday, undoubtedly played some of his classic scenes with a hangover is a hard thing to imagine when one sees him on-screen. No one was more tightly wired or alert. "I'm acting the way I've always wanted to be," he once said of his screen persona. Real life was the hard part.

"Why all this adverse publicity about Lee Tracy's bad habits?" a fan once wrote to *Modern Screen*. "All we know is that he's a great actor." Many decades later, the hapless drinker is history, while the actor— delightful, extraordinary, irreplaceable—is all there's left to know.

• • •

THE PRE-CODE ERA was one in which audiences wanted to believe in fixers, those guys with the banter and the angles to sell anything, snow anybody, and solve any problem. Tracy made a career playing such fellows. He didn't play all of them.

Douglas Fairbanks, Jr., remembered today as a patrician and a swashbuckler, was completely at home in *Love Is a Racket* as a big-city gossip columnist, doing all those things that gossip columnists naturally do: He hobnobs with celebrities, attends openings, and he covers up a murder because he thinks his girlfriend did it. Actually, his girlfriend's mother did it, but, in any case, covering up a homicide was all in a day's work.

Fairbanks once said that his favorite thing about living in the twentieth century was the speed of it—the ability to travel by air, talk by phone, send telegrams, take trains, drive fast, talk on the radio. Actors who excelled in these fixer roles exuded a comfort with the speed and tools of twentieth-century life. They played men who were not intimidated by the size and impersonality of urban life and saw the big city as a playground in which to romp.

Journalism was a natural profession for such characters. As reporters never kept set hours, they could be on the job or at home as the plot required. Gangsters, businessmen, and socialites traveled in a confined circle. But reporters, at least in the movies, gained entrance into all spheres, acting as roving proletarian spies or ambassadors, talking all the way. Pre-Code movies never portrayed journalists as quiet writer types. They rarely seemed to write at all. Their job was to talk fast, into a telephone, while an unseen rewrite man on the other end did all the work.

In 1931, Frank Capra's *Platinum Blonde* had shown blithe reporter Robert Williams talking his way into marriage to a wealthy heiress (Jean Harlow), then talking his way out of it when he could no longer stand life in his wife's shadow. Williams, who was airy and hard-nosed by turns, had a one-of-a-kind way of speaking lines—breezy and distracted, yet focused. An unmistakable original, Williams is one of film history's regrets. After a handful of talkies and this one starring role, he died of a ruptured appendix at age thirty-four.

Some movies touched on the abuses of the press, but in a casual way, chalking them up to exuberance, the rough-and-tumble nature of the profession, or a single reporter's ruthlessness—as in the case of *Is My Face Red?* (1932), with Ricardo Cortez as yet another Walter Winchell spin-off. The Edward G. Robinson film *Five Star Final,* which had arrived in 1931, was in a different category. It looked at press abuse as systemic, not isolated. And it dealt with the media's intrusion into the lives of average people: A tabloid newspaper resurrects an old murder case for a sensational "Where are they now?" exposé that results in several ruined lives and a pair of suicides.

Robinson played the managing editor of a New York tabloid, who hates his job but likes his pension plan. Plagued by guilt, he has an obsessive compulsion for hand washing, but that works about as well for him as it did for Lady Macbeth. He also has to endure the disapproving looks of his secretary (Aline MacMahon), who is both his conscience and the film's moral voice. When the tabloid resurrects the case—twenty years earlier, a woman was acquitted for killing in self-defense—someone points out that the story will sell papers. The secretary answers, "You can always get people interested in the crucifixion of a woman."

Robinson assigns the story to a reporter, played by Boris Karloff, one of the few slow-talking journalists of the era. To infiltrate the home of the now-married and middle-aged defendant, Karloff dresses as a minister. When Robinson sees Karloff in the clerical garb, he sneers, "You're the most blasphemous-looking thing I've ever seen. It's a miracle you're not struck dead." Yet the movie takes pains to make sure that no one's hands are clean. Robinson's self-disgust doesn't absolve him. His redemption comes only at the end, when he sees the disaster he helped create and follows his conscience. If the movie has a main villain, it's the publisher, a rich, self-righteous phony who embodies the duplicity of the industry. Before Robinson says good-bye to his job and his pension—and goes off with his secretary—he leaves the boss with the kiss-off: "I want you to know that every human being who works for you knows what a diseased hypocrite you are."

Though reporters could travel in all social spheres, journalism was, all the same, presented as a low-down profession, whose denizens moved in rowdy, hostile packs. "Once again . . . Warner[s] has seen fit to portray newspapermen as a group of moronic hoodlums," complained the *New York American* when *The Strange Love of Molly Louvain* opened. In *Picture Snatcher* (1933), James Cagney played a mug who is released from Sing Sing and goes right into a job as a photographer for a New York tabloid. The social milieus of prison and journalism were about the same.

Like reporters, the publicists and promoters in pre-Code movies were idea men, masters of mass manipulation. The difference was that they didn't travel in packs and they tended to have more class, or at least more polish. In *High Pressure* (1932), William Powell is sobered up following a bender and hired to promote a process that makes rubber out of sewage. He sets up a glorious facade with a suite of offices, inspires a sales team, and sees the stock rise—only to find out that the process doesn't work and that its inventor is insane. Still, the movie myth of guys like these was that they were invincible. Somehow, they always got out of trouble.

In *The Dark Horse* (1932), the magnificent Warren William, of whom we shall hear more, played an expert in running political campaigns. "He's the dumbest human being I ever saw," he says of his own candidate, but he surmises that this could work to their advantage: The voters will mistake the candidate's stupidity for honesty and plainspokenness. In *The Dark Horse*, it was axiomatic that even the electoral process was open to the machinations of sleazy individualists like William. But better they than the unbalanced or wholly malevolent.

Pre-Code audiences enjoyed watching charlatans work their cons and wiggle out of trouble. "The public is like a cow, bellowing, bellowing to be milked," Cagney says in *Hard to Handle* (1933). "And if you're smart, you'll get yourself a bucket." He played a publicist who, faced with prison for having sold a series of worthless grapefruit farms, increases demand for the product by promoting the "eighteen-day grapefruit diet." He tells one grapefruit distributor, "You're making it possible to bring happiness and peace of mind to the tortured fat people of the universe!"

Made on Broadway (1933) was so clumsily written that it stated flat out what other movies merely showed. Robert Montgomery starred as a promoter who is described in the opening scene as "the greatest press agent, the best fixer, the smartest guy at figuring angles this town has ever seen." Enter Montgomery in a derby and spats, a sophisticated New Yorker with his hand in everything—politics, law enforcement, finance, business. Women love him. "The dames you've almost loved would reach from here to Chicago, laid end to end," his valet grumbles. To which he replies, "What a quaint expression."

The rest of the movie was a jumble, but the opening, at least, gives us the early-thirties vision of ultimate success—a man with a smooth facade and lots of connections, living on the fringes of the law.

WITH MOVIES ABOUT opportunists in vogue by 1932, John Gilbert's starring in *Downstairs* (1932) must have seemed like a reasonable career move. Pictures had become increasingly cynical by 1932, and they would get even more cynical before the Code intruded in mid-1934. Yet nothing could have prepared audiences for *Downstairs*, a movie that had the misfortune of being ahead of its time by about forty years.

Leading up to *Downstairs*, Gilbert's talkie history had been a series of disappointments and humiliations. Howard Hawks had hoped to cast him in *The Dawn Patrol* in 1930, a movie that could have helped him, but MGM's Louis B. Mayer refused to lend him out to Warners. Meanwhile, at MGM, Gilbert watched helplessly as roles originally intended for him went to other people. Nature, hating a vacuum, had seen fit to bestow upon MGM Clark Gable, who emerged to replace Gilbert as the studio's alpha male. In what might have been the worst blow, Gilbert was given the lead in *Red Dust* (1932), only to see it yanked from him and handed to Gable.

In 1932, Irving Thalberg—perhaps feeling guilty for doing exactly squat to stop his supposed friend's slide into oblivion—agreed to let Gilbert make a movie from his own scenario. It was one Gilbert had been carrying around since the silent days. Set in Central Europe, *Downstairs* was the story of a chauffeur who moves into a wealthy household and proceeds to seduce, blackmail, and steal from everybody. It was the story of a black-hearted scoundrel, a smiling, irredeemable rogue who lies and calculates every waking minute. On the few occasions when he lets loose with a real emotion, it's made of nothing but sneers and bile.

One can only wonder at the psychological implications of Gilbert's writing such a story for himself at the height of his silent glory. Had the notoriously self-destructive Gilbert harbored a dark impulse to kill his career—or at least his heroic image? In the 1920s, such a movie would have seemed to arrive from Pluto. By 1932, the presence of unpleasant protagonists in film suggested that maybe the times had caught up with the story.

For his director, Gilbert was given Monta Bell, with whom he had collaborated on a number of silents, including *Man, Woman and Sin* (1927). Bell, with his caustic irony, was ideal for *Downstairs*. He had a particular affinity for class issues, and virtually all his extant films demonstrate an anger toward the oblivious cruelties of privilege. In Bell's hands, Gilbert's despicable chauffeur was bound to emerge full strength.

Warner Bros. movies had a warmth, a swift pace, and a gallows humor—an overall style that, in itself, expressed a kind of philosophy and gave its most anarchic subject matter an understandable, crazy-world context. But *Downstairs* was an MGM film. As such, it expressed its mad reality within a reasonably paced, naturalistic framework, which only made the film's perversity stand out in greater relief. This was no heightened reality, but human nature in action, according to Gilbert and Bell.

Karl (Gilbert) starts his new job and quickly gets the lay of the land. The master of the house (Reginald Owen) is a selfish hypochondriac; his wife is an adulteress. Karl embarks on a three-pronged quest for power: He blackmails the mistress, seduces the pretty young maid (Virginia Bruce), who is married to the butler, and plots to steal the life savings of the fat old cook, who keeps her money rolled up in her stocking.

With the maid, he's self-effacing and sneaky, overstepping himself and retreating, waiting for his moment, his eyes dark and his smile steady, pouring the wine and pouring the wine until she's drunk and ready for anything. Gilbert is the perfect villain. His thoughts are always clear. Because his eyes never lie to us, it's fun to watch him lying.

His scenes with the cook are a hoot for the opposite reason. With her, he worries less about letting his personality slip through, and that personality is appalling. Apparently, they've been sleeping with each other. He calls her "grandma" and tells her, "With a face like yours, you oughta pay plenty." In a scene that makes viewers wonder if they're actually seeing what they're seeing, Gilbert talks to her as he picks his nose and his ears with his pinkie, then wipes it on his shirt. Such was Gilbert's plan for getting back in the public's good graces. Good plan, wrong century.

Today, we can see the humor of *Downstairs* as expressing dark truths about human lust and avarice. But in its time, the picture—which was just a bit weirder and nastier than anything else the era produced—was hated by critics, who saw it as a needless wallow in unpleasantness. It would take another world war to make people jaded enough to embrace *Downstairs*, and by then, the movie would be forgotten.

Indeed, it was forgotten almost as soon as it came out. In 1932, it came and went, just one more nail in Gilbert's coffin. Not until the nineties did a widespread audience get to discover it on television (thanks to Turner Classic Movies) and see the dark little masterpiece that Gilbert and Bell had made.

For Bell, *Downstairs* was the last important film, expressing a bleak vision of Depression economics as seen through the veneer of Austrian society. For Gilbert it was even more—a personal statement about his own stardom and a real parting shot. Through the protagonist, Gilbert got to present his own seductive power as something calculated, joyless, and dangerous—and to show the people who fell for it as gullible and ridiculous. Perhaps that's why the film failed: Audiences and critics registered the insult without quite grasping it.

Gilbert would go on to make a few more pictures, including *Queen Christina*, the Garbo classic. But this was his last, best chance to transform himself from an old-style great lover to a new-style roguish lover, and it didn't work. Perhaps nothing would have worked.

At least this once, Gilbert got to thumb his nose on the way down.

9

"No Longer a Man's World"

MODERN MEN LIKED modern women. Pre-Code movies consistently presented admirable and heroic characters who—even when they looked like old-fashioned he-men—were broad-minded, tolerant, and appreciative when it came to women. These fellows weren't necessarily easy to get along with, but at least they weren't virtue-obsessed or judgmental. Except in Greta Garbo movies, which were in their own category, heroes did not barge out in a huff when they heard the heroine wasn't a virgin.

The pre-Code era, a great age for men, was also *the* great age for women in American cinema, a fact that should not be overlooked. In this period, there was a rich array of talented and charismatic actresses making films that reflected the expanding role of women in modern America. Their movies dealt with changing mores regarding sex, romance, and marriage, and they showed women in the workplace, sometimes as educated professionals. The films, which echoed the public's changing attitudes, would grow yet more freethinking and daring until the ax of censorship fell in July 1934.

Men's films reflected those same changes. That men and women were equal partners in the adventure of life was not something asserted by these movies, but something so understood as to need no asserting. Anyone looking for a rare pocket of film history in which male-female relationships were presented as healthy, sane, and lively should look no further than the years 1929 to 1934.

Yet in acknowledging this, it's important not to sweep a few facts under the rug. One item too big for any rug is the era's indelible image of James Cagney hitting Mae Clarke in the face with a grapefruit in *The Public Enemy* (1931). Even if we counter that by saying that the jolly relationship between William Powell and Myrna Loy in *The Thin Man* (1934)—or Astaire and Rogers in *Flying Down to Rio* (1933)—was more in the spirit of the era than the grapefruit incident, there are yet other moments to account for: Cagney's dragging Mae Clarke by the hair in *Lady Killer* (1933); Chester Morris working over Jean Harlow in *Red-Headed Woman* (1932), though she seems to like it; and the comic climax of *Bureau of Missing Persons* (1933), in which Pat O'Brien beats up greedy ex-wife Glenda Farrell, offscreen, as we hear the sounds of crashing and breaking.

Certainly, in a way that's lost to us, Depression audiences seemed to get a kick out of the sight of men and women physically fighting, whether it was Norma Shearer and Robert Montgomery's knock-down-drag-out in *Private Lives* (1931) or bad guy Gable's one-punch knockout of Barbara Stanwyck in *Night Nurse* (1931). Audiences, for that matter, also enjoyed the sight of women fighting one another. Yet even if we see some of these encounters as manifestations of an underlying assumption that women could give as well as they got, that was clearly not the whole story.

Cagney himself was self-conscious about his image as a woman-beater and would always go out of his way to assure people he wasn't really that sort of guy. In an early interview, for *Movie Classic* in October 1931, he ruefully read from his fan mail. Fourteen- and fifteen-year-old girls were apparently writing in to say that they hoped he was "as nasty and brutal" in real life, because they "adore[d] nasty and brutal men" and could "love him to death." In 1933, he told a reporter, "I can't . . . sock a woman on screen without feeling nauseated. Fact is, I've developed a technique of my own that makes for realism but wouldn't hurt the pollen on a butterfly's wing." Two years later, as if to atone, he gave a woman reporter from *Modern Screen* jujitsu lessons. When she pointed out that she hardly looked like a wrestler, Cagney answered, "Do I?"

In these early years, Cagney was both a tough-guy actor and a romantic icon. Critic Irene Thirer wrote in 1932, "The lad isn't tall, isn't handsome, isn't romantic. He's cute, and he has a grand sense of humor." Apparently, that was enough. Reporter Gladys Hall claimed that Hollywood's actresses invariably mentioned Cagney "as their idea of sex appeal, and they mean sex appeal." Glenda Farrell called him "the most vital man I've ever known. Physically vital. Mentally vital. Emotionally vital." Mae West gave a characteristically terse explanation of Cagney's appeal, "It's because he always looks as though he's just about to spring."

It would be a mistake to pretend that Cagney's appeal was in spite of his brutality rather than partly because of it. In April 1932, the *New York World-Telegram* went so far as to write, "James Cagney gained his large following because he was rough on women. . . . No screen hero ever was rougher on the fair sex than Cagney and none ever dominated them more than Gable."

The freedom of pre-Code cinema, so heartening to encounter, is evident not just in its willingness to endorse the era's most open-minded attitudes toward sex and relationships but also in its low-down acceptance of some of the more inconvenient and embarrassing aspects of sexual attraction. With popular expression not limited by some 1932 equivalent of political correctness, movies could delve into the squishy, messy terrain of lust—or just play with the silliness of it all. In *Blood Money* (1933), Frances Dee had her most amusing early role, playing a nymphomaniac heiress whose single-minded attraction for brutes frightens big bruiser George Bancroft. She wants a tough guy, she tells him, so she can "follow him around like a dog on a leash."

In 1932, *Picture Play* magazine asked women to write in about what they found attractive about Clark Gable. One fan called him "the most deliciously ugly man I've ever seen." Another wrote, "Clark Gable's thrilling because no girl would feel safe with him for a minute." Of the dangerous men of pre-Code, Gable was the most sexually dangerous. As we saw earlier, his brutality to Norma Shearer in *A Free Soul* (1931) lifted him out of supporting roles and captured the imagination of fans. From then on, writers were comparing his allure to that of Rudolph Valentino, who had died in 1926. Asked by a reporter if he hoped to incite the same screaming, hysterical feminine adulation that had attended the earlier icon's career, Gable had the perfect answer. He said, "I should think it would be sort of repulsive."

In matters of style, Valentino and Gable were completely different. Valentino was smooth and Continental; Gable, rough and American. Yet they had one thing in common, apart from their appeal. They played men who accepted and understood women as sexual beings. In the case of the Latin lover Valentino, this would be expected, but Gable often played American lugs, hard guys with some pretty narrow ideas, generally speaking. Yet in the pre-Codes, once Gable was a star, these narrow ideas didn't extend to women and sexuality.

Before he was a star, Gable could appear in a minor role in *The Easiest Way* (1931), refusing to let his sister-in-law (Constance Bennett) set foot in his house because she was a fallen woman, the mistress of a wealthy man. After *A Free Soul*, he became, in comparison, a paragon of sophistication. In *Sporting Blood* (1931), his true love was Madge Evans, the drunken mistress of his boss. In *Possessed* (1931), he was a wealthy power broker, whose true love was his mistress, played by Joan Crawford. In *Red Dust* (1932), his character's moral journey consisted of realizing that the playful, wise-talking prostitute, played by Jean Harlow, was just the girl for him. And in *Strange Interlude* (1932), he was in love with a promiscuous neurotic (Shearer), with whom he then had a child, though she was married to another man.

As a figure of fantasy, Gable was all purpose. His allure was irresistible. He was dangerous enough to impose his will, thus relieving a woman of responsibility for her actions. And he was broad-minded enough that when it was all over, he'd still respect her, maybe even respect her more for taking a chance. On-screen—and off, too—Gable preferred worldly, sexually sophisticated women.

He wasn't the only one. In *Roar of the Dragon* (1932), an adventure about white tourists trapped in revolutionary China, he-man Richard Dix played a drunken captain who falls in love with Gwili Andre, who has been the sex slave of a war lord. In James Whale's *Waterloo Bridge* (1931), Kent Douglass was a sensitive young soldier who wants to marry Mae Clarke and doesn't care that she has been a streetwalker.

Perhaps soldiers and prostitutes understood each other, both of them victims of gender. In *Rain* (1932), William Gargan was an easygoing sergeant who falls in love with the notorious Sadie Thompson (Joan Crawford). Her past doesn't faze him. "Them that kick highest always seem to settle down the hardest," he says. A year later, Miriam Hopkins gave Gargan a second opportunity to be forward-thinking, in *The Story of Temple Drake*, in which she confesses on the witness stand that she lived with a murderous gangster.

In pre-Codes, good guys didn't get worked up about a woman's virtue—villains did. So in *Faithless* (1932), good guy Robert Montgomery is only awed by his wife's sacrifice when he finds out she turned tricks in order to support him through a life-threatening health crisis. In contrast, Herbert Marshall rejects Dietrich in *Blonde Venus* (1932) for doing more or less the same thing, "It would've been better, Helen, if you'd let me die." He is clearly the villain, and on the off chance there might be any doubt, director Josef von Sternberg lights Marshall as a figure of shadows and menace.

The willingness of early-thirties heroes to be sanguine, not only about their wives' sacrificial sexcapades but also about a fair quotient of premarital misadventure, allowed for a cheerful approach to male-female relationships. It's a pleasing thing, for example, to see Warren William, as a blue-blooded banker in *Gold Diggers of 1933*, going gaga over chorus girl Joan Blondell, whom he first regarded as "cheap and vulgar." Later, when she playfully throws his words back at him, he tells her, "Every time you say 'cheap and vulgar' I'm going to kiss you."

The movies were keeping pace with the public. As Frederick Lewis Allen wrote in *Only Yesterday* (1931), his snapshot social history of the 1920s:

> One began to hear of young girls, intelligent and well-born, who had spent week-ends with men before marriage and had told their prospective husbands everything and had been not merely for-given, but told there was nothing to forgive; a little "experience," these men felt, was all to the good for any girl. . . . There was an unmistakable and rapid trend away from the old American code toward a philosophy of sex relations and of marriage wholly new to the country, toward a feeling that the virtues of chastity and fidelity had been rated too highly. . . .

We can see this new philosophy play out in *Woman Accused* (1933). Cary Grant, in an early role, wants to marry Nancy Carroll, but she says she can't because she once lived with a man. Grant replies by sticking out his hand and saying, "Shake." They shake hands and forget it, and in no time he's wooing her with the kind of lines that Grant made famous, "I'd go miles and miles on my hands and knees over broken bottles just for a little kiss."

There's a mutuality about sex, as it's spoken of in these films, that comes as a surprise to anyone familiar with movies made under the Code. In pre-Codes, sex was understood as something men and women did together, not something men did *to* women. *A Farewell to Arms* (1932)—essentially a love story set against a World War I background— featured Gary Cooper and Helen Hayes as an ambulance driver and a nurse who meet at a party. Since this is wartime, they don't even wait till the first date—they have sex immediately, in the garden, while the party goes on inside. The next day Cooper shows up at the military hospital where she works and, stammering as only he can, tells her, "I'd hate to have you feel that it wasn't important to me . . . about us."

After July 1934, movie heroes would have to cultivate an interest in virgins, but in the pre-Codes sophisticated women were the ideal, and innocence was almost never an aphrodisiac. A rare exception came in Cecil B. DeMille's *The Sign of the Cross* (1932), in which Fredric March played a Roman prefect who falls in love with a virtuous Christian girl, played by Elissa Landi. Over the course of the film, he does everything he can to tempt her with the pleasures of pagan life, and when nothing works, he chucks it all and becomes a Christian.

Yet, looked at from another angle, even *The Sign of the Cross* wasn't really against the pre-Code pattern. Reverse the sexes, and March's role was typical, very much in the tradition established by Greta Garbo and upheld by other leading ladies of the era. He played a sexually active man who has never known love, a big slut given a choice between two lovers—a decadent, cynical lover (Claudette Colbert), who represents his past, or a virtuous one (Landi), pointing the way to a life-changing direction. Like the boring leading men of Garbo's films, Landi in *The Sign of the Cross* has no worldly power, no leverage at all but moral example. That example suggests to him a love beyond sex, beyond human imperfection, an example so strong that he becomes a martyr. It says something about the halfhearted spirituality of the times, that when called upon to craft a Christian epic, the best DeMille's writers could come up with was a guy version of a Garbo movie.

IN INTERVIEWS, MOST actors went out of their way to praise modern women, often at the expense of more traditional ladies. In one interview, Richard Barthelmess managed a loony segue from extolling the femininity of working women to expounding on the mental power of great loose gals of history:

> I believe the economically independent woman can be, and usually is, as feminine as the old-fashioned wife and mother who rocked the cradle with one hand and had hysterics with the other. . . . Look at the famous women of history. Dubarry, Maintenon, de Lienclos, Nell Gwynn. True, they were courtesans. But certainly they were all feminine to the nth degree and certainly, also, they were powerful mentally. They knew how to make their brains serve their bodies and their bodies serve their brains. . . . This is no longer a man's world. It may have been once upon a time, but that time is gone.

Gable, when asked what he liked in women, said he liked, according to Gladys Hall, "modern women, self-reliant women, women with minds of their own . . . not clinging vines nor cute little things." The comment calls to mind the scene from *Susan Lenox: Her Fall and Rise* (1931) in which Gable, pestered by a cute clinging vine, finally scoops her up and throws her over a stairway landing. Gable had a way of making his preferences clear.

Of the young leading men, only Ramon Novarro was willing to stick up for tradition. Presenting himself as a gentleman of the old school, he expounded on his ideas about women and romance in a 1930 interview. "The women of America are starved for romance," he said, "and they have brought it on themselves. Women have insisted on being 'equal' to man. . . . Women have thrown away, with their own hands, their own mystery."

In making such remarks, Novarro was, in essence, placing himself in opposition to the modern tide, announcing a determination to be old-fashioned. He was probably sincere, though one might doubt the intensity with which Novarro, a gay man, fretted over womanly mystery. Perhaps upholding the old verities in the face of faddishness seemed a decent strategy. But movie stars who embody unfashionable notions, then and ever since, are invariably doomed to decline.

To watch a succession of Novarro's films, in chronological order, is fascinating. MGM tried everything, but nothing helped. In *Son of India* (1931), he was an Indian diamond merchant, in love with a lovely white woman (Madge Evans). Novarro goes through the movie abject and forlorn, and then in the final shot, he gives her up, kneeling before her like a sexless, pathetic specimen. What was MGM thinking, and how did Novarro allow that to be shot?

MGM also tried him as an Italian-American college football player in *Huddle* (1932), again pathetically abject in the face of Madge Evans's beauty (at least in the early scenes). The movie wasn't bad, but by now the fans smelled blood. A 1932 letter to *Picture Play* offered the kind of friendly advice that could keep an actor up nights, "Tone down the adolescent behavior or else take an inch off the jowl line."

By 1932, Novarro's old style of romance came across as less principled than fearful. It was as if his characters were resorting to old-fashioned courting as a way of insulating themselves from the disconcerting reality of their women's complexity. So, in a change of pace, he was cast in *The Barbarian* (1933). In his early talkies, Novarro had played a cuddly nuisance. Now he played a smirky, sadistic one, an Egyptian who rapes an American woman (Myrna Loy). The assault (off-camera) was meant to be understood as romantic, evocative of Valentino, but the film left a bad taste. Things got even worse in *Laughing Boy* (1934), in which he played an American Indian who accidentally kills his wife (Lupe Velez) with a bow and arrow.

The winning formula for Novarro should have been obvious: Cast him opposite a modern woman and don't have him slaver, don't have him rape her, and, by all means, don't let him near a bow and arrow. Just have him act like an adult man with an adult woman. That happened exactly twice in Novarro's talkie career: Once, when it was too late, in *The Night Is Young* (1935), his last starring role at MGM; and earlier, in the movie *Daybreak* (1931), made when there was still hope.

In *Daybreak*, Novarro was, as usual, a playboy in the grand manner— a bit too grand at times—but for once he was neither boyish nor innocuous. He played a fellow so macho that he lets his gay valet wear his underwear. ("I think they're beautiful," the valet says.) And his lover was played by the lovely and bizarre Helen Chandler, whom he first seduces in a Viennese beer garden. In her characteristically plaintive yet detached way, Chandler tells him that when she first met him, she wondered "what I'd give you for breakfast." For once, it was good to see Novarro interacting with a complicated woman. When he accidentally insults her, she leaves him to become a glamorous sophisticate. "I've only lately learned to appreciate your viewpoint," she tells him, ". . . about finding love where you like it." No one would call *Daybreak* a searing exploration of sexual politics, but it showed Novarro at his romantic best, finally holding his own with a woman of his time.

Chandler had the "mystery" that Novarro, in his interview, claimed was lacking in American women. It was a mystery of complication, not of innocence. To bring a smile to the face of an ingenue—how could that be a legitimate challenge for a world-class screen lover? Any handsome fellow with a decent line could sweep a naïve girl off her feet. What Novarro never quite realized, and what MGM somehow never discovered for him, was that in this bold new era, ingenues did not make romantic heroes look good. Sexy, daring leading ladies did.

It wasn't necessary to be a he-man like Gable. The pre-Codes saw another type of leading man emerge, one who was relaxed, well mannered, and comfortable in a woman's milieu. William Powell is best known today for his *Thin Man* series, and for his crisp speech and precise gestures, which often took on a faint trace of self-mockery. But in his early talkies, at Paramount, he played seducers and gigolos. In *Charming Sinners* (1929), he's an old friend of Ruth Chatterton whom he tries to take from her cheating husband. In *Ladies' Man* (1931), he lives off the gifts of wealthy women and has his downfall when a mother and daughter fall in love with him. Before he can go straight and marry the woman he really loves, the wronged husband/father kills him.

Powell hated playing the *Ladies' Man*. "He was just weak. Passive. . . . He hasn't any of the characteristics of parts I like to play," he complained to *Screenland*. Indeed, the gigolo was more pitiable than enviable, soiling himself in affairs with unattractive, gullible victims. "It sounds trite," Powell told *Screenland*, "but I am a very unhappy person."

In the middle of 1931, Powell moved from Paramount to Warner Bros. and had reason to be happy in his first assignment there, *The Road to Singapore* (1931). It took the seducer character Powell had established and turned him into a hero. "[Powell] saunters through the picture with bored, heavy-lidded detachment," wrote critic Harriet Parsons, "yet conveying always a suggestion of fascinating danger." He played Dawltry, the most notorious man in Khota, a British community in the tropics. Scorned by decent society for having broken up a marriage, he spends most of his evenings getting drunk in the local club. Here and elsewhere, Powell had a way of picking up a highball glass as though handling a precision tool.

The Road to Singapore was a film about one thing only—a man's effort to break up yet another marriage. Dawltry wants Philippa (Doris Kenyon), the new wife of the town doctor, a fussy workaholic played by Louis Calhern. Will Hays, upon seeing the finished film, wrote a letter in protest to producer Jack Warner, which accurately summed up the film's story and point of view, "The picture portrays the relationship and the characters who represent decent and conventional society in a most unfavorable light and clearly attempts to create sympathy and justification for an adulterous affair without any attempt to show that this is wrong or immoral." Certainly, there's no husbandly wickedness to justify the wife's behavior. The doctor isn't mean to his wife, just boring. Confronted with an interesting case, he asks Philippa, a former nurse, if she'd like to work with him on it. She answers, "I came here to be a wife, not a nurse." The film embraces those who loll about all day, drinking and lusting, and makes a mockery of the hardworking professional.

The maturity of the actors added to the sense of seriousness, that these were no kids involved in a flirtation. Powell was thirty-nine, and Kenyon was thirty-four. From early in the movie, as we see her fanning herself as she reclines on a daybed, her legs spread, we understand that here in the tropics a womanly sexuality percolates. The adult nature of the lust is emphasized by the unsuccessful attempts by Philippa's teenage sister (Marian Marsh) to seduce Dawltry. He's not interested in a kid.

The Road to Singapore suggested not only that physical attraction made its own rules but that it had a right to, that to submit to such impulses was to be in harmony with nature. The film's most impressive shot begins with Philippa sitting longingly on her porch at night, listening to the tribal drums beat-beat-beat out a tribute to the goddess of love. The camera tracks from her porch through the woods, past the trees, and through the village, finally coming to rest on Dawltry, who is also listening. The two are of one mind, while the graceful shot suggests that the distance between their bodies can be just as easily surmounted.

Robert Montgomery was another actor comfortable in a women's milieu. His one-of-a-kind screen image allowed him to play callow young men and sophisticates, by turns, and also men who somehow managed to be both: childish professionals, immature rich kids, boyish snobs. After a stage career in New York, he arrived at MGM in 1929, appearing as an embodiment of carefree twenties youth in *So This Is College* and, opposite Shearer, in *Their Own Desire*.

Something slightly shifty about Montgomery's essence made it easy to accept him as a drunk who goes to bed with his best friend's wife in *The Divorcee* and as a convicted drunk driver who turns stool pigeon in *The Big House* (both 1930). From the beginning, Montgomery specialized in portraying nonachievers. Yet his flops, wastrels, petty thieves, and sodden playboys were always pleasant to be around. Montgomery played fully nonproductive members of society, men who were silly, easily rattled, and yet deeply confident, in a childlike way, of their own beauty.

Over the course of 1930, MGM came to recognize Montgomery's value as a romantic lead. Then again, who else did the studio have? Chester Morris was good, but he never caught on completely. Gable would not be signed by the studio for another year. Silent stars Gilbert, Novarro, and an impish comedian named William Haines were sinking fast, and the studio's great male star, Lon Chaney, was dead. Anyone who could hold up a suit at MGM might have had a chance in 1930, and Montgomery was more than a suit. He was both a handsome lead and a comedian, and at a time when the package wasn't typical. Until Cary Grant came along, Montgomery held the patent.

He was cast opposite Joan Crawford in *Untamed* (1929) and *Our Blushing Brides* (1930). He graduated to Garbo in *Inspiration* (1931), a disastrous pairing, but his role as the usual prudish Garbo boyfriend was impossible. Playing prudes was not Montgomery's strength. He was debonair and hardly seemed tortured by conscience or scruples. In *The*

Easiest Way (1931), he left Constance Bennett when he discovered her living with another man, but the film ended with the possibility that he might return. That's as ambiguous as things got. After that, Montgomery became the ideal costar in women's pictures. He didn't care whom his women slept with.

In *Strangers May Kiss* (1931), he wants to marry Shearer, even after she has had a series of meaningless affairs in every European capital. In *The Man in Possession* (1931), he proposes to Irene Purcell, who has had a shady past with at least one wealthy suitor. He reached the apex of tolerance in *Letty Lynton* (1932), choosing to overlook not only Joan Crawford's life with a previous lover but also the fact that she murdered the guy. And in *When Ladies Meet* (1933), he makes it his mission to take Myrna Loy away from her married lover, Frank Morgan.

Montgomery was a drunk in *Strangers May Kiss*. He played more than his share of drunks—usually polite, always boyish. In *Private Lives* (1931), it was his petulance that made him boyish. In *Another Language* (1933), he was a perpetual child, a married man unable to escape or even recognize the manipulations of his selfish mother (Louise Closser Hale). It was an unflattering role and produced one of his best pre-Code performances.

Taken together, Montgomery's pre-Codes give us a picture of a certain kind of young American man—born to relative comfort, having come of age in the tolerant atmosphere of the twenties; dapper, pleasure-loving, sometimes shallow, sometimes unconventional—dimly, if at all, aware of the rules, and following only his heart. His heart always led him to women.

Montgomery played men who needed women. He didn't need them in the Gable way—needing them and not knowing it—or the Cagney way, needing them but knowing they'd always be around. Montgomery's characters *knew* they needed women. They needed girlfriends, lovers, mommies, wives, and nurses, and when they found a woman who was all those things, they wanted her. It was the one thing they knew. Often, it was their one saving grace.

MAURICE CHEVALIER, A star of musicals, occupies a singular position as a leading man. Though musicals, after an early talkie heyday, had become box-office roadkill by 1931, Chevalier enjoyed and grew in popularity. At Paramount, working with some of the studio's—indeed history's—finest directors (Rouben Mamoulian, George Cukor, Ernst Lubitsch), he made films that were startling in their daring. Time and again, Chevalier sang about sex and little else. And he played men who did more than sing about it.

Offscreen, Chevalier's moodiness and reserve were remarked upon by journalists. *Vanity Fair* described him as "taciturn, aloof and more than a little cynical." Perhaps he gave too much in performance to have much energy left for real life. On-screen, he was the ultimate extrovert, throwing himself into songs with enormous gusto, playfulness, and a flamboyance that stayed just within the border of complete foolishness, but only just within it.

If an erection had a personality, it would act like Chevalier in films such as *The Smiling Lieutenant* (1931), *One Hour with You* (1932), and *Love Me Tonight* (1932). His energy is relentless. He exudes insinuation. Chevalier's humor, his appeal, and, undoubtedly, his Frenchness allowed the characters he played to escape judgment for a level of sexuality that would have made any other leading man appear immoral and unsavory.

In *The Smiling Lieutenant*, he played a Viennese guard forced into marriage with a foreign princess (Miriam Hopkins). Yet he continues to see his lover (Claudette Colbert) and refuses to sleep with his wife. The film's ending, in which the wife transforms into a siren and the lover goes away forever, has been criticized as an unfortunate concession to morality. In fact, this jarring ending—we root for Colbert all along—takes the movie out of the realm of fairy tale. That Chevalier can be desolate at losing his lover and then, minutes later, be delighted to see his wife in a negligee is in itself a wonderful commentary on the nature of the Chevalier hero and of male sexuality in general. The smiling lieutenant is quite simple, after all. It doesn't take much to keep him smiling.

The Smiling Lieutenant could not have been made except in the pre-Code era, nor could it be rereleased after it. In 1936, Paramount would request permission to rerelease it and would get back from Production Code chief Joseph Breen a letter demanding twenty-seven cuts, which, if implemented, would have turned the film into a short subject.

In *One Hour with You*, Chevalier continued in his merry pre-Code vein, in a film that treated adultery with Continental nonchalance. He played a happily married doctor, who is relentlessly and shamelessly pursued by his wife's best friend, Mitzi (Genevieve Tobin). Faced one night with the choice of sleeping with his wife (Jeanette MacDonald) or Mitzi, he looks into the camera, singing and weighing his options, unable to decide whether or not to go out or stay home, "But this I know—we can't all three be satisfied."

A few years later, a comic hero might flirt with romantic possibilities but would stay true. (In 1924, in *The Marriage Circle*, the silent version of the same story, the husband never gives in to temptation.) But in *One Hour with You*, our hero goes off and spends the night with Mitzi. Unbeknownst to him, Mitzi's husband has hired a detective, and Chevalier soon finds himself on the brink of having his infidelity exposed. Whereupon he sings Richard A. and Leo Robbin's "Now I Ask What Would You Do?" asking the men in the audience if they'd have done anything differently. Wouldn't they have "kissed her"? Certainly they wouldn't have "treated her like" a "sister." "I ask you, what would you do?" he sings, and then shrugs miserably. "That's what I did, too."

"All of these [songs] seem quite risqué," wrote the Studio Relations Committee, whose job was to get Hollywood movies past the state censor boards, uncut and intact. "But bearing in mind that Chevalier will do them, we do not suggest any changes." Such was Chevalier's charm—to get Continental sophistication past people whose mission was to stamp out sophistication at the source.

When the material or the situation was less than ideal, Chevalier could bring it off. In *Love Me Tonight*, he sings "Mimi" to a princess (MacDonald) who is not named Mimi. "I shall call you Mimi!" he says. It's as good an excuse as any. When the material was ideal, Chevalier soared. In the glorious Rodgers and Hart's number "Isn't It Romantic?", from the same film, the Chevalier character, a tailor, imagines his future marriage. His wife will make onion soup for him, kiss him around the clock, and scrub his back in the shower.

Apparently he anticipates lots of sex and lots of "kiddies," "We'll help the population—it's a duty that we owe to France!" Chevalier sings the line with his mischievous smile, and in that moment embodies the splendor of the era and much of what's wonderful about its films—the zest, the playfulness, and the wholehearted embrace of the physical and romantic sides of love.

At his best, Chevalier suggested a man at peace with himself, one who had the wisdom to understand that the little recreations of life were indeed the substance of life, the Continental understanding that play was serious. On the heels of a social and sexual revolution, Chevalier—whose screen portrayals harmonized lust with an unmistakably warm humanity—assured audiences that sex wasn't bad and couldn't be tragic. In a less direct way, he served the same function and provided the male equivalent of that other great Paramount star, Mae West.

American musical stars were less energetic, more down-to-earth. Bing Crosby, who made his name on radio and in recordings, introduced his offhand, casual personality to movie audiences through cameo roles in feature films and through a series of musical-comedy shorts he made for producer Mack Sennett starting in 1931. With Sennett, Crosby got to perfect his comic skills, though he was such a natural, his skills needed little honing. To see one of those early two-reelers today is to realize Bing was Bing from the beginning—natural, relaxed, and willing to place himself in ridiculous situations, with never any true loss of dignity. It's also to appreciate his ease and grace, while imagining just how revolutionary his manner must have seemed in 1931, barely a year or two removed from the love-me-or-I'll-die antics of Al Jolson. Crosby represented virtually a new kind of consciousness.

In *Going Hollywood* (1933), he played a crooner. Hungover for a recording session in his apartment, he breezes about, singing "Beautiful Girl," mixing a hangover cure as a technician follows him around with a microphone. He is cool, perhaps the first male star to be cool in the modern sense. It's doubtful any man since has ever seen *Going Hollywood* without wishing he could be as smooth and unflappable as Crosby.

Crosby would make his most important contributions during the Code era. So would Fred Astaire, though Astaire's one pre-Code movie with Ginger Rogers, *Flying Down to Rio* (1933), has its distinct magic. She played a singer, and he played an accordion player/choreographer for a musical group that flies down to Rio for an engagement. They weren't the stars of the film. They were in supporting roles, playing a couple of pals who like to hang out on the road.

The duo's extended dance—to the "Carioca"—pleased audiences and led to the Astaire-Rogers vogue. But, of course, it was also their rapport, the appeal of a male-female partnership, that captured audiences' fancy. Astaire-Rogers made visual, indeed iconic, the era's reverence and affection for the notion of men and women working together as equals.

It was the closest thing the pre-Code era had to something sacred. In a frenzied and increasingly desperate world, heroes could lie in business, rob banks, and kill rivals. But once a movie established a woman as a man's partner, that was it. It was the one higher value that saved a man from a savage's self-interest, the one relationship that couldn't be violated without an audience's demanding consequences.

10

Warren William and the Money Changers

ARREN WILLIAM IS one of the singular joys of the pre-Code era. Mention his name to people who've seen his movies, and everyone smiles. For those who don't know him, he's a discovery waiting to be made, an obsession waiting to take hold. To see one William movie is to want to see another, and to see two is to want to see all of them. There has never been a film star like him, nor one who regularly made the kind of movies he made.

In Warren William, all things bright and sleazy about the era come together in a persona at once magnificent, confident, and fraudulent. In film after film, William was the ultimate scoundrel lover—the no-good charmer that John Gilbert tried to create in *Downstairs* (but got tripped up on the charm part). He was also the ultimate fixer, the ultimate liar, the ultimate manipulator. "Don't worry about anything until it happens," he repeatedly tells an underling in *The Match King* (1932). "Then *I'll* take care of it."

William's best work was confined to the pre-Code era. Unlike Robinson, Cagney, or Fredric March, who had outstanding careers for decades, William's heyday was from 1932 until the Code's enforcement in mid-1934. His career continued—he worked steadily until his untimely death in 1948—but the great screen personality he created in his early films just wasn't translatable in an era of censorship. Only a relatively uncensored cinema could have allowed a phenomenon like William to occur, and only a public toughened up by the Depression could have had the mordant humor to respond to his movies.

For those two years, William played mountebanks and big-shot frauds of every stripe. He also gave the era's most indelible portraits of the crooked big businessman. "There is no actor who can talk big money quite as effectively before the camera as Mr. William," the *New York Journal* wrote in 1933. In between talking money, William usually got around to finding time to sexually harass his employees, rob financial partners, drive subordinates to suicide, or even commit murder.

To say his films were cynical isn't enough. They were exuberantly cynical, gloriously cynical. Yet as such, they suggested, in their strange way, an embrace of life in all its madness and variety. In the world of William's films, he was the hero. He was often the villain, too, but he did two things heroes did—he overcame obstacles and achieved his goals. Usually, his goals were purely selfish, but that just made the whole spectacle more absurdist and fun. He was "the master charlatan of the screen," wrote the *New York Post* in 1933, an actor who "brought villainy to a high place in pictures without any noticeable diminution in his own popularity."

Tall, sharp-nosed, and slick, William looked like a fun house–mirror image of John Barrymore, with a vitality that made him appealing. He was as unstoppable as the life force and as relentless. He was relentless with women, too. There was always something of the wolf dressed as granny in his smile. Innocents might be taken in, but never the audience, who, once tipped off, could sit back and enjoy the inexorableness of his technique.

A classic William seduction scene takes place in *The Mind Reader*

(1933), in which he played Chandra the Great, a psychic medium who is absolutely 100 percent fake. He becomes attracted to a young woman (Constance Cummings) who believes in his extrasensory powers, and as they sit on a garden bench together, he begins to make his move. Over the course of a long take, all the while smiling in his eerie way and maintaining an easy flow of conversation, he touches her arm casually; idly fingers the material of her dress; extends his arm over her shoulder, without touching her; and then, first with one finger, then two, puts his hand on her shoulder. Finally, he drops his other hand onto her thigh, as if distracted. He is still smiling, still nodding, and the encirclement is complete. She is engulfed.

William played rogues who inspired loyalty in their women and made us understand that loyalty by being more interesting than any-body else. In *Skyscraper Souls* (1932), he played a visionary builder struggling to maintain financial control over his crowning accomplish-ment, the world's tallest skyscraper. He finagles, schemes, and cheats, with the help of his loyal secretary and mistress (Verree Teasdale). But ultimately he cheats her, taking up with *her* secretary (Maureen O'Sul-livan), and that's where he goes too far. "A man needs youth, Sarah," he explains to her. "Without it, life is stale and meaningless." So she shoots him, and then she jumps off the top of his building.

For all his drive, there was often an element of self-mockery about William. That quality was apparently present in his real-life demeanor, as well. Gladys Hall, upon meeting him for the first time, said, "He looked perpetually amused and a little bit tired of it all." On-screen, he could be the show-off, the huckster, the bombastic orator, the essence of confidence and capitalism. And then, as often happened in his films, the bottom would fall out, and we'd find him drunk in a speakeasy, hair askew, dead eyes peering through a cloud of cigarette smoke, a mess.

If William's smooth frauds had a weakness, it was a very human one. On some level, they believed their own lies. And when they were sincere, they seemed to want to make the fraudulent part real. It's probably why audiences found it easy to love him. However cynical his characters may have been, William was never *ultimately* cynical, as in hate-filled or nihilistic. His frauds and crooks were, at heart, fantasists. In his distinctly pre-Code way, William was a romantic.

The man who'd grow up to become, in Hall's words, "dangerous, debonair and devastating," a "romantic menace," was born Warren William Krech in Minnesota in 1895. His father was a newspaper publisher, and it was assumed the son would follow him into the business. Instead, after serving in World War I, William turned to acting. Among the stage roles he originated were the male leads in *Let Us Be Gay* (later a talkie with Norma Shearer and Rod La Rocque) and *Twelve Miles Out* (later a silent vehicle for John Gilbert).

In 1923, already an established Broadway lead, the romantic menace married, and he stayed married until his death twenty-five years later. Though he projected something quite different on-screen, the real Warren William seems to have been neither power mad nor sexually driven nor even particularly ambitious as an actor. He was, above all, intellectually curious, an amateur inventor who, in his free time, spent hours on end in his workshop. "It's all very paradoxical," William once said, "because my one aim in life, my one philosophy, is to save myself the slightest unnecessary exertion." He invented an apartment on wheels—the 1930s equivalent of a Winnebago—so he could shower and get made up on the way to the studio. "I can sleep an extra hour when I am working," he explained.

He applied for a patent for a circular showboat, a kind of floating theater-in-the-round, but found that someone else had gotten there first. He did, however, manage to patent a device described as "a vacuum cleaner for lawns." On his property, he built a revolving doghouse, so that the same patch of grass would not get worn out by the dog's running in and out. He also tended to his two and a half acres of citrus fruit and raised prizewinning hens. Once a New York newspaper reported that William went to a meeting about research into the many uses of sawdust.

As a Broadway actor, William tried for years to get a Hollywood contract. He once said he could have made a living making screen tests. After he became an established star, *Variety* wrote that "he almost went bald combing his hair in different styles to please scouts." Finally, he signed with Warner Bros. in 1931.

It took a few films for the studio to realize what it had. In *Expensive Women* (1931), he played a charming composer who meets his future sweetheart in a bathroom, when the two enter through separate doors at a party. ("When two are brought together by a bathroom, they sort of belong together," he says.) In *The Woman from Monte Carlo* (1932), he was the other man in a romantic triangle with Lil Dagover and Walter Huston, but any leading man would have done as well.

Under 18, released in January of 1932, first hinted at the pleasures to come. William played a rich playboy who spots poverty-stricken Marian Marsh and turns on the charm. He buys her lunch, gives her presents, and invites her to his apartment. The film is interesting for reasons besides William. In its depiction of Marsh's family, it paints a grim portrait of working-class life. (Marsh's sister, played by Anita Page, has an abusive husband who won't work, and at one point Marsh uses money she gets from William to pay for her sister's abortion.) But William's role wasn't central, and for once he doesn't succeed in his seduction.

With *Beauty and the Boss*, released in April of 1932, the William persona began to come into focus. It was the first time he played a businessman—in this case, a banker with a weakness for women. Not wanting to get distracted during business hours, he resolves to find a male secretary, then settles on frumpy, starving Marian Marsh instead. *Beauty and the Boss* was a woman's story—the duckling turns into a swan, and a marriage proposal follows—but William's portrait of the driven man of the world was commanding.

The Mouthpiece (1932), released the following month, put him over as a star. He played a crooked lawyer, and, like every other pre-Code lawyer, this one had his reasons. But the movie raised the stakes by having his reasons be strong and his crookedness know no bounds. We first see him as a prosecutor, making a grand summation that will send an innocent man to the chair. When William finds out the man was innocent, his world collapses, and he becomes a mob lawyer, devoted to getting anybody and everybody off—for a fee.

The Mouthpiece gave William a flashy role that provided a foundation for his screen image. The lawyer was bombastic in the courtroom, and in his off hours, when depressed, he'd hit the skids, drinking. He was an audacious trickster. In the film's best scene, he gets a murderer off by drinking the poison that was the main exhibit for the defense. When the jury sees that no harm has come to him, it returns a not guilty verdict; whereupon, he walks across the street, where paramedics have been standing by, and has his stomach pumped. In these aspects, *The Mouthpiece* looked toward the future. Its connection with past William films was that it cast him opposite an all-too-innocent leading lady—Sidney Fox, as a secretary whose rectitude encourages him to reform.

The idea of an innocent defeating the monster by the mere example of her innocence—that was the Chaney pattern and had no business in a Warren William film. The William atmosphere was too lighthearted, too careless for complete moral certitude. When William was defeated, it could never be because universal laws had been broken, but because he had screwed up. In his future pictures, William's women would hold their own without being saints, and try to temper his mischief, sometimes succeeding, sometimes failing. In this way, no matter what kind of cad William played, the male-female relationships in his films are always satisfying from a modern perspective. Their give and take feels real.

If *The Mouthpiece* introduced William as the magnificent scoundrel—
"We like him because we can't help it," wrote one critic—*Skyscraper
Souls* moved this scoundrel into the world of business. (William traveled in worlds which the public understood to be the scoundrel's natural habitat). *Skyscraper Souls*, about various people working in a New
York skyscraper, was based on the novel by Faith Baldwin. But the film
made a vast improvement on the novel by transforming the lead character, David Dwight, from a successful lawyer to a driven, obsessive
banker, the man who financed the building and will do anything to
hold on to it.

Dwight is not the temperate man of business the previous generation
might have extolled. He tears through life, doing as he pleases. He
makes a date with one woman, then drops her for another, "Sorry, my
dear, but I've suddenly developed spinal meningitis." He gets to keep
his building through the help of a wealthy friend, then colludes with a
corporate pirate to break the friend's business and own the building free
and clear. When his friend confronts him, he doesn't apologize, "If I
double-crossed somebody else for you, I wouldn't be a double-crosser.
I'd be a financial genius. . . . You'd love it. You'd love me. I'd be your
pal, your leader. But I put one over on you, so I'm a double-crosser. It's
all in the point of view, gentlemen."

Such behavior should have made him an unlikely candidate for sympathetic treatment. But in the pre-Code era, the worst crime—with the
possible exception of embezzlement—was hypocrisy. In *Skyscraper
Souls*, William was a buccaneer, a self-aggrandizer, and a cheat, but he
knew the game he was in and admitted it. His honesty about his own
dishonesty made him fun to watch, and illuminated for audiences what
they had come to suspect about business ethics—that they didn't exist.
Dwight was also a creator. He'd been told his skyscraper could never be
built. "But I had the courage and the vision, and it's mine, and I own
it," he says. "It goes halfway to hell, and right up to heaven, and it's

beautiful!" In *Skyscraper Souls,* William played the businessman as ruthless artist. At one point, his estranged wife compares him to the Renaissance sculptor Cellini.

William had made the film on loan-out to MGM, and it served to help cement the pattern for him at his home studio, Warners, whose mischievous, low-down personality best suited his talents. At Warners, his opportunists and schemers would have an artistic drive as well, but with a difference. At MGM, he'd played a man who connived and bamboozled people as a way of serving his art. At Warners, cheating *became* his art. He played men for whom deceit itself was a special talent. He played, in the fullest sense of the term, the most amazing bullshit artists who ever lived.

His films had their own tone and point of view. *The Match King,* based on the rise and fall of a ruthless Swedish match manufacturer, called for an actor with a multitude of distinct characteristics. The role required a seductive, charming actor whom audiences could accept as a lothario; an actor with an ability to overwhelm people with torrents of pompous bravado; an actor with a sense of irony, who could bring out the script's humor; an actor the audience could accept as a murderer; an actor appealing enough for viewers to root for, in spite of themselves; and an actor who could blow his brains out at the end of the picture without in any way saddening the audience.

No other actor could have fit the bill. Without William, *The Match King* would have had to have been a serious drama or a comedy with a different ending. Or it would have had to have introduced an additional character, a detective on the trail, for example, and made *him* the protagonist. William's versatility as an actor—and the dimension of the image he'd created—was broad enough to cast a wide net and capture all kinds of truths normally separated from one another by neat genre categories.

In this fictionalized biography of Swedish tycoon Ivar Kreuger,

William played Paul Kroll, an immigrant working as a maintenance man at a Chicago baseball stadium. Not happy sweeping sidewalks, he enters into a scheme with his boss to rob their employers, then seduces the boss's wife and takes all her money. He puts her in a cab, telling her that he'll meet her on the train. He waves and smiles until she's out of range, then gets on the next boat to Sweden.

In Sweden, the cycle begins again, but on a grand scale. He bluffs his relatives into giving him control of their troubled match factory, convincing them that he's a big American businessman with "vast holdings in Chicago." No one could say "vast" like William. His booming voice suggested empires. From there, he gains control of the match business in a succession of European countries, each time leveraging his properties to buy more. When a harmless eccentric invents a reusable match, he suppresses the invention by having the man thrown into an insane asylum. Later, with his business struggling, he buys fake securities from a counterfeiter, then drowns the counterfeiter.

Along the way, he seduces women he believes can help his business, until he falls in love with a screen actress named Marta Molnar (Lili Damita as a stand-in for Greta Garbo). And when the romance doesn't work out, William actually makes us feel sorry for him: After all this hard work, bluffing, breaking, and killing people, isn't he entitled to a little happiness?

At a time when audiences wanted to believe in personalities big enough to force their will on monolithic power, on businesses and governments who presented formidable and insurmountable fronts to the average imagination, William was an inspiration. His characters had no altruism; they were only out for themselves. But at a time when so many people were up against it, was that so bad? With legitimate avenues to success cut off by the Depression, William was the fantasy figure of a guy who could start off cleaning sidewalks and, through sheer guile and inventiveness, end up creating an empire. If, by the finish, he ended up back in the gutter, well, that was reassuring, too—proof not that goodness triumphs in the end (his enemies were usually as bad as he was) but, rather, that it doesn't pay to work so hard.

Employees' Entrance (1933), William's next film, cast him as an American businessman. His previous businessmen had been Europeans, though he never used an accent. The picture, about the goings-on at a massive department store, was Warners' answer to *Skyscraper Souls*. William was the boss and, as in the earlier picture, he lived in the building. He lived his work.

Employees' Entrance was equal parts sex and business. The sex part involved a hungry young woman (Loretta Young) whom the ruthless businessman Anderson (William) hires as a model. Then, when he's sure she can't say no, he has her spend the night. Later, he manages to have sex with her again by getting her almost paralyzed with drink. The sequence remains startling today: At an office party, he gives her the key to his apartment, ostensibly so she can sleep it off. Minutes later, he takes the elevator upstairs, and there we see him walking down the hall toward her door with a look of dead-eyed calculation. When he gets there, one expects, at first, that he won't go through with it. It's tantamount to rape. She's practically in a coma.

The business aspect of *Employees' Entrance* involved a man's absolute determination to keep a huge commercial enterprise thriving despite the Depression. Anderson is a slave driver, demanding new ideas from his board. When an older executive timidly expresses misgivings, he fires him, and soon the man jumps out a window. Our hero is unfazed. "When a man outlives his usefulness, he ought to jump out of a window."

"But he's worked here thirty years," a shocked assistant says.

"Well, send him a wreath," Anderson replies. He is a monomaniac and an egomaniac, but his drive is arresting and becomes admirable. In the end, his store thrives; he retains control, and anytime he needs to amuse himself, he just calls Polly (Alice White), a hard-boiled girl who is as jaded and mercenary as he is.

William was becoming a subgenre all to himself. Every six to eight weeks, a new Warren William film would hit the screen, each time showing him behaving in a way just a bit more appalling and frisky than the time before. When *The Mind Reader* was released in April 1933, critic John S. Cohen commented that William was now "ahead of everyone out west in the number of portraits in his own rogues gallery." With *Mind Reader* and also with *Bedside* (1934), which arrived the following winter, William's movies cut loose from any sensible moral landscape and entered into a zone in which everyone was slightly mad. The attitude of these films wasn't pessimistic, but cheerful and fatalistic, jaded but engaged. And gleefully peculiar: For a visual kick, it was hard to beat the sight of William in a turban, looking into a crystal ball in *The Mind Reader.*

As Chandra the Great, William not only fleeces the suckers who come to see his mind-reading act, but for one dollar, he dispenses advice through the mail, exerting a blithely destructive impact on people's lives. He also meets a very young woman (Constance Cummings), who idolizes him, so he takes her on tour, despite a friend's (Allen Jenkins) word of caution, "Did ya ever hear of that guy Mann? He's got an Act, and he ain't even in vaudeville."

In *The Mind Reader,* William's genius for crookedness is understood to be a talent, a legitimate God-given gift, like a knack for music. So when he gets married and goes straight, it's as if Heifetz had thrown away his violin. "A guy with your con, your larceny, selling brushes," his friend gripes. "Love, marriage, honesty—now there's a combination guaranteed to get anybody in the poorhouse." That's essentially the movie's point of view. His genius is too good to waste. He goes back into business as Dr. Munro, a fake mystic who specializes in telling New York society wives if their husbands are cheating. He's so *not* on the level that director Roy Del Ruth actually films him on a slant.

When an accidental shooting death forces him to leave the country, Dr. Munro ends up in a carnival in Juárez. There, a newspaper article informs him that his wife has been charged with the murder. To be stuck in a carnival in Juárez, with nothing to do but get drunk or turn yourself in—that's down-and-out, William-style.

In the early thirties, in between playing his trademark louses, William took on a number of other roles. He was, in the words of film historian William K. Everson, "extremely versatile, capable of tackling virtually anything—more than Cagney, Robinson or Muni." He neither fought for parts nor seemed all that concerned with building an image. "I've never refused a part—or suggested one, either," he told an interviewer. "I just play all the roles that everyone else won't play." In *Three on a Match* (1932), he was the understanding husband of no-good wife Ann Dvorak, who loses interest in him for no reason. In an early scene, she hurries to bed and pretends to be sleeping so he won't bother her for sex. When he played nice guys, William played nice guys, without any hint of the menace he showed in his other pictures. He was good at light comedy, too—for example, *Goodbye Again* (1933), in which he played a novelist trying to keep from getting involved with an obsessive fan.

But if we're to remember Warren William, it's for the films he made playing men who'd do anything for money, for status, for power; men who presented a polished surface in order to trick people into giving them what a gangster might, clumsily, try to steal. He could do other roles, but this was the one sort of role only William could do with such panache. In *Bedside*, the William villain-hero got as low as he ever got—though one has to wonder where William might have taken him had the Code not arrived five months later.

To appreciate the skewed universe in which *Bedside* takes place, think about this: It's about a drunk, who, with a fake diploma, sets himself up as a surgeon, operates on the throat of an opera singer, and nearly kills her. Yet what are the last words of the movie? "Oh, Bob, you're marvelous!" He's marvelous?

Bedside was composed of a series of unsavory interludes made delectable by William's wolfish charm. When we first meet him, he's hungover and can't remember much about getting "lucky" with a one-night stand the previous night. He's an X-ray technician whose long-suffering girlfriend (Jean Muir) stakes him to a medical school education—but he blows the tuition on a dice game before the first day of class. It doesn't stop him: He just goes ahead and fakes his credentials.

Once established as a (fraudulent) physician, he doesn't lie low as any sane person might. This is a William hero. He craves publicity. He finds ways to make the gossip columns, to become physician to the stars. He lets it be known that he's a great surgeon, even though he doesn't know how to stitch an incision. After the operation, the opera singer starts hemorrhaging and almost bleeds to death.

"After being explored for a solid hour," wrote *Variety*, "as a gambler, drunkard, cheat and fraud, Warren William is unable in the last three minutes to rehabilitate himself in the grace of the spectator." Maybe in 1934. But many years later, we know better than to respond to *Bedside* as realism. It was a fantasy that best encapsulated William's body of work, one whose message is as deeply reassuring today as yesterday: Lack of morals, lack of ethics, lack of honest application, and lack of wholesome personal habits present no obstacle to success in America.

THE DEPICTIONS OF old businessmen, early in the pre-Code era, show the last vestiges of reverence for a generation that believed in the value of hard work and self-denial. In *The Millionaire* (1931), George Arliss embodied the old values. In other films, the kind old businessman usually had a supporting role. He might be a cantankerous old dad, such as the one played by William Holden (no relation to the famous later star of the same name) in the Joan Crawford film *Dance Fools Dance* (1931). Yet as time went on and the Depression sank in, it was hard to believe that dad knew much or that his values were going to get him anywhere. Indeed, in *Dance Fools Dance*, dad drops dead of a heart attack on the day the stock market crashes. The message was beyond implicit, bordering on ham-fisted: Your day is done, dad. It's over.

It's no coincidence that William's heyday came not at the beginning of the pre-Code era but a couple of years into it, after the Depression had transformed the public's attitude toward business. Businessmen who in the twenties had been, according to Frederick Lewis Allen, "objects of veneration" were now "objects of derision and distrust." Calvin Coolidge, president during the economic boom, reflected his era's reverence for business when he said, "The man who builds a factory builds a temple." But President Franklin Roosevelt, entering office at the height of the Depression in March 1933, saw a different situation, "The money changers have fled from their high seats in the temple of our civilization." In this new climate, the old values seemed inapplicable, naïve, sometimes hypocritical. Occasionally, a film might come along, such as Arliss's *The Working Man* (1933), in which he played a shoe manufacturer with a thing or two to teach the younger generation. But for the most part, business in pre-Code films was pretty much nasty and dog-eat-dog, a life for men with a killer instinct.

Two of the best-known films of the pre-Code era—so well known that they're rarely talked of as pre-Codes, but, rather, as thirties classics—are the MGM all-star extravaganzas, *Grand Hotel* (1932) and *Dinner at Eight* (1933). *Grand Hotel* had its origin in the German novel by Vicki Baum; and *Dinner at Eight* was adapted from the Broadway stage play by Edna Ferber and George S. Kaufman. Yet the resulting films were very much Depression pictures that shared a distaste for cutthroat business practices, and each presented a businessman as the villain.

Grand Hotel, the darker and more romantic in spirit, had Wallace Beery as a German factory owner who puts over a merger by lying about his company's business prospects. That begins the moral slide. Next thing, he's paying a young secretary (Joan Crawford) to travel (and sleep) with him, and he ends up in handcuffs, facing a manslaughter charge.

In *Grand Hotel*, only the ballerina, Grusinskaya (Greta Garbo), has money. The rest are scrambling, and the scrambling motivates most of the action. The Baron (John Barrymore) goes through the whole film trying to raise money, either by gambling or stealing. Kringelein (Lionel Barrymore), a dying bookkeeper out on a spree, wants to spend all his money before he dies—but not too quickly; hence the anxiety that surrounds that character. Meanwhile, Flaemschen, the stenographer played by Crawford, is totally for sale.

Near the end, Kringelein asks her why she even considered going with that obnoxious businessman. "Money," she answers. He replies, ingenuously, that he has money and that he "won't live long." He offers that as a point in his favor.

Dinner at Eight, the funnier and more naturalistic of the two pictures, was another film all about money. Two kinds of businessmen were contrasted here—the old style and the new style. Lionel Barrymore played Jordan, a genteel older gentleman with an established shipping line, a devoted staff of aging employees, and an office in an old downtown building. In other words, he's finished. Wallace Beery, as a mining tycoon named Packard, played one of the new breed: confident and ruthless, gregarious and deceitful, a *nouveau riche* blowhard.

In the end, only one thing saves Jordan from Packard's manipulating the market and wiping him out, and it's not Jordan's superior intelligence or virtue, nor the dedication of his cherished employees. Jordan is saved because Packard's floozy wife (Jean Harlow at her best) aspires to use Jordan as her entrée into polite society. Thus, Jordan is saved by happenstance, by absurdity, by chance in an unstable world. Or, to put it another way, he is saved because he is in a comedy. And the audience knows it.

Survival in business usually required getting modern, adjusting one's morals, and learning how to fight. That was John Barrymore's journey in *Topaze* (1933). He played a meek French schoolmaster, Professor Topaze, who starts off the film believing in all the verities he passes on to his students, such as "Ill-gotten gains are not worthwhile." His naïveté attracts a group of crooked businessmen, who use him as the front man for their fake health elixir. Horrified when he finds out he has been promoting a phony product, he soon realizes that business and government run entirely on lies, and he gets wise. He turns ruthless in business and ends up rich and respected, with a pretty young mistress (Myrna Loy) who'd have had nothing to do with him had he stayed broke.

Topaze, about facing the truth about a corrupt world, came with a Continental twist. Forced to confront the emptiness of his illusions, Topaze doesn't become bitter. He becomes a happy, full-fledged adult for the first time in his life.

IN THE PRE-CODE era, almost any movie about a rich man was a movie about a guy who eventually goes broke. Most of these films were critical assessments of the business life, though *The Conquerors* (1932) was intended as an inspirational tale, a pep talk to a nation that badly needed to believe in the resiliency of its entrepreneurial spirit. The result proved to be unintentionally laughable: *The Conquerors* was about three generations of a business family that keeps losing its money.

It starts in the 1870s, with Richard Dix as a bank clerk who loves the boss's daughter. There's a panic, and the bank is wiped out. So Dix goes out west with his new wife and starts his own bank. Everything is great for about a generation—then, oops, another panic, and now he's wiped out again. But why worry? He picks himself up, dusts himself off, and

goes on banking. And everything's swell until—oh no!—the stock market crash of 1929. Time to cash in the grandson's trust fund. . . .

The intended message of *The Conquerors* is clear: Americans never
quit, and no matter how many times an American businessman is
knocked down, he'll get back up. But the scenario could just as easily be
interpreted to mean the reverse, that no matter how many times an
American businessman gets back up, sooner or later he's going to get
clobbered again. The picture, which flopped at the box office, shows
the impossibility of making a sincerely optimistic business movie during
a depression. Audiences, upon leaving *The Conquerors*, would have felt
well advised to keep their money in their mattresses.

Edward G. Robinson starred in two of these dark business epics, but
at least their pessimism was intentional. In *Silver Dollar* (1932), he
played Yates Martin, a real-life nineteenth-century businessman who,
on his way to the screen, was translated into another of those smiling,
cigar-smoking Robinson characters who come into wealth and just love
spreading it around. He makes a fortune in silver, builds the Denver
opera house, buys himself a Senate seat, but then—look out—President
Cleveland puts the country on the gold standard. He's wiped out, and
before he can recover, he dies.

Such is success in America. A man, touched by fortune, goes
through life believing in his own specialness and glory. Then bad fortune strikes, and the thing that kills him isn't lack of money; it's disillusionment, the stumped face in the mirror, and a world devoid of color
and light. This is so many American stories. It's what F. Scott Fitzgerald
was writing about at the time and what he, indeed, became. Robinson
played one such disillusioned man in *Silver Dollar*—and also in *I Loved
a Woman*, which followed a year later.

In the latter film, Robinson loses his money and his mind, too. *I
Loved a Woman* took the form and structure of a big-scale success
story—fifty years in the life of a meatpacking tycoon—but its point, in

the end, was that the hero threw away his life. Robinson starts off the movie not wanting to take over dad's meatpacking business. He wants to study art, see? But when the old man dies, he does take it over, and along the way he acquires a wife he doesn't love (Genevieve Tobin) and a mistress who's unfaithful (Kay Francis). He sells the army tainted meat during the Spanish American War and almost goes to jail. World War I makes him rich, but legal trouble forces him to flee the country.

In the end, what does he have to show for his effort? His body is failing, his mind is gone, and he's mumbling to himself. He could have experienced the glories of art school, but instead he flushed his life down the toilet. Imagine the regret: To have stumbled through life as a millionaire entrepreneur when he could have had a degree in art history! The pre-Code disdain for business knew no bounds.

Even *Turn Back the Clock* (1933)—framed as a fantasy going on inside the mind of a sleeping man—was antibusiness. Lee Tracy, when given a second chance, chooses money over love and ends up in a miserable marriage and facing indictment and ruin. He's relieved to wake up and find that he's middle-class again.

Pre-Code businessmen, when they actually managed to be successful, were often presented as the moral equivalent of gangsters—and not lovable ones, either. In *The Ruling Voice* (1931), Walter Huston looks respectable, but he leads a racket called "the System," which extorts protection money from grocery stores. The result is that people are going hungry. In *Cabin in the Cotton* (1932)—a Richard Barthelmess film about the abuse of tenant farmers—a sharecropper is lynched by wealthy planters. "There may be just a hint of social revolution in [Barthelmess's] assault on the rapacious landowners," noted the *Herald Tribune*.

There was more than a hint in *Success at Any Price* (1934), based on the play *Success Story*, by John Howard Lawson (later blacklisted as one of the Hollywood Ten). It presented a man's phenomenal rise in business as a consequence of his stunted moral and emotional nature. It was, in a way, a transparent leftist diatribe. Yet it crystallized the era's antibusiness sentiment and was precisely the sort of movie that could not be made once the Code was enforced. The Code arrived just three and a half months after the release of the picture.

Douglas Fairbanks, Jr., in one of those young tough-guy roles he excelled at, played Joe Martin, who, on the day of his gangster brother's funeral, decides to go straight and make his fortune within the system. His girlfriend (Colleen Moore) gets him an entry-level job in an advertising company, where she works as a secretary. When Joe, a lout with a chip on his shoulder the size of a piano, finally gets a chance to make good, his talent is recognized, and he begins his climb.

Joe is driven. He has nothing but his work, his anger, and his hunger. He meets his boss's mistress (Genevieve Tobin) and decides he wants her—just like Scarface wanted *his* boss's mistress—as a symbol of his arrival. "If I had a million dollars, I'd buy you," he says.

She understands. She is all about money, too, and sold her soul long ago. "I know how you feel," she tells him. "Anything you can't get makes you sick and sour."

To make his million, he buys stock and sells short, rides employees to the breaking point, and ultimately pulls a power play, squeezing out the boss who gave him a chance in the first place. "We cleaned up on Wall Street with tricks that would make a gunman blush," he says. "There are no ethics in this town. It's kill or be killed. Get what you can." It's not until his expensive, worthless wife (Tobin) betrays him that he sees his harsh life as having no meaning, no connection, no value, and no hope. It's for these kinds of moments that characters in movies always keep a revolver in their desk. *Success at Any Price* ended with a tableau of male fragility, Fairbanks is resting his head on Moore's lap as they wait for the ambulance to arrive.

In their depiction of the business world, pre-Code movies were turning their gaze on the arena in which most men spent their working lives. "Something is missing here," these films were saying. "Something about this is antithetical to life." Warren William's films made those observations in a comic or melodramatic context, while others were more heavy-handed. In either case their point was that the business ethic, taken to the extreme, was poisonous to human interaction. The ruthless quest for riches comes between Walter Huston and his daughter (Loretta Young) in *The Ruling Voice*. In other films, it comes between old friends; mainly, it comes between men and women.

In *The Public Enemy*, when James Cagney collapses in the street, muttering, "I ain't so tough," he wasn't announcing his physical condition as much as he was saying so much of it is bluff, so much of it's for nothing. In a similar way, most business movies of the era didn't hesitate to depict the pain, the bewilderment, and the soft inner core of men. Commerce might have built the skyscrapers, but commerce alone couldn't keep men from wanting to jump out of them. To an extent that would not be seen again until the 1970s, pre-Codes emphasized men's need for a life of more than endless struggle.

Love Hurts

PRE-CODE HEROES WEREN'T required to be stoic. Some, like Barthelmess and Gary Cooper, had a natural reserve that rarely ever broke, even under the stress of strong emotion. But most actors of the era played men who were, in one form or another, extroverts. It was possible to tell when they were happy and even more easy to see when they were miserable.

When Edward G. Robinson in *Smart Money* (1931) sees that his right-hand man (James Cagney) has been killed in a freak accident, he doesn't grieve by getting all tight-lipped and going off into a little room to drink, stare at the floor, and smoke a pack of cigarettes. That kind of male behavior may have been big in the forties, but in the thirties, Robinson just did what anyone might do in real life. He lets out with animal-like moaning. What's the point in pretending it doesn't hurt?

The fragility of men. The emotional nakedness of men. The deep needs of men. Pre-Code movies were able to show some of the more vulnerable aspects of the male experience—and do it in a way that didn't seem sappy or calculated to advertise an actor's sensitivity.

The pre-Codes came blissfully before all that nonsense—before the age of bottled-up, emotionally withdrawn heroes of the forties and before the inevitable backlash, a generation later, that for a brief time threatened to elevate spineless weakness and weepiness to the level of nobility. Pre-Code actors, and the writers who wrote for them, just showed men acting like men. Sometimes it wasn't flattering, and yet these portrayals are heartening in the way that seeing the truth usually is.

John Barrymore was an actor who revealed a touching sensitivity in his pre-Code films. A renowned Broadway idol—distinguished in both light comedy and Shakespearean tragedy—he had enjoyed a successful silent-film career and entered talkies at a turning point in his castability. He was forty-four when he starred in Warners' first Vitaphone feature, *Don Juan* (1926), a silent film with a recorded musical score. By the time he made his talkie debut, as a dashing soldier in *General Crack* (1930), Barrymore was forty-seven, in his twilight years as a romantic leading man.

Like a lot of flamboyant actors, even fabulously handsome ones, Barrymore had always liked costumes and character parts. Roles that called for limping and wearing fake noses, false beards, and wigs tended to awaken in him an unseemly gusto. At Warners, in his first talkies, the erstwhile matinee idol established himself as the studio's resident grotesque in roles such as Ahab in *Moby Dick* (1930), in which he had a peg leg, and *The Mad Genius* (1931), in which he had a clubfoot. He also had the title role in *Svengali* (1931), wearing a stiff wig and beard to indicate a fellow too busy hypnotizing Trilby to bother taking baths.

These Warner Bros. films didn't do much at the box office, but Irving Thalberg at MGM, rightly guessing there might yet be life in Barrymore as a romantic lead, signed the actor and started casting him in more congenial roles—among them the ones he's most remembered for today. He was a gentleman thief in *Arsène Lupin* (1932), cast opposite his older brother, Lionel, who played the policeman out to put him in jail. As with most pre-Codes about crime, the criminal was the hero.

Arsène Lupin contains a scene like something out of a James Bond film, in which our hero finds a beautiful naked stranger (Karen Morley) waiting in his bed. Barrymore reacts to this pleasant surprise as though it's more pleasant than a surprise. He's been around. But this romance, and Barrymore's air, jaded but kindly, were just warm-ups for his next film, *Grand Hotel* (1932).

It's his movie. *Grand Hotel* may be the original all-star extravaganza, with Garbo, Crawford, Wallace Beery, Lionel Barrymore, and Lewis Stone all taking big chunks of hotel scenery between their teeth and chewing it to pieces. But it's Barrymore's film more than anyone else's, partly because he just happens to have the one role that intersects with every other character, but mainly because his understanding of the man he plays—a kindhearted but rather useless Baron—is complete.

In Vicki Baum's novel, the Baron was a young man who sneaks into the ballet dancer Grusinskaya's room to steal her pearls—and, when she returns unexpectedly from the theater, he has to improvise a reason for his being there. He romances her, and his pretended love becomes the truth. The scene in *Grand Hotel*—the result of long story conferences that included producer Irving Thalberg, director Edmund Goulding, and others—took a more unambiguously romantic direction: The Baron sees Grusinskaya, falls completely in love, and his gentleness and sincerity, not to mention his handsome profile, persuade her to let him spend the night.

The actors make such a scene possible—Garbo because it's easy to believe someone could fall in love with her instantaneously, and Barrymore for a variety of reasons. He was a good-enough actor to make us believe he had fallen in love; he was dashing enough for an audience to accept him as a worthy surrogate, and he was suave enough that no woman would show him the door. Watching the scene today, our eyes are on Garbo, but we're listening to Barrymore. His voice, ardent but mellow, is the music that heightens the picture, "Let me stay, just for a little while. Oh, please let me stay. . . ."

Barrymore plays the Baron as a middle-aged man who has spent too many years living like a beautiful boy. He still has the charm of a beautiful boy, plus the gallantry and tenderness of an older man, and this combination makes him lovable, even adorable—yet at the same time slightly pathetic. We see him in an early scene, making funny faces for the amusement of a stenographer (Joan Crawford) whom he manages to pick up. He's good at it. She starts off an indifferent stranger, and two minutes later he's patting her on the rear end. But he's too old for this. Sure, there are worse ways to be fifty than to be picking up Joan Crawford, but one senses, on Barrymore's end, the exhaustion behind the seduction. Another day, another stenographer.

Our appreciation of Barrymore's Baron is only enhanced by knowledge of Barrymore's life. At the time of *Grand Hotel*, he was in his third marriage (with one more to go). He was a compulsive ladies' man, and also a romantic who claimed to be looking for the one great love. Given that he was known as much for his dissipation as for his talent—he was a heavy drinker his entire adult life—it's surprising he accomplished as much as he did and that his looks held on for so long. We can read Barrymore's life story into that of the Baron, a grand fellow with fatal weaknesses. It's all there in his performance—in his playfulness, jauntiness, air of disappointment, and hard-earned sensitivity to human weakness.

Some men see so much of life they become cynical. Barrymore, in *Grand Hotel* and elsewhere, had the manner of man who has abused himself beyond that stage. He has passed through cynicism, arriving again at hope, a second childhood of idealism at once gnawing, perplexing and bracing. Old before his years yet wide-eyed with curiosity—with old age and youth in a contest for his face—Barrymore embodied a painful question: Is a second chance possible?

Often it wasn't. "If one lives for the moment," he warns his daughter (Helen Chandler) in *Long Lost Father* (1934), "the years are apt to slip by and leave you suddenly empty-handed." It's a recurring theme. In *Long Lost Father*, he has to leave his newly found daughter in order to stay a step ahead of the police. In *Reunion in Vienna* (1933), he spends the movie trying to rekindle a long-ago romance with a former love (Diana Wynyard), finally giving up and leaving her to her husband. He realizes the truth: "You're no longer the woman I love. You're a wife."

Dinner at Eight (1933) shamelessly exploited the Barrymore legend, casting him as a former screen star known for his superb profile. Larry Renault was not quite like Barrymore—Renault, we're to understand, never really had talent, just looks. But the character traded on the Barrymore themes of dissolution and attempted rebirth. Renault, a desperate alcoholic, is a man who has gone through scores of women, only to find that he himself is the one used up. Now he has a fresh young girlfriend (Madge Evans) who loves him, and he has hopes for rekindling his career, if not in movies, then onstage. But he's a wreck, no feelings left to give, no talent to draw on, no money to spend. Barrymore gives the story of this inflated ham the impact of tragedy, while delivering a performance extraordinary in its technical proficiency. Over the course of one long scene, he goes from relatively sober to completely sloshed, passing through every stage in between.

The question, "Is a second chance possible?" was also present in *A Bill of Divorcement* (1932), which had nothing to do with dissipation. Barrymore played a sensitive composer who, years before, while fighting in World War I, lost his sanity. After years in an asylum, he wakes up mentally fragile but lucid and returns to his home after some fifteen years away. When he sees his daughter (Katharine Hepburn, in her film debut), he thinks she's his wife. When she gently informs him otherwise, he says, with the playful wonder that was always endearing about Barrymore, "Daughter? Daughter? My wife's not my wife, she's my daughter."

In *A Bill of Divorcement*, Barrymore was a study in vulnerability. He looks exhausted. He's stooped and collapsed in his walk, a gentle man with a child's enthusiasm. Years of his life are covered in darkness, a darkness he fears piercing. He just wants everything to be as it was, but the film is uncompromising on that score. His wife (Billie Burke) has divorced him and desperately wants to remarry. He is reduced to acting like a begging child in her presence, and that can't work. As in other Barrymore films, the time is past and nothing can be done.

Counsellor at Law (1933) was a change of pace, though not completely outside the Barrymore pattern. In a role created on the New York stage by Paul Muni, Barrymore was George Simon, a Jewish lawyer in New York, slightly shady, but so is everybody. He engages in insider trading and barely gets out of trouble (through extortion) for faking an alibi for a client. He is also a liberal, or at least a civil libertarian. He takes on the case of a young Communist who was beaten up by police. "A fine joke that is," he says. "The cops beat up a kid for making a speech and then they arrest him." But the Communist holds him in contempt, calling him a "renegade and a cheap prostitute" and his wife "a pampered parasite."

Counsellor At Law, based on the play by Elmer Rice and adapted by the author, was too sophisticated to endorse a naïve young ideologue's view of a complicated middle-aged man. But one does sense something out of balance in the counselor's life. He has married a gentile society woman who treats him with barely concealed contempt, and he tries to be a father to her two brats (by a previous marriage), who look down on him. On some level, he seems to believe these people are better than he is. He has adopted values that are bound to hurt him.

Barrymore played the counselor as a lawyer's lawyer, an intense personality who does three things at once and drums his fingers on the desk when he can't find something else to do. Barrymore wisely didn't try to be too Jewish, choosing instead to inject a certain speed, a New York-type urgency, into his manner.

Eventually, Simon falls into line with the lot of Barrymore heroes by realizing he has made a mistake in life. His wife is unfaithful. He's alone. He's middle-aged, shattered, on the verge of suicide, but for once in a Barrymore movie, a second chance presents itself. It comes in the form of his first love, his work, and a probable future wife in the wings, his secretary (Bebe Daniels), who knows him better than he knows himself.

LOVE HAD A way of bringing out the frailty of men, and not all of them were lucky enough to look like John Barrymore. In *The Devil and the Deep* (1932), Charles Laughton played a British Navy Commander, who is suspicious of his wife's fidelity. He's more than a typical jealous fellow. He seems to have something wrong with his brain. "I can't forget what the brain specialist told you," his wife (Tallulah Bankhead) says tactfully, "that no doctor on earth can help you if you won't help yourself." Contemplate, for a moment, the license that mere mention of a "brain specialist" might do for an actor of Laughton's flamboyance. It was a blank check.

The Commander torments his wife with his baseless conviction that she is having an affair with his lieutenant. The lieutenant, played by Cary Grant, is too handsome to keep around, so Laughton has him dismissed, and who does the Navy send in his place? Gary Cooper. Now that's bad luck. If only the Commander had known he was in a Paramount movie— Paramount had a particularly deep bench when it came to handsome leading men. Even the hitherto faithful wife can't pass up Gary Cooper.

In *Devil and the Deep*, Cooper is stiffer and more finicky than usual, but Laughton does enough acting for ten pictures, switching, with barely a second's warning, from leering-grinning vindictiveness to screaming rage to bottomless self-pity. "It must be a happy thing to look like you do," he whines to Cooper. "I suppose women love you. I never had that. It must be a happy thing." At the point the adultery is confirmed, the three players are onboard Laughton's submarine; whereupon, he orders that they ship out immediately and proceeds to sabotage the vessel. When we last see Laughton, water is flooding into his compartment and he is laughing and laughing, then drowning and laughing, and finally just drowning. Nothing like an attractive wife to aggravate an insane man's brain problems.

Edward G. Robinson, another actor who was less than pretty, often played men with woman trouble, whether he was a gangster, a businessman, or an average Joe. He just had that kind of face. In real life, even as a young actor making his name on Broadway, Robinson was never much of a ladies' man, and his own first marriage, which would end in divorce in 1956, after twenty-nine years, was troubled. If it was Robinson's lot never to be adorable, he used that to his advantage in his work, playing a series of smiling men who fall in love and get their guts ripped out. That spectacle was never more painful than in Mervyn LeRoy's *Two Seconds* (1932).

The picture got its title from its flashback structure: What we're seeing is a man's life flashing through his mind as he sits in the electric chair—the two seconds between the juice being turned on and the lights going out forever. Robinson played the man in the hot seat, but he wasn't a gang leader or a career criminal of any kind, just a fellow who hooked up with such a vicious woman that one day he snapped and killed her.

Early in the picture he goes to a dime-a-dance club, and unlike any other movie from the period, the women are neither beautiful nor comically homely, but just subtly unattractive, rather like the chorus line in Bob Fosse's *Cabaret* a generation later. Robinson is mild and bashful with Shirley (Vivienne Osborne), a taxi dancer he meets there. He is much more relaxed, a man's man, when at his construction job, working with his best friend (Richard Arlen). To Shirley, he's a sap waiting to be taken. He gives her money for her (nonexistent) sick parents in Idaho. Later, she gets him drunk and tricks him into marriage.

When his friend points out that the new wife is a no-good floozy with a scandalous past, Robinson comes to her defense. "What she's done before we got married, that's off, see? You and me ain't been no lilies ourselves." That's typical Robinson, who is always tolerant of his woman's past, either out of innate good nature or from delight at having any woman at all. A year later, in *Tiger Shark*, he would persuade Zita Johann to marry him by assuring her he didn't expect a virgin, "I'm not an angel myself. Nobody put any wings on Mike."

Two Seconds starts off routinely downbeat but soon deepens into something awesome and unique. When Robinson finds out his wife is seeing another man, he falls into despair and unravels, while she never stops taunting him. "Ooh, I don't know what keeps me from killing you . . ." he groans. "I hate you." On the page, those words barely register. But Robinson says them with unfathomable misery and a sense of revelation: He really does hate her. He feels the full moral and emotional import of that realization, and so does the audience.

The best is saved for last. After he has killed the wife and been found guilty, he stands before the judge, awaiting sentencing. The judge asks if he has anything to say, and what follows is remarkable. On a stark set, expressionist in its barrenness, Robinson looks up at the judge and starts to speak. LeRoy films Robinson from above, from the judge's viewpoint, and he keeps the camera running for an unbroken two minutes and forty-one seconds. Robinson, mentally frazzled, coming apart, tries to explain to the judge that, if anything, he should have been sent to the chair *before* he killed his wife, not after. Because then he was a rat, see? "Don't you see? You're killing me at the wrong time. If you'd've killed me when I was a rat, I'd've thanked you for it, but you didn't. But now that I've squared everything off, you want to kill me. It ain't fair. It ain't fair to let a rat live and kill a man. No, it ain't reasonable. It don't make sense."

The thinking is twisted. The passion takes him over the edge. He cracks before your eyes. This is Robinson, great American actor, in the most intense minutes of his film career. He endows the speech with the shape and size of melodrama but maintains the precision of a ballet dancer. Remaining true to his core and so in control, he goes to a deep place, without fear, hesitation, or bluffing, using himself unflinchingly. No movie star ever looked like Robinson, and he's beautiful.

Two Seconds was not a cheap movie made to justify the notion of men killing cheating wives. The era did produce one of those—*The Kiss Before the Mirror* (1933)—in which Gloria Stuart played a frisky adulterous for about ninety seconds, before husband Paul Lukas walks in and blasts her and her lover. (The rest of the film involves lawyer Frank Morgan's defending Lukas, all the while contemplating murdering his own wife. Nancy Carroll, for *her* infidelity.) *Two Seconds* was in another class. It was a movie about male frailty, about a lonely man's need for love and the damage an evil woman could wreak on one man's psyche.

Robinson got to go to romantic hell again in Howard Hawks's *Tiger Shark*, in which he played a one-handed fisherman (the shark got the other hand). A nonstop talker and a braggart, he claims women love him, when, in fact, they want nothing to do with him. But he does manage to marry a penniless young woman (Zita Johann), who immediately falls in love with someone else. It's the stock Howard Hawks triangle—two guys in love with one hard-boiled lady. This one is finally resolved when Robinson, in a jealous fury, falls into the bay and is devoured by a shark. His need for love is what really devours him.

On the rare occasions that Robinson did end up happily attached, he usually suffered painful betrayals along the way. In *Hatchet Man* (1932), his young wife (Loretta Young) prefers a younger man, and Robinson only gets her back when the man proves to be a cad. In *Dark Hazard* (1934), he played a gambler who marries a small-town aristocrat (the always-fickle Genevieve Tobin), who considers him common. This wife also ends up being unfaithful, but for once, Robinson has another woman in reserve—the boisterous and lovable Glenda Farrell, who loves gambling and dog racing as much as he does.

The Robinson formula was so ingrained that he had romantic trouble even in the comedy *The Little Giant* (1933). Always gullible with the ladies, even when playing a former mob boss, he loses his head over a society girl (Helen Vinson), who pretends to be interested so that her family might swindle him. Robinson pursues her with his usual openheartedness. In one scene, he compliments her perfume, and when she invites him to smell it up close, he presses his nose up against her breast (a true pre-Code moment). He is touchingly sincere and unguarded as he practices his marriage proposal with the help of his secretary (Mary Astor). Fortunately, though the crooked society woman wants nothing to do with him, the honest secretary does.

ROBINSON AND LAUGHTON weren't the only men to get banged up by love. *Central Airport* (1933), the most apolitical of Richard Barthelmess's pre-Code films, was like a parable built on that theme. He played a flier who has an affair with a female daredevil (Sally Eilers), who suggests that maybe they ought to get married. "Well, just because you're hungry, you don't have to buy a restaurant," he replies. Sounds reasonable enough. But soon she marries his younger brother, and from then on, every time we see Barthelmess, he has a new injury. At one point, he shows up with a cane and an eye patch and sardonically alludes to leaving "an eye in Nicaragua, a heel in China, a couple of ribs in Chile. It's been a habit wherever I go. I leave 'em something to remember me by."

Charlie Chaplin was the original love victim. There's probably nothing left to be said about the remarkable ending to *City Lights* (1931), with its close-up of Chaplin's face, one of the transcendent moments in world cinema. After sacrificing everything to restore a blind girl's sight, he suffers the embarrassment of being seen by her, in all his poverty and humility, after having led her to believe that he was a rich man. It's a moment of utter emotional fragility and hopelessness—and of hoping in the midst of hopelessness.

Spencer Tracy had a curious history with women in the pre-Codes. Though today he is remembered as a kind of curmudgeonly feminist, for his on-screen and offscreen partnership with Katharine Hepburn, he was often, in the early thirties, just a hard case with women, not as cute as Cagney nor as tenderhearted as Robinson. In *Goldie* (1931), he played a loutish sailor who stays loutish through to the finish. Even in Frank Borzage's *Man's Castle* (1933), in which he's a hobo who takes in waify Loretta Young, his blustering becomes hard to take, though in the end he softens up and marries her.

Tracy's hardheaded heroes saw in women the possibility of emotional entanglement, even destruction. Tracy's intelligence as an actor enabled him to suggest that his wariness had little to do with what he knew about women and all to do with a perceived susceptibility within. As the gangster in *Quick Millions* (1931), he lets his illegal empire crumble because of his attraction to a socialite (Marguerite Churchill). In *20,000 Years in Sing Sing* (1933), he goes to the chair for a murder his girlfriend (Bette Davis) committed. In this litany of misery, Raoul Walsh's *Me and My Gal* (1932) is a gemlike anomaly, with Tracy and costar Joan Bennett exhibiting a light touch in a genial romance about a cop and a waitress. More in the Tracy pattern was *The Power and the Glory* (1933). He played a railroad tycoon, a pounding-smashing-driving type. But when he finds out that his wife (Helen Vinson) has a lover and that his child isn't his own, he has trouble walking. He makes it to his office and commits suicide.

Love even hurt Warren William. The late pre-Code *Smarty* (1934), one of the most peculiar items in the William filmography, teamed him with Joan Blondell, but an unusually flighty Blondell, in a role originally intended for Genevieve Tobin. Blondell and William are married, and one night, over dinner, with friends present, she needles him mercilessly. "You make me absolutely impotent with rage," he grumbles. To which she replies, "You mean diced carrots?" Whereupon, he leaps up and smacks her before he even knows what he's done.

Diced carrots? The reference returns later in the movie, when the wife tells a friend that diced carrots refers to "a little intimate married secret" between her and her husband—an incident of impotence, most likely, since the phrase "impotent with rage" brought about her mentioning it. Jokes about impotence, albeit silly, veiled ones, are not something one expects in a 1934 movie.

Pre-Code actors who didn't get routinely put through the romantic ringer still played men who cared very much about love and were unembarrassed about showing their feelings. In *Tonight Is Ours* (1933), Fredric March and Claudette Colbert, a queen, prepare for one night together, knowing that she has to submit to an arranged marriage the next morning. They try to keep their spirits up, but he can't manage it, and he turns away, heartsick. Fresh and handsome in most close-ups, March could make it seem as though he were staring into an abyss just by looking down.

In *All of Me* (1934), March played a building engineer who proposes to Miriam Hopkins, but she is reluctant to tie the knot, worried it might spoil their happiness. "I'm not offering you happiness," he answers with unaffected tenderness. "I'm offering you love." The March hero was always looking for something true and deep, even in *Death Takes a Holiday* (1934). No sooner does Death (March) take human form than he starts looking for a woman with whom he can share his deathless, death-filled existence. "I've been caught in this web of flesh," he says. "Caught and tortured." Take away the death gimmick, and *Death Takes a Holiday* was pretty much a straight love story about a man searching for the one woman who might overlook his unappealing traits—in this case, that he's a supernatural being who goes around killing everybody.

The only time March failed as a romantic lead, or looked faintly embarrassed carrying it off, was when cast in a period picture that lacked a modern hook, something to ground it in the real-life behavior of men and women. In *The Affairs of Cellini* (1934), one of the last pre-Codes, he's amusing but not exactly convincing as the notorious Renaissance sculptor, and, a year after the Code came into effect, he looked ridiculous and uncomfortable as Vronsky to Garbo's Anna Karenina. The grand manner was not for March, who once said he had "no desire, which most actors have, to dress up and act in costume" but preferred "modern things with a puckish humor to them."

The March romantic hero was, at his best, a potential husband. In this sense, March was projecting what he was. His own marriage to actress Florence Eldridge was fairly stable (despite some philandering on his part) and lifelong, beginning in the twenties, when he was a touring stage actor, and ending with his death in 1975. A stable marriage was rare enough in Hollywood. Yet more rare was the way March presented himself in publicity, from the beginning, as a domesticated man. In one of his first Hollywood interviews, he said, "Florence and I have been hunting down an orgy since we arrived. So far, no good. We have come to the conclusion that they must start after we leave." While other stars may have alluded to their spouses, March consistently presented himself as a very married man, usually choosing to be interviewed at his home, most often with Eldridge either present or walking in and out of the room, making comments.

Surprisingly—though perhaps this boded well for the long haul—neither presented the marriage as an idyllic or sizzling love match. Eldridge complained about "Freddie's" tendency to force reading material on her, and she once implied that not being overly attracted to one's spouse made for a steady marriage. As for March, he told *Movie Mirror* in 1932, "Love is friendship plus sex." The partnership aspect was emphasized. "I don't know what I'd do without Florence, my wife," he said the same year. "I read my scripts over with her, I almost rehearse certain scenes, talk over with her about this one or that one."

That "friendship plus sex," in which a woman helps a man reach his artistic potential, was rather like what March had in *Design for Living* (1933), only March had to share Miriam Hopkins in a threesome with Gary Cooper. The picture was one of March's personal favorites. It also provided Gary Cooper with one of his best pre-Code showcases, not least because it took Cooper out of his usual milieu and put him in the hands of a director, Ernst Lubitsch, who could pry him free of his idiosyncrasies.

"I want to do stories that are credible," Cooper once said, "that fit my personality and don't clash with people's beliefs about me." Not surprisingly, this caution sometimes led to dull performances and an over-reliance on self-conscious mannerisms. But in *Design for Living*, Cooper picked up the pace, reacting without censoring himself or framing his responses to accord with some narrow self-image. He has a wonderful flicker of a moment when he discovers that Hopkins and March have betrayed him. "To think that I loved you both," he says, hesitating just a fraction of a second on the word *loved*, as if embarrassed. A fraction of a second more and it would have been precious and all too Cooper-like. As it stands, it's spontaneous, a man letting down his guard and admitting his hurt in honest pre-Code fashion.

Screenwriter Ben Hecht's complete transformation of Noël Coward's play made the film version sexier and more risqué, though it did eliminate one element suggested in the play—that the men had some kind of homosexual attraction for each other. That's in no way present or implied by the film, and yet knowing the original play does make one particularly aware of the scene in which the two men sit together, getting drunk. The movie seems to come to a halt while the men bond over drinks, and one wonders where this affectionate camaraderie may be headed. Nowhere, it turns out.

Pre-Code cinema did find room for overtly gay characters. Though they were usually presented as comic relief—in Fox comedies, for example, a "pansy" character became almost obligatory—at least they were acknowledged to exist and were recognized by the other characters as part of the social landscape. As eccentrics, perhaps, but not freaks.

Cliff Edwards, in Buster Keaton's World War I comedy *Doughboys* (1930), played what may have been the first gay in the military. In *The Public Enemy* (1931), Cagney was fitted for a new suit by an effeminate tailor. In *Blood Money* (1933), tough guy George Bancroft meets a suit-wearing lesbian at a bar, who calls him a "big sissy" (though the movie later backs off and says that the woman only dresses that way for laughs). In *Parachute Jumper* (1933), Douglas Fairbanks, Jr., and Frank McHugh share an apartment, and though they're both straight, they sometimes lisp in a sort of gay caricature. It was enough to make critic Jerry Hoffman complain in his review about "entirely too many flashes of masculine women and feminine men in movies lately."

A typical bit along that line occurred in *Crooner* (1932), in which David Manners starred as a radio-singing heartthrob. One night, as he sings, the camera pans the audience, where, at one table, sits an effeminate man and a butch-looking woman wearing a monocle. The man says, "I think he's superb!" And the woman answers, "I think he's lousy!"

As is often the case with gay characters in movies, there were ironies in that scene. Odds are, the bit player who got to gush over Manners was straight, while Manners, a solid leading man who played opposite some of the best actresses in the business (Stanwyck, Loretta Young, Colbert, Hepburn, Kay Francis), was himself rumored to be gay. One unquestionably gay leading man was William Haines, a boyish silent actor whose wise-cracking persona was rendered obnoxious by the addition of sound. Haines's popularity quickly faded, though his design talent soon turned him into one of Southern California's most in-demand interior decorators.

Aside from Garbo's *Queen Christina* (1933), which was a fairly obvious and entirely glowing portrait of a bisexual, the presentation of homosexuality in pre-Code films was never particularly positive. Yet the increasing visibility of gay characters, not to mention the decreasing ambiguity with which they were presented, is notable. In the British historical saga *Cavalcade* (1933), which won the Oscar for Best Picture, the passage from pre–World War I simplicity to modern-day decadence was presented through a nightclub scene. As the song "Twentieth Century Blues" is sung, the camera pans the audience, and we see two women holdings hands, and a man slipping a bracelet onto the wrist of another man. At least that's what audiences saw in 1933. Two years later, in order to get permission to rerelease the film under the Code, the lesbians were permanently cut from the original negative, though the gay men still appear in existing prints.

WHEN WE WATCH pre-Code movies with an eye to their chronology, we can't help but see an era heading more and more toward a sophisticated urban sensibility. "The farmers have moved from the corral into the drawing room," commented *Motion Picture Classic* in 1931. "Mentally they'd rather mix cocktails than drink hard cider." The homogenizing of mores was accelerated by the speed with which small localities were getting new movies. In the silent days, it would often take a full five years for a movie to make it from the first-run urban houses all the way to the tiny rural bijous. But with the coming of sound, most bijou owners went out of business rather than install expensive sound equipment, forcing rural people to drive twenty or thirty miles to the nearest city to see a movie. Distributors found that viewers in the boondocks enjoyed more or less the same urbane fare as big-city audiences. As far as entertainment was concerned, America had become one big country.

Yet despite a preponderance of sensitive or savvy men, there was still the occasional trace of an old-fashioned sensibility, found in a certain kind of male character that occasionally turned up in pre-Codes—the confident bumpkin, resentful of and condescending toward women, with outdated notions he didn't care to revise. Charles Starrett played one in *Fast and Loose* (1930), a beefy auto mechanic, opposite Miriam Hopkins in her first film. Regis Toomey played another in *Under 18* (1931), opposite Miriam Marsh. Such characters make for some of the most unsatisfying pre-Codes, since the men are invariably insufferable, and yet the movies intend for us to like them. They were a holdover from another era, and they appeared with less frequency as time went on.

Norman Foster played a number of these fellows. His presence in a film rarely boded well. In most films, he played a self-righteous dunce, a half-wit boyfriend or husband with traditional and wholly unexamined values; someone not remotely as intelligent or as talented as his partner; yet someone who, all the same, assumes it's his inability to grasp subtleties that enables him to see the big picture. In *Playgirl* (1932), he marries Loretta Young, who has no idea he's a gambler until he loses all their money. He also loses all his money in *Skyscraper Souls* (1932), only this time in the stock market. In *Professional Sweetheart* (1933), he was an even bigger bumpkin, a hick who kidnaps his celebrity wife and drags her back to his farm in Kentucky. In the latter case, however, the movie was more or less intended as farce, a clash between two caricatures—city girl, country boy.

Foster's most cheerless distinction was in costarring with Loretta Young in the most atypically backward film of the entire era, *Weekend Marriage* (1932). Young and Foster played a couple in a two-career marriage, but Foster wants his wife to stop working. She excels in her job. He fails in his. She gets promotion after promotion. He gets fired—and arrested in a speakeasy raid. She is a success, and he's a waste of space; yet when she has a great opportunity in St. Louis, he refuses to relocate, and she has to go by herself.

In any other pre-Code, she would have divorced her husband and married a coworker—in this case, George Brent, who was considerably more prepossessing than Foster. Instead, *Weekend Marriage* went off the tracks: Young races home when she hears the husband has pneumonia, and upon her arrival, she has to endure a lecture by the family doctor that her husband's illness is *her* fault, that her success has emasculated him, practically killed him. The "happy" ending that results is that she agrees to quit her rewarding, high-paying job and stay at home, even though her husband is an unemployed loser and the world is in the midst of the worst economic slump in modern history.

To be fair to Foster, it should be said that he had a talent for playing weak men, and when movies didn't try to make those weaknesses into virtues, he could be effective. In *Alias the Doctor* (1932), he was in his element as a drunken, irresponsible medical student who performs an illegal operation on his girlfriend, then lets his brother (Richard Barthelmess) take the rap. Later, Foster made a successful career for himself as a film director, his most lauded effort being the noir film *Journey into Fear* (1942).

Today when we see misogynistic pre-Codes, it's clear that we're seeing films and leading men that were outside the pattern of their day. The men in such films represented a type recognized as outmoded, a type anyone at the time might reasonably have assumed was on the verge of extinction. It's the bitter irony that, just a few years later, after the enforcement of the Code, most Hollywood heroes would end up having to endorse old-fashioned values—and that endings like the one in *Weekend Marriage*, anomalous by pre-Code standards, would become enshrined as formula.

12

Remember My Forgotten Man

THE GREAT DEPRESSION ushered in an era of escapist entertainment—or so goes the fable. Of course all movies are, in some sense,
escapist, or else who would bother to see them? The whole point of
going to movies is to escape, even if it's to escape to someplace worse.

The implication, however, that movies made at the height of the
Depression were particularly escapist because times were especially
rough is wrong. As we've seen, the opportunity provided by the coincidence of talkies and relaxed censorship ushered in an unprecedented
era of soul-searching. Gangster films, political films, (anti)war films,
films about business, and horror films, not to mention feminist women's
films, challenged conventional mores and questioned the value of
American institutions. The collapse of the stock market and a deepen-
ing Depression, if anything, only helped fortify the trend.

Today, when thinking of supposedly escapist Depression-era entertainment, some might picture the classic opening to *Gold Diggers of
1933*, with Ginger Rogers leading a scantily clad Busby Berkeley chorus
line in the song "We're in the Money." Indeed, the scene does exem-
plify the era, though to understand its spirit, you have to remember how

the number ends: A sheriff enters and closes down the dress rehearsal because the producers have gone broke.

Musicals, whose popularity had waned early in the pre-Code era, came back with a vengeance in 1933, after Warner Bros. figured out two things—how to make a musical for movies, and how to make one that captured the present moment. In *Gold Diggers of 1933*—as well as in *42nd Street* (1933), which preceded it, and *Footlight Parade* (1933), which followed it—characters don't sing unless they're really singing. (That is, songs never function, as in opera, to emphasize the emotions of characters who, in a realistic convention, would be thinking or talking.) And the Depression, with its hardship, cynicism, and gallows humor, is always present.

The musical, *42nd Street,* is about showbiz that's a world away from the "let's put on a show" cornfests that would later be made in the late thirties and early forties. Everything about it is tough. The director Julian Marsh (Warner Baxter) has lost his money in the stock market crash and needs to direct a hit, even though he has already had one breakdown and the tension could kill him. Everything goes wrong. The leading lady (Bebe Daniels) sprains her ankle and has to be replaced, on the spot, by a novice (Ruby Keeler). By the time the show finally goes up, the director looks like he's been on a three-day drunk, followed by a beating. Show business is not for sissies.

The title song is tough, too. The melody has an ominous quality, the lyrics are cynical, and Busby Berkeley's dance number includes a murder, something passed off as just one more event in the insane parade of "naughty, gaudy, bawdy, sporty 42nd Street"—a litany that rhymes, appropriately enough, only when sung with a New York accent. When the movie is not tough, it's vulgar, though in the best way. Musical mainstay Dick Powell, whose insolent touch saved him from being just another smirky juvenile, sings "I'm Young and Healthy" to chorus girl

Toby Wing. His spring-loaded body language and on-the-make facial expressions eliminate any doubt about what a demonstration of masculine good health might consist of, "If I could hate ya I'd keep away/ But it ain't my nature—I'm full of vitamin A." The number concludes with the camera cruising between the legs of a dozen chorus girls.

Less than a year later, by the time the last in the classic pre-Code trio, *Footlight Parade,* arrived in theaters, the Great Depression toughness was still an element, but the despair had lessened. James Cagney played a producer of Broadway shows whose business goes bust when the talkies come in. So, with the usual Cagney resilience, he makes a thriving business of producing musical "prologues," short stage shows for movie theaters. In the "Shanghai Lil" number, Berkeley's choreography places Cagney in a couple of seedy bars and an opium den, prime pre-Code territory. But it ends with soldiers marching and pictures flashing of the American flag, President Franklin Roosevelt, and the eagle that symbolized the National Recovery Administration. Optimism, like the economy, was attempting a comeback.

Gold Diggers of 1933, which came between *42nd Street* and *Footlight Parade,* is the best of Warners' trio of near-great musicals from 1933, the Depression film par excellence, and one of the best exemplars of its era. The sights, the sounds, the feeling of the early thirties are embedded in this movie's molecular structure. Take a single cell and clone it, and you'd find yourself in Times Square, smelling the hot air from the subway grating and watching the Checker cabs go by. Since Berkeley's unmistakable choreography makes its signature stamp on all three films, there's a tendency to think of them as his alone. But *Gold Diggers* was directed by Mervyn LeRoy, who had already chalked up a string of uncompromising time-capsule-worthy pictures: *Little Caesar, Five Star Final, Two Seconds, Three on a Match,* and *I Am a Fugitive from a Chain Gang.*

Gold Diggers is structured like a dream—the kind of dream in which the dreamer believes, at one point, that he's awake, but he's still dreaming. The dream behind *Gold Diggers* is simple—it's the audience's dream of being "in the money."

A director (Ned Sparks) wants to make a movie about the Depression—about hungry men "marching, marching, marching"—and finds that the young composer (Dick Powell) he hires to write the show is also wealthy enough to produce it. The young man puts up the money, but his family is appalled and dispatches his older brother—played by Warren William—to rescue him from his scandalous Broadway life. Instead, William and the family's business attorney (Guy Kibbee) fall in love with showgirls. Broadway values are embraced by the upper crust, and everyone shares in the bounty.

For most of its running time, *Gold Diggers of 1933* is an enormously likable, slightly naughty backstage musical comedy. About ten minutes before the finish, all the plot issues are resolved. The gold diggers (Joan Blondell, Aline MacMahon, and Ruby Keeler) are happily matched, the show is going well, and the movie is seemingly over. But then along comes Al Dubin and Harry Warren's "Remember My Forgotten Man" number to wipe out the audience and transform everything that went before.

Blondell appears onstage as a prostitute walking a bleak urban street. Under a streetlight, while somehow managing not to blink over the course of a long close-up, Blondell recites the song's lyric, which is not addressed to the audience, but to the government. The song presents an argument for the government's doing something to help Americans hard hit by the Depression. The case made is similar to that which had been made by the Bonus Army the previous summer—that the people not only need it but *deserve* it. Didn't they "cultivate the land?" Didn't they go to war? If a citizen has an implicit obligation to come to the government's aid in a time of need, why not the other way around?

The number makes yet another argument: What about the women? After all, leaving American men to rot amounts to doing the same to American women, "Forgetting him you see/ Means you're forgetting me/ Like my forgotten man." If the mean daddy that is the federal government expects men to fend for themselves, does it also expect women to do the same? The song suggests that even if the government finds it distasteful to come to the aid of able-bodied men, helping them might be a good idea, if only to prevent the blossom of American womanhood from having to peddle itself on the street.

This is heady stuff for a musical comedy. An audience that, a few reels earlier, was watching Dick Powell and Ruby Keeler sing "Pettin' in the Park" is confronted suddenly with a polemical, emotional plea for an aggressive government response to the Depression. As the recent election of Roosevelt proved, this was a sentiment shared by a majority of Americans, but it was also opposed by a large minority. It was rare for a movie to express any idea that would not readily be accepted almost unanimously. This was vigorous, adventurous filmmaking.

The number gets yet more daring when, following the recitation of the lyrics, Blondell stops a cop from rousting a derelict. She comes to the man's aid by pointing at the war medal on the inside of his jacket and staring down the cop. The look on her face is one of utter contempt and hatred. So much for supporting your local police.

The rest of the music sequence pounds home the song's message and shows those "marching, marching, marching" men that the director promised earlier. First, they march to France in World War I. Then they stumble along on breadlines. The statement is startling in its starkness. Finally, Blondell appears again, center stage, surrounded by the chorus, repeating the refrain, "Forgetting him, you see . . ."

The number ends there, but the ending is a double punch. As the chorus sings its last note, the Warner Bros. logo appears, and the theme is repeated by an unseen horn section. Ten seconds after the musical within the movie is over, so is the movie. It's an ending that can rock a viewer sitting alone with the TV set decades later. Just imagine what it must have been like in 1933—to find yourself summarily tossed back into the real world, the one with no theme music and no Joan Blondell, but maybe somebody selling apples on the street corner.

To experience that ending is to realize that *Gold Diggers* has weaved a persuasive and happy dream. We might have thought the dream was over when the "We're in the Money" number was interrupted in the first scene, but what came after that was nothing like real life. Rather, we saw a Broadway where the rich come to the rescue, where art is unstoppable, talent recognized, and love able to build bridges across class. Only in the last minutes does the movie tell the whole truth, and with that realization, the viewer is jolted from the dream into the waking world.

By ending the movie with the conclusion of the musical, the filmmakers were also saying, in effect, "Their ending is our ending, too. Everything you've seen has led to this message. The musical within the movie is fiction. But the musical about the Depression has been made in earnest—and that's what you've been watching. And here's our corporate logo to show we mean it."

This was an important film, and astute critics realized it at the time. As the *New York Herald Tribune* wrote, "*Gold Diggers of 1933* might represent the American screen's first coming to appropriate sentimental grips with economic misery."

FILMS IN WHICH the Depression figured prominently were rare until late 1932. *Stolen Heaven*, released in February 1931, was an early one to show that President Hoover's assertion that no one ever went hungry in America wasn't exactly accurate. Phillips Holmes played an unemployed man who is so desperate that he steals twenty thousand dollars from the factory that once employed him. A young woman (probably a streetwalker) takes him in, and the fellow, hardly a criminal type, describes his efforts to make good in a world where following the rules no longer works:

> I tried to get ahead. Did everything. Worked hard. Went to night school. . . . Never did me any good. I got fired from my job the same as anyone else. Do you know what it's like to stand in a breadline? Do you know what it's like to be willing to work your head off, not to be able to get a job, pushing a broom or carrying a tray or anything else? After a little while of that, you begin to get desperate.

His plan now—to go on a spending spree with the money and then commit suicide—is an idea she can appreciate. "You just wanted a chance at life," the woman (Nancy Carroll) says. ". . . It wasn't money you stole. It was music, lights and friends and good things to eat." Implicit was the assumption that everyone deserved at least a fighting chance at happiness and material comfort.

American Madness, released in the summer of 1932, dealt directly with financial panic. Walter Huston played a bank president who espouses a liberal lending policy, believing that the only way to end a depression is to get money circulating. False rumors that the bank is insolvent leads to a run on the bank by depositors, which threatens to put it out of business. But, as would often happen in Capra films, things get unbearably bad, only to get blessedly better. *American Madness*, which opened seven months before Roosevelt's inaugural, showed that the only thing investors had to fear was fear itself. It's a story of average people banding together, with a sense of community, to overcome that fear. In the months to come, movies would get considerably more cynical.

By the beginning of 1933, the Depression was an open topic in movies. It may have been a case of Hollywood's finally catching up with the story, or a matter of events reaching such critical mass that the movies could no longer ignore it. Or perhaps Roosevelt's election in November 1932 had something to do with it. Studios no longer had to fear angering the Hoover administration by depicting bad times. And with audiences feeling a bit more optimistic about the future, producers felt freer to show the present reality. As the *Syracuse Herald* put it in June of 1933, "With the public mind definitely turned toward hope . . . the industry can now afford to come clean and let the public in on the fact that, for some years, one out of every ten Americans has not known where his next meal was coming from."

I Am a Fugitive from a Chain Gang was filmed in the summer of 1932 and released in mid-November. Technically, it's not a Depression movie. It takes place mainly in the twenties, before the Depression, and the Wall Street crash doesn't figure into the story at all. Yet everything about the picture—the clothes, the cars, the mood, the attitude—reads early thirties. Economic hardship is present from the start, and familiar pre-Code themes soon emerge: the corruption of entrenched power, the inadequacy of small-town life, and the creativity of the independent spirit.

Paul Muni played a man who returns home from the Great War wanting nothing but self-fulfillment and freedom. "I learned that life is more important than a medal on my chest or a stupid, insignificant job," he says. He resolves to become an engineer, but his aspirations are regarded by family and friends with suspicion and even hostility, as though he threatens to provide an example of liberty and happiness that might make others discontented with their own lot. From the beginning, then, the movie establishes Muni not just as a victim of circumstances but as a forceful individual of vision and enterprise, whom a narrow-minded America will sooner or later find a way to stop.

He goes off to make it, traveling the country, piecing together work here and there, at other times walking along the train tracks, with nowhere to live and nowhere to go. In a nod to the Bonus Army, he tries to pawn his war medals, but the pawnbroker shows him a whole case full of pawned medals, each one a promise broken. Mistakenly implicated in an armed robbery, he ends up on a chain gang. The first time he manages to escape, he makes a life for himself as an important engineer in Illinois, until his spiteful wife (Glenda Farrell) turns him in. The second time he escapes, he blows up a bridge and becomes a fugitive.

Based on the autobiographical book by Robert E. Burns, *I Am a Fugitive from a Chain Gang* took one man's hard-luck story and turned it into a treatise on how contemporary America could wreck a guy. First send him to war. And if that doesn't kill him, stifle any impulse he has for a rewarding existence. If that fails, set him loose in an economy in which there's no work, then rig the political justice system. And, finally, create prisons designed to kill people if they stay and kill them if they try to escape. In *I Am a Fugitive*, few things connected with authority have any value or integrity—even the church, or at least that's implied. The protagonist's brother, a well-meaning minister (Hale Hamilton), gives him nothing but bad advice and eventually commits an indiscretion that sends him back to prison.

In pre-Code Depression films, moral precepts took a backseat to practical necessity. It might be criminal to blow up a bridge, but some things just have to be done. Likewise, hungry people were not expected to starve rather than steal. Like Saint Thomas Aquinas, the films saw nothing immoral in a hungry person's taking food in order to keep body and soul together (as Joan Blondell does when she steals two hot dogs for herself and her boyfriend in 1932's *Central Park*). The moral license granted by the Depression resulted in outrageous behavior in many films.

In *Parachute Jumper* (1933), Douglas Fairbanks, Jr. played a jaunty former navy pilot who, broke and hungry, is happy to do anything for money. He is hired by a crooked importer (Leo Carillo), who asks, "Do you object to cracking, or should I say 'denting,' the law a little here and there?"

"*What* law?" Fairbanks says.

"The one we all laugh at," the new boss replies.

Fairbanks ends up shooting down American Border Patrol planes in the process of smuggling narcotics in from Canada. His act is mitigated somewhat by the fact that he thinks he's smuggling liquor and that he mistakes the Border Patrol for rival bootleggers. Even so, it's a fairly extreme act for a good-guy protagonist.

Nineteen thirty-two was the depth of the Depression, the nadir. By the middle of 1932, industry was operating at half of its 1929 capacity and wages were down a full 60 percent from their 1929 high. Even without knowing the particulars, one could tell from the movies released in early 1933 that something was very wrong. *Parachute Jumper*, released in January, may have been lighthearted and snappy, but between the frames, it was clearly the product of a heartsick, disoriented country. An explicit expression of the same turmoil can be found in another early 1933 film, this one about a party hack who becomes president, nearly dies in a car wreck, and then is reborn as a visionary leader. In *Gabriel Over the White House*, President Hammond (Walter Huston) represented the era's collective fantasy of the ideal president. The picture is a fascinating document from a brief but distinct juncture in American history, a time when problems seemed so insoluble that the prospect of a dictator was attractive.

The film was based on a futuristic political novel by a British author, Thomas Tweed, about a president who becomes possessed by the angel Gabriel and solves all the world's problems, circa 1950. In bringing the book to the screen, the filmmakers—producer Walter Wanger, director Gregory La Cava, and screenwriter Carey Wilson—not only streamlined the story but made it more immediately relevant by having it take place in the America of 1933. Daringly, Hammond, at the start, is not just presented as a mediocrity but as an identifiably Republican sort of mediocrity. He supports Prohibition and calls unemployment a "local problem." After he is conked on the head, he becomes more than willing to use federal power.

The movie makes excellent use of Huston's range. As an actor, he tended to look powerful and resolute when stern, and vapid or demented when smiling. Accordingly, in the beginning of the movie, he smiles a lot. Later, in his great man incarnation, he is serious and talks in a brisk monotone, as though channeling a force speaking through him. It's strange, all these decades later, how Huston's portrayal of President Hammond still taps into an American viewer's yearning for a strong and benevolent leader. Advised to call out the military when the Army of the Unemployed is about to march on Washington—yet another pre-Code reference to the Bonus Army—Hammond says, "I refuse to call out the Army on the people of the United States."

Instead, he meets the marchers and congratulates them for arousing "the stupid, lazy people of the United States to force their government to do something before everybody slowly starves to death." He enlists the men in an "army of construction," sets aside billions to stimulate purchases, to shore up banks, and to protect homeowners against foreclosures. He also solves the gangster problem (with tanks), the Prohibition problem (through repeal), and the problem of world peace (by scaring European leaders with American air power). He is able to get so much done because he dismisses Congress, fires his cabinet, and threatens to declare martial law. In the same year that Germany elevated Hitler, *Gabriel Over the White House* made an alarmingly seductive case for an American dictator.

Before the picture was released, forces within the film industry were worried that it might be too incendiary to unleash on an angry public. MGM mogul Louis B. Mayer, an active Republican, was appalled to

198 • Dangerous Men

realize his studio had made a film that was an unmistakable repudiation of the Hoover administration. James Wingate of the Studio Relations Committee was afraid it might "foment violence against the better elements of established government" and cause protestors to descend on Washington en masse. In February 1933, Will Hays—fearful of government intervention in the film industry—expressed concern about two bills introduced in the New York legislature to prevent the certification of any motion picture that would "tend to undermine public confidence in public officials and their conduct of office."

Clearly, *Gabriel Over the White House* was primed to be a national sensation, but then Mayer did one thing that changed everything. He held up the film's release until after Franklin Roosevelt's inauguration. Released twenty-seven days into the new president's term, the film was no longer a comment on the current president's inadequacies, but a political fantasy that was old news on arrival. Audiences saw President Hammond asking for special powers to combat the Depression, something that Roosevelt—a fan of the film, as it turned out—had already done weeks before. The movie was greeted with critical success but popular indifference.

THE PRE-CODE POLITICAL films are exhilarating in the way they let us eavesdrop, many years later, on a conversation between filmmakers and their audiences. Without censorship getting in the way of free expression, the movies spoke frankly but also with an added immediacy, since no one at the time ever expected these movies to last. Not meant for our eyes and ears, these films weren't intended to document a time or court approval from history. They were as fresh as headlines and, like newspapers, were designed to be ephemeral.

Just as satisfying as the kick of eavesdropping is hearing the actual sentiments expressed by the films, viewpoints that often defy their ancient provenance by sounding like something that could have been said yesterday. When President Hammond tells indifferent bureaucrats that the president will *not* allow Americans to starve—or when a homeless Frankie Darro makes a defiant speech to a judge in *Wild Boys of the Road* (1933)—we feel the surge that comes of seeing authority confronted by courageous self-assertion.

Such movie moments are of a sort to which anyone would respond. Yet seeing them becomes especially precious when we remember the institutionalized dishonesty that would reign for thirty-four years under the Code, during which rigid authority was usually presented on-screen as cuddly. Even in today's films, the truly rebellious spirit is rarely associated with heroism. The closest modern movies ever come to a wild-man protagonist is the stock maverick-cop character, who worries his superiors by using unconventional methods to get the bad guys. As we've seen in the pre-Code era, the good guys often *were* the bad guys.

In 1933, Warner Bros. took the lead in making socially conscious films. These films were not the most sexually risqué—for that, audiences could turn to MGM or Paramount product; nor were they the most raw or crude—Fox held the patent on coarseness. But they were the most socially responsive. "The studios' ventures into social criticism," critic Richard Watts would write in 1934, "have been brief and intermittent and are usually conducted under the expert guidance of the zealous Warner Bros."

Wild Boys of the Road, one of the favorite films of its director, William Wellman, was also, arguably, the most disturbing of all Depression films. Like *The Mayor of Hell*, it was about kids, but, contrary to what one might infer from the title, the wild boys weren't young hellions, destined from the start to be desperadoes, but average, suburban adolescents whose lives are thrown into turmoil by the Depression. In its disarming opening minutes, *Wild Boys* could be mistaken for a light-hearted tale of adolescent life, but Wellman was just setting the stage, creating an illusion of safety soon to be shattered.

The picture was the story of two friends, Tommy (Edwin Philips) and Eddie (Frankie Darro). Tommy's mother loses her job, and Eddie's father loses his, and neither can find work. The kids get the idea that, rather than stay and be a burden on their parents, they should take off down the road and earn their own living. "Why should I stick in school and have a good time when he has to stand in a breadline?" Eddie says of his father.

In *Wild Boys*, the Depression came home to Middle America. In dramatizing a very real phenomenon—by 1933, an estimated 200,000 children, many of them girls dressed as boys, were rail-riding drifters—the movie demonstrated just how quickly it could all go, how the middle class's financial security was like a rickety footbridge over an abyss. It showed what happens to people when they do plummet from the middle class—they keep falling, forever, and no one has any pity.

Cops roust them; railroad men throw coal at them. Each time the kids—soon there are dozens of them—arrive in a new city, they are greeted by goons carrying billy clubs. A teenage girl is raped by a brakeman. Tommy is run over by a train and has a leg amputated. If the kids go into town, every property owner reacts with a hostility bordering on blind hysteria. *Wild Boys of the Road* is no paean to the generous American heart. It's a have-nots versus the haves story, as told from the viewpoint of underage have-nots.

The Bonus Army continued to capture the imagination and weigh on the national conscience. Made a year after the Bonus Army's forced ejection from Washington, *Wild Boys* paralleled their story: The kids set up their own "republic" outside of Cleveland but eventually are driven out and dispersed. Eddie, Tommy, and Sally, a girl they befriend on the road (played by Dorothy Coonan, the future Mrs. Wellman), end up living in a New York City garbage dump. Having been chased and chased by every form of authority, the dump is the one place where American kids can be allowed to live, unmolested by the authorities.

Kids left to rot in a garbage dump—that's beyond metaphor. It's as direct a commentary as can be.

Wellman's velocity, a characteristic of his and Warners' pre-Code style, infuses *Wild Boys of the Road* with a snappy archness that keeps it from being completely depressing. In one scene, Sally takes the boys to the home of her aunt, knowing she'll take them in. In a matter of seconds, Wellman establishes the aunt's apartment as a brothel (a whorehouse piano is tinkling away), and shows the place getting raided before the hungry kids can get a bite to eat.

The ending strikes an overtly optimistic note, when the kids, arrested and beginning to harden, are taken to a judge, from whom they expect the worst. But the judge turns out to be, of all things, a New Dealer, who makes a speech about a new spirit in the land. The judge not only speaks for Roosevelt; he looks and sounds like Roosevelt—the actor Robert Barrat does his best vocal impression and even wears Roosevelt's pince-nez glasses. Clearly, he is the Santa's helper equivalent of the president of the United States, and he sends the kids home on a note of hope. This is certainly not the devastating ending that *Wild Boys of the Road* may have led us to expect, but after all the misery, it's a relief for the viewer. In any case, we understand. As Richard Watts, Jr., ably put it in a *New York Herald Tribune* analysis of social-issue films, "The safe and sane liberalism of the final scenes in these photoplays [should not] cause anyone to forget that before the more or less happy endings are reached, some pretty telling blows are struck."

UP UNTIL THE end of the pre-Code period, Richard Barthelmess used movies to address social and political issues. The movie industry had caught up with him by 1933—he was no longer alone in his concerns—but he used the trend toward social awareness to become more uncompromising in his subject matter and more strident in his approach. His last three pre-Codes—*Heroes for Sale* (1933), *Massacre* (1934), and *A*

Modern Hero (1934)—were hardly cozy entertainment. They were films driven by earnest purpose and passion. To make these films, Barthelmess was leveraging the most precious capital a film star has—his popularity—to reach the people of his time. Watts called him "Hollywood's most serious-minded citizen." The *New York World-Telegram* noted that Barthelmess "displays more courage and intelligence in the selection of his screen material" than other stars. Barthelmess wryly called himself, "the screen's champion underdog."

Heroes for Sale (also directed by Wellman) was the devastating story of Tom, a World War I soldier who gets shot up in the course of doing something heroic and gets only grief for his pains. His medal, as well as all the credit for his heroic deed, mistakenly goes to a wealthy coward from his hometown, while Tom ends up getting released from a military hospital, having gained nothing but a morphine addiction.

Barthelmess invested Tom with his patented quiet decency and moral certitude, while the story implied that, in modern America, such a decent fellow could never succeed, at least not with his integrity intact. Ideologically, *Heroes for Sale* was confused, but the one consistent element in the story was that the authorities were not to be trusted. Businessmen are heartless, and cops don't even care if they catch the right guy. In one scene, Tom tries to break up a strike by workers and is given a five-year prison sentence for Communist agitation.

Heroes for Sale does have an actual Communist character, but it's not Barthelmess. It's a zany inventor (Robert Barrat), who becomes a raging capitalist as soon as he starts making money. The Communist turned capitalist is presented as a buffoon. For him, ideology is strictly a function of self-interest—when he was poor, he wanted an equal distribution of wealth; now rich, he does not. Yet the flexible morality he practices is one shared by every other powerful character in the film. The joke is on Tom. His mistake, the misapprehension at the root of all his miscalculations, is his belief that his own government is essentially benevolent, when it is, in fact, as cold and pragmatic in its morality as the buffoonish inventor.

Heroes for Sale is a film whose viewpoint is hard to nail down. Tom, the hero, is both an all-American patriot and something of a socialist. When he becomes rich, he gives all his money to feeding the poor and lives the life of a wanderer. Yet, in the end, he's extolling Franklin Roosevelt's inaugural address and telling a fellow hobo that the Depression "may be the end of us, but it's not the end of America." "If we didn't know better," commented the *Baltimore Sun*, "we would suspect that the American Legion, the American Civil Liberties Union, and Comrade Stalin of Moscow collaborated in writing *Heroes for Sale*." That's how ideologically jumbled the picture was.

Yet a case can be made that the film's ideological confusion accurately captured its historic moment—a quality that must be factored into any assessment of its worth. After all, if Tom had no set ideology, neither did the new man in the White House, who'd moved in only months before, having no fixed plan, just a willingness to improvise. "Take a method, and try it," Roosevelt had said. "If it fails, admit it frankly, and try another. But by all means, try something." At heart, *Heroes for Sale* was not about capitalism versus socialism, or even about the virtues of a benevolent pragmatism over a cold-blooded pragmatism. It was about a people in such despair for so long that they were in a state of philosophical bewilderment, just looking for any reason to hope.

SINCE PRE-CODES—OR at least a certain kind of socially conscious pre-Code—began with Barthelmess, it makes sense to end with him. We move to the year 1934, which dawned with movies more explicit, more frank, and more intelligent than they'd ever been—and, alas, would be, for another generation. By 1934, virtually no adult subject, if handled with taste and restraint, was too outrageous. No social or political sentiment, if presented persuasively, was beyond expression. With *Massacre*, released in January, Barthelmess took on the government's mistreatment of American Indians. Critics recognized it immediately as a step forward.

"To denounce a government with fire and indignation requires artistry, which Richard Barthelmess possesses," columnist Joan Kennison wrote in the *Herald Tribune*. "This . . . picture is the most vigorous assault upon American injustice since *I Am a Fugitive from a Chain Gang*."

What excited critics about the film was that it seemed to herald a Hollywood that might actually serve not as a propaganda arm of power but as a watchdog against governmental abuse. The *New Orleans Tribune* considered it a "sign of the mental and emotional vigor" of the film industry that it should concern itself with "a serious detail of national affairs . . . in a fashion not likely to please politicians." The *New York Evening Post* said, "The picture may come under the head of propaganda, but if it is true, then the motion picture [industry] in this country has reason to be proud of itself." Al Sherman in the *New York Telegraph* wrote that *Massacre* proved that "the movies . . . are growing up. . . . Films can study social abuses and, too, take sides."

The *Buffalo Times* praised Barthelmess as "the chief denouncer of civic injustices in pictures." Richard Watts, Jr., who'd been the first critic to recognize the social significance of Barthelmess's work, was especially excited about *Massacre*. Calling Barthelmess the "most earnest of Hollywood's crusaders," he wrote, "As proof that the cinema is definitely, if laboriously, developing a social conscience, [*Massacre*] is of genuine value. . . . The picture gets in some of the most unrelenting blows against economic and racial oppression that the American cinema has yet struck." The sad irony is that what critics hailed as a beginning was practically an end. In less than six months, the enforcement of the Code would stop this new direction in its tracks.

So we approach *Massacre* not as the forerunner of a movement but as a fascinating original. Barthelmess played Joe Thunder Horse, a stunt rider who makes a good living and lives a thoroughly modern life. At the start of the movie, his girlfriend is a depraved white woman (Claire Dodd), who clearly gets aroused at the idea of being ravished by a savage. She asks him to put on an Indian headdress and lies back on a chaise longue. "Red skin," she says seductively.

The fun and games end when Joe gets word that his father is dying and returns to the reservation, to find his people living under appalling conditions. The physician lets sick Indians die, while the chief administrator and the undertaker are in cahoots to steal the land from their heirs. Later, the undertaker rapes Joe's sister. In retaliation, Joe ties him to the back of his car and drags him through the dust.

Throughout, the movie has respect for Indian customs. When Barthelmess, in violation of reservation policy, has a traditional Sioux funeral service for his father, the administrators—the very people who are causing the Indians to die of malnourishment and medical neglect—complain about the "pagan" ceremony. In moments like this, *Massacre* is more than a tale of individual corruption; it is a critique of the white man's treatment of the red man. The implications go even further when Joe's black valet (Clarence Muse) refers to the reservation as "the plantation." At the end, Joe has rediscovered his Indian consciousness and, instead of trading on his heritage at carnivals, marries an Indian woman (Ann Dvorak) and takes a job with the Bureau of Indian Affairs.

Barthelmess's last pre-Code film, *A Modern Hero*, released in April 1934, was the apotheosis of the era's businessmen sagas, and it followed the usual pattern: rags to riches to rags. Directed by German filmmaker G. W. Pabst (*Pandora's Box*, *The Joyless Street*), faithfully adapted from a novel by Louis Bromfield, it was the story of a poor foreigner who cashes in on the American dream, using women who can help him and cheating his partners on the way to becoming an industrial magnate. At the time when Americans blamed the greed of their business leaders for the economic debacle, the picture presented an American success story as an utterly failed life. The hero fails as a son, as a lover, as a husband, as a father, and, ultimately, as a businessman.

What distinguished this film from other pre-Code antibusiness films was Barthelmess. Unlike Warren William's businessmen, who were born piranhas, Barthelmess's essence seemed moral, so the spectacle of him cheating everyone registered as a spiritual derailment. In its tale of an ambitious immigrant who blithely, and without thinking, adopts the ethos and the standard of success of his new country, A Modern Hero suggested it was in the very nature of America to produce such people. The result for them and the country at large was the same—moral bankruptcy, followed by financial bankruptcy.

The Depression films of 1933 and early 1934 were pointing the way toward an American cinema of increasing public responsiveness and audacity. But by mid-1934, this direction was curtailed. Hollywood's movement into more serious and adult territory was halted by the enforcement of the Production Code and the installment of a regime determined to use movies to enforce fixed standards and glorify author-ity in all forms—religious, economic, governmental.

For the next generation, right and wrong were rigid entities, defined in terms that conformed to the censors' narrow morals and that most benefited those in power. The era of moral questioning was over and a mindless era of moral certainty had begun.

SO WHY GO back to the movies of the pre-Code era? What's the point of discovering and watching these films all these years later? The ques-tions are valid. After all, we're talking about a brief period that ended almost seventy years ago and counting. Most of the films are unknown and don't even attract nostalgia buffs, since there's nothing drippy or sentimental about them. Indeed, the kick of pre-Codes is the opposite of nostalgia. Watching them, we don't search for the past in the present. Rather, we discover the present in the past.

There's pleasure in that and also utility. Watching a vanished era expressing itself honestly brings a sense of privilege, as well as an almost eerie recognition that yours wasn't the first generation to be confronted by this or that feeling or situation. To see a moment on-screen so alive you can't believe it is to be, in a small way, assured of the value of moments in the face of time. Yet the very vividness of the pre-Codes also emphasizes a warning: Even vitality such as this can be squelched if a close-minded faction is obsessed, pernicious, and willing to organize.

All entrenched power depends on the illusion of unity to suppress dissent at the source, to make anyone who has the impulse to question authority feel odd, surrounded, or powerless. Simplistic dogma is offered as revealed truth, but inevitably it will collapse in the face of sophisticated thinking or even good old common sense. Pre-Code movies applied sophisticated thinking, honest observation, and common sense to the turbulent America of the early thirties and said things that are not usually said—that war is hell, that governments lie, that officials are corrupt, that it's every man for himself, that to be honest and courageous sometimes means fighting the system or subverting it. These may be healthy things for individuals to know, but they aren't what governments like to see pumped into the public consciousness. So when fanatics drove honesty off the American screen, no politician, Democrat or Republican, did anything to bring it back.

Movies reflect culture but also affect it, and we can never know for sure which is influencing the other more. Still, it's safe to say that the censors achieved their goals. Some social progress that seemed inevitable in the early thirties was stalled for decades, a fact we can attribute to a number of factors. At the very least, movies of the Code era did their part to keep everyone a happy cog in the machine by encouraging chastity and conformity and by reminding men and women of their place. For a while, it seemed to work.

It doesn't take much to see that movies made under the Code would have been better had the Code never come about. To encounter pre-Code cinema is to wonder if America might have been better, too. A society that is honest in its critique of itself is a society that maintains its aspirations for itself. For all their movies' cynicism, the dangerous men and complicated women of the pre-Code screen assumed they had the power to change their circumstances—and they had the force and the feistiness to manage it.

They represent an aspect of the American character that should never have been suppressed and would be a tragedy to lose.

Epilogue

Throughout the pre-Code era, there were would-be reformers working behind the scenes to gain control over screen content. Attempts were made to incite public outrage, in the hope that consumer pressure might make Hollywood change its ways or that the government might intervene and enforce rigid censorship.

When we look at the contemporaneous arguments for and against censorship, it is curious to note that the people on both sides claimed that they were acting to promote screen realism. Reformers insisted that the movies we now know as pre-Code were presenting—and propagating—a distorted vision of American life and morals as corrupt. Others saw the era's films as being merely honest and responsible.

As they argued that their vision was more in line with reality, reformers also emphasized the positive propaganda potential of film. "Here is an instrument at last in universal terms," wrote Henry James Forman in the pro-censorship study *Our Movie-Made Children* (1933). "Send forth a great message, broadcast a vision of truth and beauty . . . [and] literally all America will be your audience."

The reformers, like all before and since, justified their appeal for censorship by claiming that movies were destroying the younger generation. *Our Movie-Made Children* quoted boys who claimed to have learned tricks of the criminal trade by watching gangster movies. In one survey, 50 percent of troubled boys interviewed claimed that they emulated Cagney, rather than Robinson, because Cagney was "tougher." At least they were watching closely.

Some of the surveys rang true. The 1933 study "The Social Conduct and Attitudes of Movie Fans," by Frank K. Shuttleworth and Mark A. May, worried that the majority of movie-watching students said they'd rather be a movie star than a college professor. Imagine that. Shuttleworth and May also found that movie-watching children tended to believe that "policeman torture or mistreat anyone suspected of a crime" and that "few or no small-town police officials are clever and efficient."

In the same study, Shuttleworth and May expressed surprise that "the movie children tend to deny that social workers are busybodies." That finding would have come as no surprise if they'd been watching movies instead of taking surveys. In the pre-Codes, authority may have been the enemy, but people who wanted to reach out and help were often presented as heroic.

The "save the children" refrain was just one argument. Another tactic of persuasion, a perennial, was to say something utterly idiotic that *sounded* like patriotism, when it was anything but. Nina Wilcox Putnam, herself a screenwriter, wrote in the July 1933 issue of *Modern Screen*: "For the sake of those respected forbears who fought and died to give us a clean country, don't let us gobble up poison! . . . When such showings affect the love life of an entire nation, we cannot watch those responsible too carefully nor call them to strict enough account." No doubt it would have been fruitless to point out to Ms. Putnam that, in fact, nobody's forbears had fought to give her a "clean" country. They had fought to give her a free country and for inconvenient incidentals such as the Bill of Rights.

The censorship, which came down like a hammer on July 1, 1934, changed movies irrevocably, but the actors of the time survived better than the actresses. Actors switched from playing criminals to cops. Self-interested individualists became, in a pinch, flag-wavers, while their girlfriends just played virgins. Sophisticated actresses, who'd made their name in sex dramas, now found themselves in dramas without sex. They lost the basis of their appeal, while actors were able to hang on.

Yet if the actors themselves survived, their pre-Code legacies suffered at the hands of censorship more than did those of the actresses. Under the Code, whenever a studio wanted to rerelease a pre-Code movie, it had to be submitted to Joseph Breen, head of the Production Code Administration, for approval. As the Production Code files at the Motion Picture Academy's library reveal, Breen tended to reject most women's sex dramas out of hand. But with the men's films, he often suggested cuts, which the studios made—not only to the prints but also to the original negatives.

As a result, there are pre-Codes today that don't exist in complete form. *The Eagle and the Hawk* (1933), for example, showed aviator Fredric March in a one-night stand with socialite Carole Lombard. In a scene that no longer exists, he wakes up the next morning in her bed.

Breen took pride in his ability as a story editor, and in 1938 he bragged about his edit of the Loretta Young–Spencer Tracy film, *Man's Castle* (1933), as though he'd done something creative. The whole movie was about a woman who becomes pregnant out of wedlock. She tells her boyfriend, who almost runs away, but he returns to her, and they marry. In Breen's edit, the marriage ceremony was lifted from reel seven and inserted into reel two, "without," as Breen put it, "any suggestion of violence to the story or to its easy flow." Or so he claimed. As Loretta Young recalled in 1998, "It ruined the whole story."

Fortunately, *Man's Castle* can be seen today in its original version. Likewise, *Frankenstein* (1931) has now been restored to its full length, though for decades it was available only in a 1937 version, in which the scene of the monster throwing the little girl into the lake was cut, among other things.

The luckiest break for posterity is that, somehow, Warner Bros. preserved the original negatives of its pre-Code films before the films were cut for reissue in the middle and late thirties. Had this not been the case, the legacy of Warren William would have been all but lost—his films were butchered in rerelease. Classics such as *42nd Street* and *Gold Diggers of 1933* were also hacked to pieces. These are just a couple of examples. In fact, we're talking about dozens of movies whose boldness and flavor would have been lost to us.

Alas, one Warners movie that was cut and has never been restored is *The Public Enemy* (1931). Though it survived the mid-thirties purge, the original negative was apparently cut for a 1953 rerelease, according to Breen's recommendations. This was done despite the fact that the film was, by then, already recognized as a classic. As a result, the scene in which Cagney's sidekick (Edward Woods) romps in bed with his girlfriend (Joan Blondell) appears to be lost to the ages.

THE ACTORS WHOSE films make up the story of *Dangerous Men*, like all people who come together in glory, went on to individual fates: George Arliss, whose career was already in decline by 1934, retired in 1937. He died in his native England in 1946, at age seventy-seven.

John Barrymore became, in his later years, a parody of himself—or, rather, of the public's idea of who he was—a drunken ham actor, a great profile gone to seed. But when given a good script, he could occasionally rouse himself. His years of alcoholism, however, eventually caught up with him, and he died in 1942, at age sixty.

Lionel Barrymore enjoyed a long association with MGM, first as a thin middle-aged man and later as a heavyset old man, confined to a wheelchair by arthritis. He gave many fine performances in his later years, including the villain in Frank Capra's *It's a Wonderful Life* (1946) and the father of a war hero in *Key Largo* (1948). He died in 1954 at age seventy-six.

Richard Barthelmess, in 1935, told a reporter, "I have said goodbye to youth." He worked only sporadically until 1942, when he quit acting and joined the U.S. Naval Reserve. He died in 1963, at age sixty-eight.

James Cagney enjoyed one of the great screen careers. He retired in 1961 to live on his farm in upstate New York, and came back in 1981 to make his last feature film, *Ragtime*. He died in 1986, at age eighty-six. President Reagan gave the eulogy.

Maurice Chevalier moved back to Europe in the second half of the 1930s. As an older man, he returned to Hollywood and made a series of notable films, including *Gigi* (1958), in which he sang "Thank Heaven for Little Girls." He died on New Year's Day of 1972, at age eighty-three.

Gary Cooper's old-fashioned heroism was more suited to the Code era than the pre-Code era. He thrived in the late thirties, forties, and fifties, making many signature films, including *Mr. Deeds Goes to Town* (1936), *Meet John Doe* (1941), and *High Noon* (1952). He died in 1961, at age sixty.

Ricardo Cortez gradually descended into B movies in the late thirties and retired from films in 1940, when he was forty-one. Following his screen career, he made a prosperous living as a stockbroker. He died in 1977, at age seventy-eight.

Douglas Fairbanks lost interest in his career and hadn't quite found something else in which to channel his restlessness when he died of a heart attack in 1939, at age fifty-six.

Douglas Fairbanks, Jr., after playing young wise guys in the pre-Codes, enjoyed a career in comedies, swashbucklers, and adventure films. He was adept at everything he attempted. He died in 2000, at age ninety.

Clark Gable's career left posterity with an aesthetic question: Do we like him better with the mustache or without it? The undisputed king of Hollywood for most of his career, Gable made few great films, but the fact that one can watch fifty Gable movies in a row without ever hitting a bad one is persuasive evidence of his personal greatness. His performance in *The Misfits* (1961), which was released posthumously, was one of his best. He died in 1960, at age fifty-nine.

Walter Huston is best remembered for his most atypical role, that of the toothless prospector in *The Treasure of the Sierra Madre* (1948), directed by his son, John Huston. He died in 1950, a day after his sixty-sixth birthday.

Al Jolson enjoyed a resurgence of popularity in the forties, when two biopics of his life were released by Columbia, *The Jolson Story* (1946) and *Jolson Sings Again* (1949). He provided new vocals for both and died in 1950, at age sixty-four.

Charles Laughton worked in British and American films for the rest of his life. His one directorial effort, *Night of the Hunter* (1955), is recognized as a classic. He died in 1962, at age sixty-three.

Fredric March was an actor's actor, onstage and in films. He won a second Academy Award for *The Best Years of Our Lives* (1946). He had a stroke during the making of his last film, *The Iceman Cometh* (1973), but returned to finish the film, at one point working while suffering with the flu. He died in 1975, at age seventy-seven.

Robert Montgomery joined the navy in World War II and served on a destroyer in the D-day invasion. Upon his return, he resumed his acting career, and directed several films, as well. He directed and hosted a television series and won a Tony for directing *The Desperate Hours*

(1955) on Broadway. He also worked in politics and was an adviser to President Eisenhower. He died in 1981, at age seventy-seven.

Paul Muni divided his time between Broadway and Hollywood. His last film was *The Last Angry Man* (1959). He died in 1967, at age seventy-two.

Ramon Novarro made a few films after 1935, some in Mexico and some in the United States. He was murdered in 1968 by two hustlers in Hollywood. He was sixty-nine.

William Powell had a bout with colon cancer in the late thirties, but he survived and worked steadily thereafter. His last film was *Mister Roberts* (1955), in which he played the wise doctor. In 1982, when he turned 90, he released a statement saying he felt more like 190. He died in 1984, a few months shy of his ninety-second birthday.

Edward G. Robinson enjoyed a distinguished career and worked steadily until his death in 1973, at age seventy-nine.

Lee Tracy's career never quite recovered from the Mexico City incident. As his film career gradually faded, he found work mainly in theater and, in his last two decades, television. He had a late-career break, appearing onstage as a former president in Gore Vidal's *The Best Man*. He repeated this gem of a role in the 1964 film version and was nominated for an Oscar. He died in 1968, at age seventy.

Spencer Tracy came into his own in the late 1930s and was thereafter regarded as one of America's greatest actors. He died in 1967, at age sixty-seven.

Warren William worked steadily, usually playing authority figures in his later years. He died of a blood disease in 1948, at age fifty-three.

Appendix I
Dangerous Men on Television and Video

It would be cruel to incite interest in movies that can't be seen. The good news is that most of the pre-Codes mentioned in these pages are either available on video or can be seen on television.

Pre-Code films in the Turner Library, now owned by Warners, are the movies most available. The library consists of MGM, RKO, and Warner Bros. titles. Turner has prints of all its films and most are available for theatrical rental.

Twentieth Century–Fox has made a number of the old Fox pre-Codes available for theatrical rental, and so has Columbia. Columbia pre-Codes also occasionally turn up in theaters and on television.

The idea of a studio actually keeping prints of its films might sound unremarkable. In fact, there is no existing print for many extant pre-Code and classic titles. The potential to strike prints is there—materials exist—but the studios don't bother. And so when great theaters like the Roxie Cinema or the Castro Theatre in San Francisco, or the Brattle in Boston, or Film Forum in New York want to hold a pre-Code festival, they must rely on private collectors. These collectors are true keepers of the flame and deserve credit and appreciation, but it shouldn't have to be so hard for theaters.

Right now, the least available pre-Code films are the ones owned by Universal. If Universal only owned Universal, well, that would hurt, but we could deal with it. But Universal also owns the pre-Code Paramounts, and Paramount is just indispensable. That's where William Powell, Maurice Chevalier, Gary Cooper, Fredric March, and Charles Laughton did much of their work, as did high-powered actresses such as Nancy Carroll, Ruth Chatterton, Claudette Colbert, Jeanette Mac-Donald, Carole Lombard, Kay Francis, and Miriam Hopkins.

For years, Universal was known, to those of us who care, as an Evil Empire among film libraries. Fortunately, in recent years, something of a thaw has set in. More titles have hit the video market and prints of some classics have made their way to theaters. Still, if Universal is no longer the Evil Empire, it remains, as of this writing, at the early Gorbachev stage, with no Yeltsin yet on the horizon.

The following list is limited to the pre-Code films mentioned in the book, with a handful of cited films from after the Code also included:

Ace of Aces can be seen on TCM.
The Ace of Hearts can be seen on TCM.
Advice to the Lovelorn is not available.
The Affairs of Cellini has not been made available.
Alias the Doctor can be seen on TCM.
Alibi is on video.
All of Me, owned by Universal, has not been made available.
All Quiet on the Western Front is available on video.
Another Language can be seen on TCM.
Arsène Lupin can be seen on TCM.
Bad Company can be seen on TCM.
The Barbarian can be seen on TCM.
Beast of the City can be seen on TCM.

Beauty and the Boss can be seen on TCM.

Bedside can be seen on TCM.

Ben-Hur is available on video.

The Big House is available on video.

The Big Parade is available on video.

A Bill of Divorcement is available on video.

The Black Pirate is available on video.

Blessed Event is available on video.

Blonde Crazy is available on video.

Blonde Venus is available on video.

Blood and Sand is available on DVD.

Blood Money has not been made available.

Bombshell is available on video.

Broken Blossoms is available on DVD.

Broken Lullaby, sometimes known as *The Man I Killed*, has been shown on American Movie Classics.

Bureau of Missing Persons can be seen on TCM.

Cabin in the Cotton is available on video.

Call of the Flesh can be seen on TCM.

Cavalcade is available on video.

Central Airport can be seen on TCM.

Central Park can be seen on TCM.

Charming Sinners, owned by Universal, has not been made available.

The Conquerors can be seen on TCM.

Counsellor at Law has not been made available.

Crooner can be seen on TCM.

Dance Fools Dance is available on video.

Dark Hazard can be seen on TCM.

The Dark Horse can be seen on TCM.

The Dawn Patrol can be seen on TCM.

Daybreak can be seen on TCM.

Death Takes a Holiday is available on video.

Design for Living is available on laser disc.

The Devil and the Deep, owned by Universal, has not been made available.

Devil-May-Care can be seen on TCM.

Dinner at Eight is available on video.

Disraeli is available on video.

The Divorcée is available on video.

Dr. Jekyll and Mr. Hyde (1921) is available on DVD.

Dr. Jekyll and Mr. Hyde (1931) is available on video.

Doctor X is available on video.

Doorway to Hell can be seen on TCM.

Doughboys is available on video.

Downstairs can be seen on TCM.

Dracula is available on video.

Drag is, alack, a lost film.

Duck Soup is available on video.

The Eagle and the Hawk is available on TCM.

The Easiest Way can be seen on TCM.

Employees' Entrance is available on video.

Expensive Women can be seen on TCM.

Faithless can be seen on TCM.

A Farewell to Arms is available, in a restored print, on DVD.

Fast and Loose can be seen on TCM.

The Finger Points can be seen on TCM.

Five Star Final can be seen on TCM.

Flesh and the Devil is available on video.

Flying Down to Rio is available on video.

Footlight Parade is available on video.

42nd Street is available on video and DVD.

The Four Horsemen of the Apocalypse can be seen on TCM.

Frankenstein is available on video.

Freaks is available on video.

A Free Soul is available on video.

Gabriel Over the White House is available on video.

The Gaucho is available on video.

Gentleman's Fate can be seen on TCM.

Going Hollywood is available on video.

Gold Diggers of 1933 is available on video.

The Good Bad Girl has not been made available.

Goodbye Again can be seen on TCM.

Good Intentions is not available.

Grand Hotel is available on video.

The Green Goddess can be seen on TCM.

The Guilty Generation has not been made available.

The Half-Naked Truth can be seen on TCM.

Hard to Handle can be seen on TCM.

The Hatchet Man can be seen on TCM.

He Who Gets Slapped is available on video.

Heartbreak has not been made available.

Hell's Angels has been shown on American Movie Classics and TCM.

Heroes for Sale is available on video.

High Pressure can be seen on TCM.

His Glorious Night has not been made available.

Huddle can be seen on TCM.

The Hunchback of Notre Dame is available on video.

I Am a Fugitive from a Chain Gang is available on video.

I Loved a Woman can be seen on TCM.

In Gay Madrid can be seen on TCM.

Inspiration is available on video.

The Iron Mask is available on video.

Is My Face Red? can be seen on TCM.

Island of Lost Souls is available on video.

The Jazz Singer is available on video.

The Kiss Before the Mirror has not been made available.

Ladies' Man, owned by Universal, has not been made available.

Lady Killer is available on video.

The Lash is occasionally shown on TCM.

Laughing Boy can be seen on TCM.

Laughter, owned by Universal, has not been made available.

Letty Lynton has not been made available.

The Lights of New York can be seen on TCM.

Little Caesar is available on video.

The Little Giant can be seen on TCM.

Long Lost Father can be seen on TCM.

Love is available on video.

Love Is a Racket can be seen on TCM.

Love Me Tonight is available on video and laser disc.

The Mad Genius can be seen on TCM.

Made on Broadway can be seen on TCM.

Mammy can be seen on TCM.

The Man in Possession can be seen on TCM.

Man, Woman and Sin has not been made available.

Man's Castle sometimes turns up in repertory theaters.

Manslaughter, owned by Universal, has not been made available.

The Mark of Zorro is available on video.

Massacre can be seen on TCM.

The Match King can be seen on TCM.

The Mayor of Hell can be seen on TCM.

Men Must Fight can be seen on TCM.

Merrily We Go to Hell, owned by Universal, has not been made available.

The Millionaire can be seen on TCM.

The Mind Reader can be seen on TCM.

Moby Dick can be seen on TCM.

A Modern Hero can be seen on TCM.

The Mouthpiece can be seen on TCM.

My Sin, owned by Universal, has not been made available.

The Night Is Young can be seen on TCM.

Night Nurse is available on video.

The Nuisance can be seen on TCM.

One Hour with You is available on laser disc.

Our Blushing Brides can be seen on TCM.

The Pagan can be seen on TCM.

The Painted Desert can be seen on TCM.

Parachute Jumper can be seen on TCM.

The Pay Off has not been made available.

The Penalty is available on DVD.

The Phantom of the Opera is available on video.

Picture Snatcher can be seen on TCM.

Platinum Blonde is available on video.

Playgirl can be seen on TCM.

Possessed is available on video.

The Private Life of Don Juan is available on video.

Private Lives is available on video.

Professional Sweetheart can be seen on TCM.

The Public Enemy is available on video.

Queen Christina is available on video.

Rain is on DVD.

Reaching for the Moon is available on video.

Red Dust is available on video.

Redemption can be seen on TCM.

Red-Headed Woman is available on video.

Reunion in Vienna can be seen on TCM.

The Road to Singapore can be seen on TCM.

Roar of the Dragon can be seen on TCM.

Robin Hood is available on video.

The Royal Family of Broadway can be seen on TCM.

The Ruling Voice can be seen on TCM.

Say It with Songs can be seen on TCM.

Scarface is available on video.

The Secret Six can be seen on TCM.

The Sheik is available on video.

The Sign of the Cross is available on video.

Silver Dollar can be seen on TCM.

The Singing Fool can be seen on TCM.

Skyscraper Souls is available on video.

Smart Money can be seen on TCM.

Smarty can be seen on TCM.

The Smiling Lieutenant is available on laser disc.

Smilin' Through is available on video.

So This Is College can be seen on TCM.

Son of India can be seen on TCM.

Son of the Gods can be seen on TCM.

The Son of the Sheik is available on video and DVD.

Sporting Blood can be seen on TCM.

Stolen Heaven, owned by Universal, has not been made available.

The Story of Temple Drake, owned by Universal, is not available.

Strange Interlude is available on video.

The Strange Love of Molly Louvain is available on video.

Strangers May Kiss can be seen on TCM.

Street of Chance is not available.

Success at Any Price can be seen on TCM.

Susan Lenox: Her Fall and Rise is available on video.

Svengali is available on video.

The Taming of the Shrew (1929) is available on video.

Their Own Desire can be seen on TCM.

The Thief of Bagdad is available on video.

The Thin Man is available on video.

The Three Musketeers is available on video.

Three on a Match can be seen on TCM.

Thunderbolt has not been made available.

Tiger Shark can be seen on TCM.

Tol'able David is available on DVD.

Tonight Is Ours, owned by Universal, has not been made available.

Topaze can be seen on TCM.

Turn Back the Clock can be seen on TCM.

Two Seconds can be seen on TCM.

Under 18 can be seen on TCM.

The Unholy Three (1925) is available on video.

The Unholy Three (1930) can be seen on TCM and also on laser disc.

The Unknown can be found on video and on TCM.

Untamed can be seen on TCM.

Upperworld can be seen on TCM.

The Virginian is available on video.

Viva Villa can be seen on TCM.

Washington Masquerade can be seen on TCM.

Washington Merry-Go-Round, from Columbia, turns up occasionally in theaters.

Waterloo Bridge (1931) can be seen on TCM.

Way Down East is available on video.

Way for a Sailor can be seen on TCM.

Weary River can be scene on TCM.

Weekend Marriage can be seen on TCM.

West of Zanzibar can be seen on TCM.

What Price Glory? is available on video.

When Ladies Meet can be seen on TCM.

The Widow from Chicago can be seen on TCM.

Wild Boys of the Road can be seen on TCM.

Wings is available on video.

The Woman Accused has not been made available.

The Woman from Monte Carlo can be seen on TCM.

A Woman of Affairs is available on video.

The Working Man can be seen on TCM.

Young Nowheres is, alas, a lost film.

Appendix 9
A Short History of the Code

Any pressure group with a desire to seize control of motion picture content would do well to study the machinations of the Code's sponsors, for these fellows were indeed artists. They cleverly worked the press. They bided their time. They wormed their way into positions of authority. They played factions off against one another, and eventually, when the moment was right, they pounced.

Indeed, to read about the history of the Code, from the standpoint of wishing it had never happened, is frustrating, because things did not have to go the way they did. With a little less luck, the forces of repression might not have succeeded. After all, it was really rather a small minority who wanted Hollywood censored.

Film censorship is about as old as the medium itself. For our purposes, the story of censorship begins in 1922, when Hollywood, hit by a couple of widely publicized scandals—the Fatty Arbuckle murder trial and the William Desmond Taylor murder case—needed something to counteract the call of concerned citizens for government censorship of movies.

The film industry was afraid of two things. They were afraid that the federal government might intervene and exert control over their product. More immediately, they were afraid that all the states and even the cities might adopt censorship boards. The prospect of these boards represented a potentially expensive problem for the picture industry. It could have meant the studios having to edit and tailor each print to the needs of each locality.

To offset this looming possibility—and dissuade public officials from assuming the pleasant and rather easy job of censor—the studios got together and formed a trade protection organization, the Motion Picture Producers and Distributors of America. They hired, as the organization's president, Will Hays, who stepped down from his position as Postmaster General in the Harding administration.

It was Hays's task to put out the fire. He went to local officials all over the country and more or less said, *You* don't have to censor the movies. *We* will censor ourselves. We will adopt standards that will be suitable for everyone, so that no one anywhere will have to worry about censoring anything. And you don't have to trust the producers—just trust *me*, and I will make them bend to your lofty moral standards, which I share. Hays's approach worked. By the time he was through, only seven states had installed censorship boards. Seven was a lot better than forty-eight.

Hays was ideal for the job. The movie moguls were for the most part Jewish, many of them immigrants, and from urban, hardscrabble backgrounds. They needed someone like Hays, who was folksy and Protestant, a Republican from Indiana, who could speak the language of the American heartland. At the same time, Hays was no crusading fanatic. As the head of the MPPDA, he worked for the studios and was committed to looking out for their interests.

Hays developed guidelines—Dos and Don'ts, don'ts and be carefuls— and served as the industry's front man. In 1927, he created the Studio

Relations Committee, an advisory body whose job was to review scripts and finished films and advise studios as to what might need to be cut in order to get movies past the state boards.

Meanwhile, as the twenties wore on, films, reflecting the culture for which they were made, became increasingly daring, and the introduction of sound loosened standards further. This prompted a contingent of Catholics from Chicago to take action. In 1929, Daniel Lord, a Catholic priest, Joseph Breen, a Catholic advertising man, and Martin Quigley, the Catholic editor of the trade paper *Exhibitor's Herald* organized with Catholic leaders in various other cities in the belief that movies needed a new and more stringent set of guidelines. Lord wrote a draft of the Production Code in late 1929, and the following February the heads of production of the major studios met with Hays and the Chicago contingent. In the end, the moguls all signed on and agreed to make films in accordance with the guidelines provided by this new Production Code.

For the studios, it was just a public-relations ploy. They had no intention of abiding by the Code. It was too narrow a document. According to the Code, sympathy could never be accorded the criminal. Lust was to be banned. And nonmarital romance could not be made to look attractive. The limits the studios were putting on their artistic expression were enormous, except they weren't, not really. They forgot the Code as soon as they signed it.

But Breen and his contingent did not forget. For the next four and a half years, they would nurse an aggrieved sense of betrayal, and they'd use the Code as their rallying cry as movies got more adult, more political, and more outrageous.

The term *pre-Code*, strictly speaking, does not mean "before the Code" but "before the enforcement of the Code." During what we call the pre-Code years, the Studio Relations Committee had the job of applying the Code's strictures to movie content, but the SRC had no real power, and Jason Joy, who ran the committee, had little will to censor movies anyway. His correspondence makes it clear he liked movies and was no social reformer. Under Joy and James Wingate, his successor, movies got increasingly more risqué. This direction was in no way impeded by the selection of Joseph Breen to head the Studio Relations Committee in December 1933.

Breen had spent most of the pre-Code years as a public-relations man for Will Hays, which meant he worked, in effect, for the studios. When he was elevated to the position of SRC chief, he still worked for the studios, but he used his position to undermine his employers. Powerless to censor movies by fiat, he worked behind the scenes, encouraging, in one instance, the cardinal of Philadelphia to threaten a boycott of the film industry in order to demonstrate Catholic power. The cardinal went further and actually called for a boycott.

Breen's hand was strengthened in April 1934, when the Catholic cardinals went ahead and organized in the way that he and others had been encouraging for years. They formed the Catholic Legion of Decency, a rating board that told Catholics at Sunday Mass which films they could see and which they could not. The studios, terrified at the possible loss of 20 million Catholic viewers, many of them in America's largest cities, panicked.

Breen had spent four years doing everything he could to orchestrate the crisis. Now he presented himself as a peacemaker. Reasoning that he was the man best positioned to mediate between the studios and the church, he asked Will Hays to transform the Studio Relations Committee from an advisory body into an enforcing agency. Acceding to his wishes, Hays created the Production Code Administration, with Breen in charge, and gave it the power to ban outright any film that did not meet the requirements of the Code (and Breen). The studios, willing to do anything to protect their investment, went along with it.

In fact, had the studios waited longer, they might have realized that the Catholic Legion of Decency was not hurting their business, but helping it. According to a study by Hays in the summer of 1934, whenever a film was banned by the Legion, ticket sales went up—even among Catholics. However, before the studios realized this, the Code was already in effect, and with the Depression easing, the money was beginning to flow again. With profits increasing, the studios saw no need to rock the boat, and so a system, hastily arrived at during a time of manufactured crisis, remained in place for thirty-four years. For about thirty of those years, the Code remained a powerful force.

Most movie books, particularly older ones, describe Breen as a feisty Irishman, a pugnacious, two-fisted character who talked tough and beat the studios at their own game. It's as if he were Jimmy Cagney. He was no Jimmy Cagney. His correspondence reveals him as a driven anti-Semite, consumed by a mission to save America from the Jews, whom he considered "scum," and the Jewish moguls, whom he called "lice."

In 1983, the Production Code files were made public—they are stored at the Motion Picture Academy's library. Contrary to the propaganda that Breen was a talented story editor, the files reveal a record of destruction. His letters are the movie equivalent of missives from a lunatic locked inside the Louvre for nineteen years with a sledgehammer, a blowtorch, and permission to "improve" on anything he sees.

Breen retired in 1954, but the Code remained in force, somewhat weakened by the influx of foreign films, which needed no Code seal in order to be seen in art houses. Still, it was at least strong enough in the early 1960s to make sex comedies confusing. For example, in *Breakfast at Tiffany's* (1961), why do men give Holly Golightly fifty dollars every time she goes to the ladies' room? And why then? You wouldn't know from watching the movie.

The Code was eventually dismantled in 1968, and a rating system, which exists to this day, was put into place.

Acknowledgments

I have to begin where the book began, with the people who made the movies, the men in front of the cameras, of course, but also the people behind them. Over the course of writing this book and reading novels that were adapted into pre-Code movies, I found myself surprised and impressed by the skill of the early Hollywood screenwriters, who could take inert novels (such as Cleo Lucas's *I Jerry Take Thee, Joan*) and turn them into dramatic, nuanced, adult films (such as *Merrily We Go to Hell*). These screenplays were not hackwork. They were art made on an assembly line.

I'm indebted to the many writers whose books and articles helped form my understanding of this period and its movies. These writers include Jeanine Basinger, Gregory Black, Richard Corliss, William K. Everson, Scott Eyman, Paula Fass, Corey Ford, Gladys Hall, Molly Haskell, Michael Kimmel, Tom Pendergast, Andrew Sarris, Richard Schickel, Peter N. Stearns, David Stenn, David Thomson, Frank Walsh, and Kevin White.

Of course, no one should ever write a film book without seeing the actual films (besides, it's been done). Accordingly, I owe a debt to Rebecca Peters Thompson for lending me scores of Paramounts on video, and to Mark Vieira for lending me all the Foxes. On the big screen, I saw many of these films for the first time at San Francisco's Roxie Cinema, thanks to Elliot Lavine and Bill Banning. I saw others at San Francisco's Castro Theatre, thanks to Anita Monga.

Of course, anyone who loves this era owes a debt to Bruce Goldstein, whose seminal festivals at New York's Film Forum in the 1980s popularized the term "pre-Code," introduced its glories, and invited us to look at the era's films as a kind of genre. I saw *Gabriel Over the White House* for the first time thanks to his 1988 festival—and could not believe my eyes.

It's hard to imagine this book existing at all were it not for the existence of Turner Classic Movies. Not only could I not have otherwise seen many of the movies, but even had I managed it, why write a book about art that no one else can look at? Now, entire eras and genres once incomplete or mostly lost to the ages are back and being examined on millions of TV screens. Thanks to Roger Mayer for fighting for film preservation back when it was considered eccentric; to Dick May, the universally esteemed vice president in charge of preservation for Warners; and to Ted Turner, who has done more to bring classic movies before the public than any person in history.

The book was researched at a variety of institutions. I am especially grateful to Barbara Hall and the staff of the Margaret Herrick Library at the Academy of Motion Picture Arts and Sciences for providing access to Production Code files, fan magazines, the Gladys Hall collection, and many other treasures, including a series of enormous scrapbooks compiled by Richard Barthelmess's mother! I am also, once again, in awe of the generosity and wise guidance of Ned Comstock, who makes research at the University of Southern California Film and Television Archive feel like a joint endeavor. It's a privilege.

Mark Vieira took time out from writing his own book to proofread a draft of this manuscript. Rebecca Peters Thompson copyedited it. They have my thanks. So does Jody Hotchkiss of Sterling Lord Literistic.

I am likewise grateful to Edith Kramer and Nancy Goldman of the Pacific Film Archive, to Kathleen Rhodes of the *San Francisco Chronicle* library, and to the staffs of the San Francisco State University library, the British Film Institute, the UCLA library, New York's Museum of Modern Art, the Stanford University library, and the Library for the Performing Arts at Lincoln Center.

I wish to give special thanks to Jim Weiss of Turner Entertainment and to Tom Karsch and Charlie Tabesh of Turner Classic Movies, all of whom have been indispensable. Thanks also to Kevin Brownlow for putting me in touch with Rick McKay, and to Rick McKay for putting me in touch with Fay Wray. Of course, many thanks to Fay Wray for sharing her memories of her first husband, John Monk Saunders, and other pre-Code colleagues. Also worthy of special acknowledgment are the contributions of Jack and Wilfong Freed, fine individuals who passed away during the writing of this book. They are missed.

For various other reasons, thanks to Mark Amarotico, Xavier Barrios, Jami Bernard, Kate Buford, Michelle Carter, Mary Corliss, Richard Corliss, Bob Eberle, Adrian Elfenbaum, Mark Fishkin, Richard Freed, Bruce Goldstein, Bob Graham, Molly Haskell, Richard Imbro, John Karle, Kay Kostopoulos, Margaret Loft, Mark Lundgren, Carla Meyer, Koren Mike, Lance Miller, Loren Nordlund, Robert Osborne, Mi-Ai Parrish, Steve Pratt, Blancett Reynolds, Carmen Romeo, Joel Selvin, Gustavo Serina, Liz Smith, Ruthe Stein, David Stenn, William Stephenson, Herbert Swope, Jr., David Thomson, Jan Wahl, Amie Williams, Diana Winston, JoAnne Winter, and Brit Withey.

Finally, like that other dangerous man, Clark Gable, I have had the way cleared for me by amazing women. Thanks to Melissa Jacobs, my former editor, for encouraging the writing of this book; and to my current editor, Sally Kim, who edited it with enthusiasm and astuteness, and protected it with zeal. By selling my first book, Jennifer Hengen, my former agent, turned me into a made guy. Eternal thanks to her for that—and, when she left the business, for referring me to Neeti Madan, who represented this book with aplomb.

Most of all, I've benefited from the advice and counsel of the lovely Amy Freed, who believed in this book from the beginning and experienced the many horrors of having a husband in deep pre-Code immersion. I can only say in my defense that no one could watch fourteen Edward G. Robinson movies in a row without going around for a week compulsively imitating him.

Bibliography

Allen, Frederick Lewis. *Only Yesterday*. New York: Harper & Brothers, 1931.

———. *Since Yesterday: The Nineteen-Thirties in America*. New York: Harper & Brothers, 1940.

———. *The Big Change: America Transforms Itself 1900–1950*. New York: Harper & Brothers, 1952.

Allen, Virginia Mae. *The Femme Fatale: Erotic Icon*. Troy, New York: Whistler, 1983.

Anonymous. *Gabriel Over the White House: A Novel of the Presidency*. New York: Farrar & Rinehart, 1933.

Arce, Hector. *Gary Cooper: An Intimate Biography*. New York: William Morrow, 1979.

Baldwin, Faith. *Skyscraper*. New York: Dell, 1931.

Basinger, Jeanine. *Silent Stars*. New York: Alfred A. Knopf, 1999.

Black, Gregory. *Hollywood Censored: Morality Codes, Catholics, and the Movies*. New York: Cambridge University Press, 1994.

Blake, Michael F. *Lon Chaney: The Man Behind the Thousand Faces*. Vestal, New York: Vestal Press, 1993.

———. *The Films of Lon Chaney*. Vestal, New York: Vestal Press, 1998.

Blanchard, Phyllis, and Carlyn Manasses. *New Girls for Old*. New York: Macaulay, 1937.

Bourne, Randolph S. *Youth and Life*. Boston: Houghton Mifflin, 1913.

Boylan, James. "Publicity for the Great Depression: Newspaper Default and Literary Reportage." In *Mass Media Between the Wars: Perceptions of Cultural Tension, 1918–1942*, edited by Catherine L. Covert and John D. Stevens. Syracuse: Syracuse University Press, 1984.

Bret, David. *Maurice Chevalier: Up on Top of a Rainbow*. London: Robson Books, 1993.

Brownlow, Kevin. *Behind the Mask of Innocence*. New York: Alfred A. Knopf, 1990.

Burnett, W. R. *Little Caesar*. New York: Literary Guild of America, 1929.

Card, James. *Seductive Cinema: The Art of Silent Film*. New York: Alfred A. Knopf, 1994.

Colman, Juliet Benita. *Ronald Colman: A Very Private Person*. New York: William Morrow, 1975.

Cross, Gary. *An All-Consuming Century: Why Commercialism Won in Modern America*. New York: Columbia University Press, 2000.

Davidson, Bill. *Spencer Tracy: Tragic Idol*. London: Sidgwick & Jackson, 1987.

Essoe, Gabe. *The Films of Clark Gable*. New York: Citadel Press, 1970.

Everson, William K. *The American Silent Film*. New York: Oxford University Press, 1969.

Eyman, Scott. *The Speed of Sound: Hollywood and the Talkie Revolution*. New York: Simon and Schuster, 1997.

Fairbanks, Douglas, Jr. *Salad Days*. New York: Doubleday, 1988.

Forman, Henry James. *Our Movie-Mad Children*. New York: The MacMillan Co., 1933.

Fountain, Leatrice Gilbert. *Dark Star: The Untold Story of the Meteoric Rise and Fall of the Legendary John Gilbert*. New York: St. Martin's Press, 1985.

Franklin, Jay. "The Next War." *Vanity Fair*, November 1930, 59.

Fussell, Paul. *The Great War and Modern Memory*. New York: Oxford University Press, 1975.

Gansberg, Alan L. *Little Caesar: A Biography of Edward G. Robinson*. London: New English Library, 1983.

Giddins, Gary. *Bing Crosby: A Pocketful of Dreams—The Early Years, 1903–1940*. New York: Little, Brown, 2001.

Hanson, Patricia King, and Alan Gevison, eds. *The American Film Institute Catalog of Motion Pictures Produced in the United States: Feature Films, 1931–1940*. Berkeley: University of California Press, 1933.

Haskell, Molly. *From Reverence to Rape: The Treatment of Women in the Movies*. Middlesex, England: Penguin Books, 1973.

Horrocks, Roger. *Male Myths and Icons: Masculinity in Popular Culture*. New York: St. Martin's Press, 1995.

Jordan, Rene. *Gary Cooper*. New York: Pyramid, 1974.

Kimmel, Michael. *Manhood in America*. New York: Free Press, 1996.

Kyvig, David E. *Repealing National Prohibition*. Chicago: University of Chicago Press, 1979.

LaSalle, Mick. *Complicated Women: Sex and Power in Pre-Code Hollywood*. New York: St. Martin's Press, 2000.

Lawrence, Jerome. *Actor: The Life and Times of Paul Muni*. New York: G. P. Putnam's Sons, 1974.

LeRoy, Mervyn, with Dick Kleiner. *Mervyn LeRoy: Take One*. New York: Hawthorn Books, 1974.

Lucas, Cleo. *I Jerry Take Thee Joan*. Garden City, New York: Doubleday, Doran, 1933.

McCabe, John. *Cagney*. New York: Alfred A. Knopf, 1997.

McElvaine, Robert S. *Eve's Seed: Biology, the Sexes and the Course of History*. New York: McGraw Hill, 2001.

McGilligan, Patrick. *Cagney: The Actor as Auteur*. South Brunswick, New Jersey: A. S. Barnes, 1975.

Macpherson, James M., ed. *"To the Best of My Ability": The American Presidents*. London: Dorling Kindersley, 2000.

Melosh, Barbara. "Introduction." In *Gender and American History Since 1890*, edited by Barbara Melosh. New York: Routledge, 1993.

Munden, Kenneth W. *The American Film Institute Catalog of Motion Pictures Produced in the United States: Feature Films, 1921–1930*. New York: R. R. Bowker, 1971.

Murphy, James E. "Tabloids as an Urban Response." In *Mass Media Between the Wars: Perceptions of Cultural Tension, 1918–1941*, edited by Catherine L. Covert and John D. Stevens. Syracuse: Syracuse University Press, 1984.

Nash, Jay Robert, and Stanley Ralph Ross. *The Motion Picture Guide, 1927–1983*. Chicago: Cinebooks, 1987.

New York Times. *New York Times Film Reviews: 1913–1968*. 6 vols. New York: *New York Times* and Arno Press, 1970.

Parish, James Robert, and William T. Leonard. *Hollywood Players*. New Rochelle, New York: Arlington House, 1976.

Pendergast, Tom. *Creating the Modern Man: American Magazines and Consumer Culture, 1900–1950*. Columbia: University of Missouri Press, 2000.

Petersen, James R. *The Century of Sex: Playboy's History of the Sexual Revolution: 1900–1999*. New York: Grove Press, 1999.

Peterson, Deborah C. *Fredric March: Craftsman First, Star Second.* Westport, Connecticut: Greenwood Press, 1996.

Robinson, Edward G., with Leonard Spigelgass. *All My Yesterdays.* New York: Hawthorn Books, 1973.

Sarris, Andrew. *"You Ain't Heard Nothin' Yet: The American Talking Film, History and Memory, 1927–1949.* New York: Oxford University Press, 1998.

Saunders, John Monk. *Single Lady.* New York: Brewer & Warren, 1930.

Scagnetti, Jack. *The Life and Loves of Clark Gable.* Middle Village, New York: Jonathan David, 1976.

Schickel, Richard. *Douglas Fairbanks: The First Celebrity.* London: Elm Tree Books, 1976.

Shipman, David. *The Great Movie Stars.* New York: Bonanza Books, 1970.

Simmons, Christina. "Modern Sexuality and the Myth of Victorian Repression." In *Gender and American History Since 1890,* edited by Barbara Melosh. New York: Routledge, 1993.

Stearns, Peter N. *Be a Man!: Males in Modern Society.* New York: Holmes and Meier, 1990.

Terkel, Studs. *Hard Times: An Oral History of the Great Depression.* New York: New Press, 1970.

Thompson, Frank T. *William A. Wellman.* Metuchen, New Jersey: Scarecrow Press, 1983.

Tomlinson, Doug. *Actors on Acting for the Screen: Roles and Collaborations.* New York: Garland, 1994.

Tornabene, Lyn. *Long Live the King: A Biography of Clark Gable.* New York: G. P. Putman's Sons, 1976.

Trail, Armitage. *Scarface.* New York: Dell, 1959.

Turner, E. S. *A History of Courting.* New York: Ballantine Books, 1954.

Vieira, Mark. *Sin in Soft Focus: Pre-Code Hollywood.* New York: Harry N. Abrams, 1999.

Walsh, Frank. *Sin and Censorship: The Catholic Church and the Motion Picture Industry.* New Haven: Yale University, 1996.

Wexman, Virginia Wright. "Hollywood, Beauty and Rouben Mamoulian." In *Dr. Jekyll and Mr. Hyde After One Hundred Years,* edited by William Veeder and Gordon Hirsch. Chicago: University of Chicago Press, 1988.

White, Kevin. *The First Sexual Revolution: The Emergence of Male Heterosexuality in Modern America.* New York: New York University Press, 1993.

Wray, Fay. *On the Other Hand: A Life Story.* New York: St. Martin's Press, 1989.

Index

Ace of Aces, 102, 105, 218
Ace of Hearts, The, 12–13, 218
Adios, 41
Adorée, Renee (in *The Big Parade*), 10
Advice to the Lovelorn, 119, 218
Affairs of Cellini, The, 181, 218
Alias the Doctor, 186, 218
Alibi, 49, 50, 218
Allan, Elizabeth (in *Ace of Aces*), 102
Allen, Frederick Lewis, 134, 161
All of Me, 180, 218
All Quiet on the Western Front, 95–96, 218
American Madness, 193
American Magazine, 113
An American Tragedy, 34
Andre, Gwili, 133
Anna Karenina, 9
Another Language, 142, 218
Aquinas, Saint Thomas, 195
Arbuckle, Fatty, 227

Arlen, Richard (in *Two Seconds*), 175
Arliss, George
    in in *Disraeli*, 27–29
    in *Millionaire, The*, 160
    in *Working Man, The*, 161
Armstrong, Robert, 45
Arsène Lupin, 169–70, 218
Arzner, Dorothy, 91
Astaire, Fred, 130, 146
Astor, Mary (in *The Little Giant*), 178
Atlantic Monthly, 3
Ayres, Lew, 45
    in *All Quiet on the Western Front*, 95
    in *Doorway to Hell*, 51, 52, 62

Baclanova, Olga (in *Freaks*), 83
Bad Company, 75, 218
Baldwin, Faith, 154
Baltimore Sun, 203
Bancroft, George
    in *Blood Money*, 109, 132, 183
    in *Thunderbolt*, 50

Bankhead, Tallulah
  in *Devil and the Deep, The*, 174
  in *My Sin*, 87
Barbarian, The, 137–38, 218
Barrat, Robert
  in *Heroes for Sale*, 202
  in *Wild Boys of the Road*, 201
Barrymore, John, 89, 149, 163,
    169–74, 212
  in *Arsène Lupin*, 169–70
  in *Bill of Divorcement, A*, 172–73
  in *Counsellor at Law*, 173–74
  in *Dinner at Eight*, 117, 172
  in *Don Juan*, 169
  in *Dr. Jekyll and Mr. Hyde*, 4, 84–85
  in *General Crack*, 169
  in *Grand Hotel*, 162, 170–72
  in *Long Lost Father*, 172
  in *Mad Genius, The*, 169
  in *Moby Dick*, 169
  in *Reunion in Vienna*, 172
  in *Svengali*, 169
  in *Topaze*, 163
Barrymore, Lionel, 213
  in *Arsène Lupin*, 169
  in *Grand Hotel*, 162, 170
  in *It's a Wonderful Life*, 213
  in *Key Largo*, 213
  in *Washington Masquerade*, 107, 108
Barthelmess, Richard, xi, 29, 30–43,
    98, 136, 168, 201–6, 213
  in *Alias the Doctor*, 186
  in *Broken Blossoms*, 33
  in *Cabin in the Cotton*, 165
  in *Central Airport*, 178
  in *Dawn Patrol, The*, 39–42
  in *Drag*, 36
  in *Finger Points, The*, 42–43, 68,
    98–99
  in *Lash, The*, 41–42

  in *Last Flight, The*, 98–101
  in *Son of the Gods*, 37–39, 41
  in *Tol'able David*, 33, 43
  in *War Brides*, 33
  in *Weary River*, 31, 35–36, 41
  in *Young Nowheres*, 36–37
Baum, Vicki, 161, 170
Baxter, Warner (in *42nd Street*), 188
Beast of the City, 75, 218
"Beautiful Girl", 146
Beauty and the Boss, 152–53, 219
Bedside, 158–60, 219
Beery, Wallace, 45
  in *Grand Hotel*, 162, 170
  in *Secret Six, The*, 68
  in *Viva Villa*, 119
Bell, Monta, 10, 126–28
Ben-Hur, 8, 219
Bennett, Constance
  in *Easiest Way, The*, 132, 142
  in *Son of the Gods*, 38
Bennett, Joan (in *Me and My Gal*), 179
Berkeley, Busby, 187–89
Best Man, The, 215
Best Years of Our Lives, The, 214
Big House, The, 141, 219
Big Parade, The, 10, 97, 219
Bill of Divorcement, A, 172–73, 219
Birth of a Nation, The, 33
Black Pirate, The, 2, 219
Blake, Michael F., 79
Blessed Event, 115–17, 119, 219
Blonde Crazy, 73–74, 219
Blondell, Joan
  in *Blonde Crazy*, 73–74
  in *Central Park*, 195
  in *Gold Diggers of 1933*, 134, 190,
    191, 192
  in *Public Enemy*, 212
  in *Smarty*, 179

Blonde Venus, 133–34, 219

Blood and Sand, 7, 219

Blood Money, 109, 131–32, 183, 219

Blushing Brides, 141

Bombshell, 118, 219

Bonus Army, 109–10, 190, 195, 197, 200

Borzage, Frank (in *Man's Castle*), 179

Bourne, Randolph, 3

Bowie, David, 29

Brattle (theatre in Boston), 217

Breakfast at Tiffany's, 231

Breen, Joseph, xii, 144, 211, 229–230

Brent, George (in *Weekend Marriage*), 186

Bright, John, 73

Broadway, 114

Broken Blossoms, 33, 219

Broken Lullaby, 98, 219

Bromfield, Louis, 205

Brooklyn Daily Eagle, 5–6

Brooklyn Standard Union, 39

Brooklyn Times, 101

Brown, Clarence, 65

Browning, Tod, 15, 79, 82

Brown, John Mack (in *The Last Flight*), 99

Bruce, Virginia (in *Downstairs*), 127

Buffalo Times, 204

Bumpkin, confident, 185–86

Bureau of Missing Persons, 130, 219

Burke, Billie (in *A Bill of Divorcement*), 173

Burnett, W. R., 42, 56

Burns, Robert E., 195

Businessmen, in movies, 149–67

   Conquerors, The and, 163–64

   Dinner at Eight and, 161–63

   Grand Hotel and, 161–62

   I Loved a Woman and, 164–65

   Success at Any Price and, 165–66

   Topaze and, 163

   William (Warren) and, 149–61, 167

Cabaret, 175

Cabin in the Cotton, 165, 219

Cagney, James, xi, xiii, 7, 8, 25, 31, 60–64, 66, 69–70, 130–31, 142, 148, 159, 210, 213

   Blessed Event and, 115

   in *Blonde Crazy*, 73, 74

   Broadway and, 114

   in *Doorway to Hell*, 62

   in *Footlight Parade*, 189

   in *Hard to Handle*, 125

   in *Mayor of Hell*, 110

   in *Millionaire, The*, 28–29

   in *Picture Snatcher*, 124

   in *Public Enemy, The*, 45, 58–59, 61, 65, 75, 94, 130, 167, 183

   in *Ragtime*, 213

   in *Smart Money*, 72–73, 168

Calhern, Louis (in *The Road to Singapore*), 140

Call of the Flesh, 26, 219

Capra, Frank, 108, 122, 213

Carillo, Leo (in *Parachute Jumper*), 196

"Carioca", 146

Carroll, Nancy, 218

   in *Kiss Before the Mirror, The*, 177

   in *Laughter*, 90

   in *Stolen Heaven*, 193

   in *Woman Accused*, 134

Castro Theatre (in San Francisco), 217

Catholic Legion of Decency, 230–31

Catholics, xii, 229, 231

Cavalcade, 184, 219

Censorship, 209–11, 227–28, 230

   See also Production Code

Central Airport, 178, 219

Central Park, 195, 219

Chandler, Helen
  in *Daybreak*, 138
  in *Dracula*, 79
  in *Last Flight, The*, 99–100
  in *Long Lost Father*, 172

Chaney, Lon, xi, 11–17, 19, 37, 50–51,
      61, 77, 84, 141, 153
  in *Ace of Hearts, The*, 12–13
  Dracula and, 79
  in *He Who Gets Slapped*, 14
  in *Hunchback of Notre Dame, The*,
      13
  in *Laugh Clown Laugh*, 13
  in *Penalty, The*, 14
  in *Phantom of the Opera, The*, 13
  in *Sea Urchin, The*, 12
  in *Unholy Three, The*, 12, 77–78
  in *Unknown, The*, 15–16
  in *West of Zanzibar*, 14, 15
  in *While the City Sleeps*, 12

Chaney, Lon, Jr., 11

Chaplin, Charlie, 62, 178

Charming Sinners, 139, 219

Chatterton, Ruth, 139, 218

Chevalier, Maurice, xiii, 218
  in *Gigi*, 213
  in *Smiling Lieutenant*, 143–45

Chicago Tribune, 42

Churchill, Marguerite (in *Quick
      Millions*), 179

City Lights, 178–79

Clarke, Mae
  in *Good Bad Girl, The*, 75
  in *Public Enemy, The*, 58, 130
  in *Turn Back the Clock*, 118
  in *Waterloo Bridge*, 133

Clive, Colin, 80, 86

Code, *See* Production Code

Cody, Lew (in *Sporting Blood*), 69

Cohen, John S., 158

Colbert, Claudette, 183, 218
  in *Manslaughter*, 89
  in *Sign of the Cross, The*, 135
  in *Smiling Lieutenant, The*, 143–44
  in *Tonight Is Ours*, 180

Columbia, 116, 214, 217

*Complicated Women: Sex and Power in
      Pre-Code Hollywood*, xii

Compson, Betty (in *Weary River*), 35

Conquerors, The, 163–64, 219

Cook, Donald (in *The Public Enemy*), 94

Coolidge, Calvin, 161

Coonan, Dorothy (in *Wild Boys of the
      Road*), 200

Cooper, Gary, xiii, 8, 30, 45, 70, 168,
      213, 218
  in *Design for Living*, 182
  in *Devil and the Deep, The*, 174
  in *Farewell to Arms, A*, 98, 135
  in *Virginian, The*, 25

Cortez, Ricardo, 8, 45, 123, 213

Counsellor at Law, 173–74, 219

Coward, Noël, 182

Cowl, Jane, 67

Crawford, Joan
  in *Dance Fools Dance*, 68, 161
  in *Grand Hotel*, 162, 170–71
  in *Letty Lynton*, 142
  in *Possessed*, 132
  in *Rain*, 133
  in *Unknown, The*, 16
  in *Untamed*, 141

Crooner, 183, 219

Crosby, Bing, 29, 145–46

Cruise, Tom, xiii

Cukor, George, 143

Cummings, Constance
  in *Guilty Generation, The*, 75
  in *Mind Reader, The*, 150, 158

Dade, Frances (in *Dracula*), 79

Dagover, Lil (in *The Woman from Monte Carlo*), 152

Daily Mirror, 114

Damita, Lili (in *The Match King*), 156

Dance Fools Dance, 66–68, 161, 219

Daniels, Bebe
  in *Counsellor at Law*, 174
  in *42nd Street*, 188

Dark Hazard, 177–78, 219

Dark Horse, The, 108–9, 124–25, 219

Darro, Frankie (in *Wild Boys of the Road*), 199–200

Darrow, Clarence, 47

Davis, Bette (in *20,000 Years in Sing Sing*), 179

Dawn Patrol, The, 39–42, 94, 98, 126, 219

Daybreak, 138, 219

Death Takes a Holiday, 180, 220

Dee, Frances (in *Blood Money*), 131

Del Ruth, Roy, 159

DeMille, Cecil B., 135–36

Depression, Great, x, xii
  Barthelmess and, 42
  Conquerors, The and, 164
  Dance Fools Dance and, 161
  Downstairs and, 128
  Employees' Entrance and, 157
  escapist entertainment and, 187
  films, 193–96, 199, 206
  gangsters and, 46, 50
  heroes and, 112–13
  Heroes for Sale and, 203
  male-female relationships and, 130
  musicals and, 188–92
  Production Code and, 231
  Wild Boys of the Road and, 199–201
  William (Warren) and, 149, 156
  Young Nowheres and, 37

Design for Living, 182, 220

Desperate Hours, The, 214–15

Devil and the Deep, The, 174, 220

Devil-May-Care, 26, 220

Dietrich, Marlene (in *Blonde Venus*), 133

Digges, Dudley (in *The Mayor of Hell*), 110

Dillon, Josephine, 67

Dinner at Eight, 117, 161–63, 172, 220

Disraeli, 27–28, 220

Divorcée, The, 141, 220

Dix, Richard
  in *Ace of Aces*, 102
  in *Conquerors, The*, 163
  in *Roar of the Dragon*, 133

Doctor X, 115, 220

Dodd, Claire (in *Massacre*), 205

Don Juan, 169

Doorway to Hell, 51–52, 62, 220

Dorfler, Franz, 67

Doughboys, 183, 220

Douglass, Kent (in *Waterloo Bridge*), 133

Downstairs, 125–28, 148, 220

Dracula, 78–80, 99, 220

Drag, 36, 220

Dreiser, Theodore, 34

Dresser, Louise (in *Mammy*), 20

Dr. Jekyll and Mr. Hyde, 4, 84–88, 90, 91, 220

Dubin, Al, 190

Duck Soup, 106, 220

Dvorak, Ann
  in *Massacre*, 205
  in *Scarface*, 76
  in *Strange Love of Molly Louvain, The*, 113
  in *Three on a Match*, 159

Eagels, Jeanne (in *Man, Woman and Sin*), 10

Eagle and the Hawk, The, 102–5, 211, 220

Easiest Way, The, 132, 141–42, 220

Edwards, Cliff (in *Doughboys*), 183

Eighteenth Amendment, 46–47

Eilers, Sally (in *Central Airport*), 178

Eisenhower, Dwight D., 215

Eisenstein, Sergei, 34–35

Eldridge, Florence, 181

Elliott, Robert (in *Doorway to Hell*), 51

Employees' Entrance, 157–58, 220

Erwin, Stu (in *Viva Villa*), 119

Escapist entertainment, 187

Evans, Madge, 172
  in *Heartbreak*, 105
  in *Son of India*, 137
  in *Sporting Blood*, 69, 132

Everson, William K., 159

Exhibitor's Herald, 229

Expensive Women, 152, 220

Eyman, Scott, 21

Fairbanks, Douglas, 4–6, 16, 24–25, 213
  in *Black Pirate, The*, 2
  in *Gaucho, The*, 5
  in *Iron Mask, The*, 2, 6
  in *Mark of Zorro, The*, 5
  in *Private Life of Don Juan, The*, 25
  in *Reaching for the Moon*, 25
  in *Robin Hood*, 5
  in *Thief of Bagdad, The*, 5
  in *Three Musketeers, The*, 5

Fairbanks, Douglas, Jr., xiii, 9, 32, 34, 214
  in *Dawn Patrol, The*, 40
  in *Little Caesar*, 55, 56
  in *Love Is a Racket*, 115, 122
  in *Parachute Jumper*, 183, 195–96

  in *Success at Any Price*, 166
  in *Union Depot*, 25

"Fairy stories", 5–6

Faithless, 133, 220

Fantasy, 6

Farewell to Arms, A, 98, 135, 220

Farrell, Charles, 105

Farrell, Glenda, 131
  in *Bureau of Missing Persons*, 130
  in *Dark Hazard*, 178
  in *I Am a Fugitive from a Chain Gang*, 195

Fast and Loose, 185, 220

Ferber, Edna, 161

Film Forum (theatre in New York), 217

Finger Points, The, 42–43, 68, 98–99, 220

Fitzgerald, F. Scott, 164

Five Star Final, 123, 189, 220

Fixers, 122, 148

Flesh and the Devil, 9, 220

Flying Down to Rio, 130, 146, 220

Fonda, Henry, 30

Footlight Parade, 188–89, 220

Ford, Corey, 47, 48

Forman, Henry James, 209

42nd Street, 188–89, 212, 220

Fosse, Bob, 175

Foster, Norman
  in *Alias the Doctor*, 186
  as director of *Journey into Fear*, 186
  in *Playgirl*, 185
  in *Professional Sweetheart*, 185
  in *Skycraper Souls*, 185

Four Horsemen of the Apocalypse, The, 8, 220

Fox, *See* Twentieth Century-Fox

Fox, Sidney (in *The Mouthpiece*), 153

Francis, Kay, 165, 183, 218

Frankenstein, 78, 80–82, 212, 221

Franklin, Jay, 97, 105

Freaks, 82–83, 221
Frederick, Pauline, 67
Free Soul, A, 65–66, 68, 132, 221
Front Page, The, 114
Fussell, Paul, 4

Gable, Clark, xi, xiii, 7, 8, 25, 45,
    66–67, 114, 139, 141–42, 214
  in *Dance Fools Dance*, 66–68
  in *Easiest Way, The*, 132
  in *Finger Points, The*, 68
  in *Free Soul, A*, 65–66, 68, 132
  in *Gone With the Wind*, 65
  in *Last Mile, The*, 67
  in *Machinal*, 67
  in *Misfits, The*, 214
  in *Night Nurse*, 66, 68, 130
  in *Painted Desert, The*, 67
  in *Possessed*, 132
  in *Red Dust*, 126, 131–33
  in *Secret Six, The*, 68
  in *Sporting Blood*, 68–70, 73, 132
  in *Strange Interlude*, 133
Gabriel Over the White House, 196–98,
    221
Gallup poll, 47, 106
Gangster films, 44–59, 75, 76, 77
  See also names of individual gangster
    films
Garbo, Greta, 12, 15, 17, 37, 77, 129,
    135, 136
  in *Flesh and the Devil*, 9
  in *Grand Hotel*, 162, 170
  in *Inspiration*, 141
  in *Love*, 9, 181
  Match King, The and, 156
  in *Queen Christina*, 128, 184
  in *Woman of Affairs, A*, 9
Gargan, William (in *Rain* and *The
    Story of Temple Drake*), 133

Gaucho, The, 5, 221
General Crack, 169
Gentleman's Fate, 23, 221
Gigi, 213
Gilbert, John, 4, 9–11, 20–25, 45,
    125–28, 141
  in *Big Parade, The*, 10, 97
  Dawn Patrol, The and, 126
  in *Downstairs*, 125–28, 148
  in *Flesh and the Devil*, 9
  in *Gentleman's Fate*, 23
  in *His Glorious Night*, 20–22, 24
  in *Love*, 9
  in *Man, Woman and Sin*, 10–11,
    126
  Red Dust and, 126
  in *Redemption*, 22–23
  Twelve Miles Out and, 151
  in *Way for a Sailor*, 23
  in *Woman of Affairs, A*, 9
Gish, Lillian, 30, 33
Glasmon, Kubec, 73
Going Hollywood, 146, 221
Gold Diggers of 1933, 134, 187–90,
    192, 212, 221
Goldie, 179
Gone With the Wind, xiii, 65
Good Bad Girl, The, 75, 221
Goodbye Again, 159, 221
Good Intentions, 50, 221
Goulding, Edmund, 170
Grand Hotel, 161–62, 170–71, 221
Grant, Cary, xiii, 45, 141
  in *Devil and the Deep, The*, 174
  in *Woman Accused*, 134
Green Goddess, The, 28, 221
Griffith, Clyde (in *An American
    Tragedy*), 34
Griffith, D. W., 33
Guilty Generation, The, 75, 221

Haines, William, 141, 183
Hale, Louise Closser (in *Another Language*), 142
Half-Naked Truth, The, 116, 221
Hall, Gladys, 64, 116, 131, 136, 150–51
Hall, James (in *Hell's Angels*), 97
Hamilton, Hale (in *I Am a Fugitive from a Chain Gang*), 195
Hamilton, Neil, 45
Harding, Ann, 90
Hard to Handle, 125, 221
Harlow, Jean
  in *Bombshell*, 118
  in *Dinner at Eight*, 162
  in *Hell's Angels*, 97
  in *Platinum Blonde*, 122
  in *Red Dust*, 133
  in *Red-Headed Woman*, 130
Hatchet Man, The, 177, 221
Hawks, Howard, 40, 75, 126, 177
Hayes, Helen, 98, 135
Hays, Will, 140, 198, 228–31
Heartbreak, 105, 221
Hecht, Ben, 114, 182
Hell's Angels, 97, 221
Hemingway, Ernest, 98, 100
Hepburn, Katharine, 172, 179, 183
Herald Tribune, 165, 204
Heroes, 112–13
Heroes for Sale, 201–3, 221
He Who Gets Slapped, 14, 221
High Noon, 213
High Pressure, 124, 221
His Glorious Night, 20–23, 221
Hitler, Adolf, 105, 197
Hobart, Rose (in *Dr. Jekyll and Mr. Hyde*), 85
Hobbes, Halliwell (in *Dr. Jekyll and Mr. Hyde*), 88

Hoffman, Jerry, 183
Holden, William (in *Dance Fools Dance*), 161
Holmes, Phillips
  in *Broken Lullaby*, 98
  in *Stolen Heaven*, 192
Hoover, Herbert, 109, 192, 194, 198
Hopkins, Miriam, 218
  in *All of Me*, 180
  in *Design for Living*, 182
  in *Dr. Jekyll and Mr. Hyde*, 86
  in *Fast and Loose*, 185
  in *Smiling Lieutenant, The*, 143
  in *Story of Temple Drake, The*, 133
Horror films, 77–88
  See also names of individual horror films
Howard, Leslie, 65
Huddle, 137, 221
Hughes, Howard, 97
Hunchback of Notre Dame, The, 13, 221
Huston, John (in *The Treasure of the Sierra Madre*), 214
Huston, Walter, xiii, 45, 214
  in *American Madness*, 193
  in *Gabriel Over the White House*, 196–97
  in *Ruling Voice, The*, 165, 167
  in *Treasure of the Sierra Madre, The*, 214
  in *Virginian, The*, 25
  in *Woman from Monte Carlo, The*, 152

I Am a Fugitive from a Chain Gang, 189, 194–95, 204, 221
Iceman Cometh, The, 214
I Loved a Woman, 164–65, 221
"I'm Young and Healthy", 188

In Gay Madrid, 26, 221
Ingram, Rex, 8
Inspiration, 141, 221
Iron Mask, The, 2, 6, 221
Irony, 4
Island of Dr. Moreau, The (Wells), 81
Island of Lost Souls, 81–82, 83, 222
Is My Face Red?, 123, 221
"Isn't It Romantic" (Rodgers and
    Hart), 145
It's a Wonderful Life, 213

Janis, Dorothy (in *The Pagan*), 8
Jazz Singer, The, 17–19, 222
Jenkins, Allen (in *The Mind Reader*),
    158
Jewell, Isabel, 120
Johann, Zita (in *Tiger Shark*), 176, 177
Jolson, Al, 37, 146, 214
    in *Jazz Singer, The*, 17–20
    in *Mammy*, 19–20
    in *Say It With Song*, 19
    in *Singing Fool, The*, 19
Jolson Sings Again, 214
Jolson Story, The, 214
Jordan, Dorothy
    in *Call of the Flesh*, 26
    in *Devil-May-Care*, 26
    in *In Gay Madrid*, 26
Journalists, in movies, 122–24
Journey into Fear, 186
Journey's End, 98
Joy, Jason, 230
Joyless Street, The, 205

Karloff, Boris, 45, 84, 86
    in *Five Star Final*, 123
    in *Frankenstein*, 81
Kaufman, George S., 161
Keaton, Buster (*Doughboys* and), 183

Keeler, Ruby
    in *42nd Street*, 188
    in *Gold Diggers of 1933*, 190–91
Kennison, Joan, 204
Kenyon, Doris (in *The Road to
    Singapore*), 140
Key Largo, 213
Kibbee, Guy
    in *Dark Horse, The*, 108
    in *Gold Diggers of 1933*, 190
King, Henry, 33
King Kong, 83–84
Kiss Before the Mirror, The, 177, 222
Kreuger, Ivar, 155

La Cava, Gregory, 196
Ladies' Man, 139, 222
Lady Killer, 130, 222
Landi, Elissa (in *The Sign of the Cross*),
    135
Langdon, Harry, 22
Langham, Ria, 67
La Rocque, Rod (*Let Us Be Gay* and),
    151
Lash, The, 41–42, 222
Last Angry Man, The, 215
Last Flight, The, 98–99, 101
Last Mile, The, 67
Latin lovers, 7–8
Laugh Clown Laugh, 13
Laughing Boy, 138, 222
Laughter, 90, 222
Laughton, Charles, 214, 218
    in *Devil and the Deep, The*, 174–75
    as director of *Night of the Hunter*,
        214
    in *Island of Lost Souls*, 81
    in *Sign of the Cross, The*, 66
Lawson, John Howard, 165
Lee, Lila (in *The Unholy Three*), 78

Leisen, Mitchell, 103
LeRoy, Mervyn, 23, 54, 70, 175–77,
   189
Lester, Richard, 99
Letty Lynton, 142, 222
Let Us Be Gay, 151
Life, 18
Lights of New York, The, 51, 222
Lingle, Jake, 42
Little Caesar, 54–57
   Gable and, 70
   LeRoy and, 23, 54–55, 70, 189
   novel by Burnett, 42, 56
   opening of, 44, 54
   pre-Code era assumptions and, xi
   Scarface and, 75
   sexuality and, 76
   Smart Money and, 72
   on video, 222
"Little Drummer Boy", 29
Little Giant, The, 71–72, 178, 222
"Little Pal", 19
Living Corpse, The, 22
Lombard, Carole, 211, 218
Long Lost Father, 172, 222
Lord, Daniel, 229
Los Angeles Times, 99
Love, 9, 222
Love, in movies, 168–86
   Barrymore (John) and, 169–74
   confident bumpkins and, 185–86
   Devil and the Deep, The and, 174–75
   homosexuality and, 182–84
   March (Fredric) and, 180–82
   Two Seconds and, 175–77
   See also Male-female relationships,
      in movies; Sexuality, in movies
Love Is a Racket, 115, 122, 222
Love Me Tonight, 143, 145, 222
Lowe, Edmund (in *Good Intentions*), 50

Loy, Myrna
   in *Barbarian, The*, 137
   in *Thin Man, The*, 130
   in *Topaze*, 163
   in *When Ladies Meet*, 142
Lubitsch, Ernst, 8, 98, 143, 182
Lugosi, Bela, 86
   in *Dracula*, 79
   in *Island of Lost Souls*, 82
Lukas, Paul (in *The Kiss Before the
      Mirror*), 177
Lyon, Ben, 45, 97

MacArthur, Charles, 114
MacArthur, Gen. Douglas, 109
MacDonald, Jeanette, 218
   in *Love Me Tonight*, 145
   in *One Hour with You*, 144
Machinal, 67
MacMahon, Aline
   in *Five Star Final*, 123
   in *Gold Diggers of 1933*, 190
Made on Broadway, 125, 222
Mad Genius, The, 169, 222
Male-female relationships, in movies,
      129–47, 153
   Astaire-Rogers and, 146
   Barthelmess and, 136
   Cagney and, 130–31
   Chevalier and, 143–45
   Gable and, 132–33, 136
   Montgomery and, 141–43
   Novarro and, 136–39
   Powell (William) and, 139–40
   See also, Love, in movies; Sexuality,
      in movies
Malkovich, John, 66
Mammy, 19–20, 222
Mamoulian, Rouben, 86, 143
Man in Possession, The, 142, 222

Manners, David, 99–100, 183

Man's Castle, 179, 211–12, 222

Manslaughter, 89, 222

Man, Woman and Sin, 10–11, 126, 222

March, Fredric, xi, xiii, 88–93, 148,
    214, 218
  in Affairs of Cellini, The, 181
  in All of Me, 180
  in Best Years of Our Lives, The, 214
  in Death Takes a Holiday, 180
  in Design for Living, 182
  in Dr. Jekyll and Mr. Hyde, 4, 84, 86,
    90–91
  in Eagle and the Hawk, The, 102–4,
    211
  in Iceman Cometh, The, 214
  in Laughter, 90
  in Manslaugter, 89
  in Merrily We Go to Hell, 91–92
  in My Sin, 87
  in Sign of the Cross, The, 135
  in Smilin' Through, 91, 93–94
  in Tonight Is Ours, 180

Mark of Zorro, The, 5, 222

Marriage Circle, The, 144

Marshall, Herbert (in Blonde Venus),
    133–34

Marsh, Marian
  in Under 18, 152, 185
  in The Road to Singapore, 140

Marx Brothers, 74, 106

Marx, Groucho (in Duck Soup), 106

Massacre, 156, 201, 204–5, 222

Match King, The, 148, 155, 222

Mayer, Louis B., 21, 126, 197–98

May, Mark A., 210

Mayor of Hell, The, 110, 199, 222

McHugh, Frank (in Parachute Jumper),
    183

Me and My Gal, 179

Meet John Doe, 213

Men Must Fight, 97, 222

Merrily We Go to Hell, 91–92, 222

Metro-Goldwyn-Mayer (MGM)
  Barrymore (John) at, 169
  Barrymore (Lionel) at, 213
  Chaney at, 13, 79
  Dinner at Eight from, 161
  Downstairs from, 127
  Gable at, 67–68, 126
  Gabriel Over the White House from,
    197–98
  Gilbert and, 9, 21–23, 126
  Grand Hotel from, 161
  He Who Gets Slapped from, 14
  Montgomery at, 141
  Novarro at, 8, 27, 137–38
  Robinson at, 52–53
  sexually risqué films and, 199
  Tracy (Lee) at, 117, 119
  Turner Library and, 217
  William (Warren) and, 155

Milestone, Lewis, 95

Milland, Ray (in Blonde Crazy), 74

Millionaire, The, 28–29, 160, 222

Mind Reader, The, 149–50, 158–59,
    223

Misfits, The, 214

Mister Roberts, 215

Moby Dick, 169, 223

Modern Hero, A, 201–2, 205–6, 223

Modern Screen, 120–21, 131, 210

Money, in movies, 71, 149, 162–63,
    166

Montgomery, Robert, xiii, 141–43,
    214–15
  in Another Language, 142
  in Big House, The, 141
  in Desperate Hours, The, 214–15
  in Divorcée, The, 141

Montgomery, Robert (*continued*)
  in *Easiest Way, The*, 141–42
  in *Faithless*, 133
  in *Inspiration*, 141
  in *Letty Lynton*, 142
  in *Made on Broadway*, 125
  in *Man in Possession, The*, 142
  in *Our Blushing Brides*, 141
  in *Private Lives*, 130, 142
  in *So This Is College*, 141
  in *Strangers May Kiss*, 142
  in *Their Own Desire*, 141
  in *Untamed*, 141
  in *When Ladies Meet*, 142
Moore, Colleen (*Success at Any Price*),
  166
Morgan, Frank
  in *Kiss Before the Mirror, The*, 177
  in *When Ladies Meet*, 142
Morley, Karen (in *Arsène Lupin*), 170
Morris, Chester, 45, 141
  in *Alibi*, 49
  in *Red-Headed Woman*, 130
Motion Picture Academy, 211, 231
Motion Picture Classic, 184
Motion Picture Producers and
  Distributors of America
  (MPPDA), 228
Mouthpiece, The, 153–54, 223
Movie Classic, 63, 130
Movie Mirror, 25, 181
Mr. Deeds Goes to Town, 213
Mr. Smith Goes to Washington, 108
Muir, Jean (in *Bedside*), 160
Muni, Paul, xiii, 159, 215
  Counsellor at Law and, 173
  in *I Am a Fugitive from a Chain
    Gang*, 194
  in *Last Angry Man, The*, 215
  in *Scarface*, 45, 75–76

Muse, Clarence (in *Massacre*), 205
Musicals, 188–192
My Sin, 86–87, 223

Nagel, Conrad, 27
Nazimova, Alla (in *War Brides*), 33
New Orleans Tribune, 204
New York American, 101, 124
New York Daily News, 101
New York Evening Post, 204
New York Herald Tribune, 39, 192, 201
New York Journal, 149
New York Post, 149
New York Telegraph, 204
New York Times, 52, 54
New York World-Telegram, 131, 202
Night is Young, The, 138, 223
Night Nurse, 66, 68, 130, 223
Night of the Hunter, 214
Nineteenth vs. twentieth century,
  2–4
Nixon, Marian (in *Young Nowheres*), 36
Novarro, Ramon, 4, 9, 25–27, 136–39,
  141, 215
  in *Barbarian, The*, 137–38
  in *Ben-Hur*, 8
  in *Call of the Flesh*, 26
  in *Daybreak*, 138
  in *Devil-May-Care*, 26
  in *In Gay Madrid*, 26
  in *Huddle*, 137
  in *Laughing Boy*, 138
  in *Night is Young, The*, 138
  in *Pagan, The*, 26
  in *Son-Daughter, The*, 26
  in *Son of India*, 137
"Now I Ask What Would You Do?",
  144
Nugent, Elliott (in *The Last Flight*), 99
Nuisance, The, 117, 223

O'Brien, Pat (in *Bureau of Missing Persons*), 130
One Hour with You, 143–45, 223
Only Yesterday, 134
Osborne, Vivienne (in *Two Seconds*), 175
O'Sullivan, Maureen (in *Skyscraper Souls*), 150
Our Blushing Brides, 141, 223
Our Movie-Made Children, 56, 209–10
Owen, Catherine Dale (in *His Glorious Night*), 20
Owen, Reginald (in *Downstairs*), 127

Pabst, G. W., 205
Pagan, The, 8–9, 26, 223
Page, Anita (in *Under 18*), 152
Painted Desert, The, 67, 223
Pandora's Box, 205
Parachute Jumper, 183, 195–96, 223
Paramount
  Chevalier at, 143, 145
  Devil and the Deep, The and, 174
  Eagle and the Hawk, The from, 102
  Mamoulian at, 86
  Powell (William) at, 139
  sexually risqué films and, 199
  Smiling Lieutenant, The and, 144
  Universal and, 218
  West and, 145
Parsons, Harriet, 139
Parsons, Louella, 120
Paterson Guardian, 38
Pay Off, The, 50, 223
Penalty, The, 14, 223
"Pettin' in the Park", 191
Phantom of the Opera, The, 13, 78, 223
Philips, Edwin (in *Wild Boys of the Road*), 200
Pickford, Mary, 5, 24–25

Picture Play, 69, 132, 137
Picture Snatcher, 124, 223
Platinum Blonde, 122–23, 223
Playgirl, 185, 223
Politics, 31, 107–10, 198–99
Possessed, 132, 223
Powell, Dick
  in *42nd Street*, 188
  in *Gold Diggers of 1933*, 190–91
Powell, William, xiii, 215, 218
  in *Charming Sinners*, 139
  in *High Pressure*, 124
  in *Ladies' Man*, 139
  in *Mister Roberts*, 215
  in *Road to Singapore, The*, 139–40
  in *Street of Chance*, 45
  Thin Man series, 130, 139
Power and the Glory, The, 179
Primitive man, 6–7
Private Life of Don Juan, The, 25, 223
Private Lives, 130, 142, 223
Production Code, ix–x, xii, 144, 206, 211, 227–31
  See also Censorship
Production Code Administration, xii, 211, 230
Professional Sweetheart, 185, 223
Prohibition, x, 46–48, 50, 197
Prostitutes, 45–46, 133, 190
Public Enemy, The
  business movies and, 167
  Cagney in, 45, 58–59, 61, 65, 72–73
  cutting of, 212
  male-female relationships and, 130
  Scarface and, 75
  sexuality and, 183
  on video, 223
  war movies and, 94–95

Purcell, Irene (in *The Man in Possession*), 142
Putnam, Nina Wilcox, 210

Queen Christina, 128, 184, 223
"Questa o Quella" (*Rigoletto*), 26
Quick Millions, 58, 179
Quigley, Martin, 229

Racism, 33, 37, 39
Racket, The, 52
Raft, George, 45, 76
Ragtime, 213
Rain, 133, 223
Reaching for the Moon, 25, 223
Red Dust, xiii, 126, 132, 223
Redemption, 22–23, 223
Redford, Robert, 31
Red-Headed Woman, 130, 223
Relationships, *See* Male-female relationships
"Remember My Forgotten Man", 190
Rennie, James (in *The Lash*), 42
Reunion in Vienna, 172, 223
Rice, Elmer, 173
Rigoletto, 26
RKO, 97, 116, 217
Road to Singapore, The, 139–40, 224
Roar of the Dragon, 133, 224
Robin Hood, 5, 224
Robinson, Edward G., xiii, 8, 31, 45, 49, 52–57, 66, 69–70, 114, 148, 159, 210, 215
  in *Dark Hazard*, 177–78
  in *Five Star Final*, 123–24
  in *Hatchet Man*, 177
  in *I Loved a Woman*, 164–65
  in *Little Caesar*, xi, 44, 54–57, 58
  in *Little Giant, The*, 71, 72, 178
  in *Racket, The*, 52

  in *Silver Dollar*, 164
  in *Smart Money*, 71–73, 168
  in *Tiger Shark*, 71, 176–77
  in *Two Seconds*, 71, 175–77
  in *Widow from Chicago, The*, 53–54
Rogers, Ginger
  in *Flying Down to Rio*, 130, 146
  in *Gold Diggers of 1933*, 187
Romeo and Juliet, 75
Roosevelt, Franklin, 161, 191, 193–94, 198, 201, 203
Roxie Cinema (in San Francisco), 217
Royal Family of Broadway, The, 89, 224
Rukeyser, Merryle Stanley, 112
Ruling Voice, The, 165, 167, 224

Saunders, John Monk, 39–40, 42, 98–99, 101–3, 105
Say It with Songs, 19, 224
Scarface, 45, 75–76, 224
Schenck, Joseph, 17
Schickel, Richard, 24
Screenland, 139
Seastrom, Victor, 14
Sea Urchin, The, 12
Secret Six, The, 68, 224
Sennett, Mack, 146
Sexuality, in movies, 3–4, 199
  Chevalier and, 143–45
  in *Dracula*, 79
  Dr. Jekyll and Mr. Hyde and, 85, 88
  in *Employees' Entrance*, 157
  gangster movies and, 46
  homosexuality in movies, 56–57, 182–84
  in *Little Caesar*, 56–57
  male-female relationships in movies and, 131–32, 134–35, 143–45

Production Code and, 211, 231
See also Love, in movies; Male-female relationships, in movies
"Shanghai Lil", 189
Shannon, Peggy (in Turn Back the Clock), 118
Shearer, Norma, 12
  in Free Soul, A, 65, 68, 132
  in He Who Gets Slapped, 14
  in Let Us Be Gay, 151
  in Private Lives, 130
  in Smilin' Through, 91–93
  in Strange Interlude, 133
  in Strangers May Kiss, 142
  in Their Own Desire, 141
Sheik, The, 7, 224
Sherman, Al, 204
Sherman, Lowell (in The Pay Off), 50
Sherwood, Robert E., 18
Shuttleworth, Frank K., 210
Sidney, Sylvia (in Merrily We Go to Hell), 91
Sign of the Cross, The, 66, 135, 224
Silent films, 1–2, 4, 17–18, 77, 169
Silver Dollar, 164, 224
Singing Fool, The, 19, 224
Single Lady, 98
Skyscraper Souls, 150, 154–55, 157, 185, 224
Smart Money, 71–73, 168, 224
Smarty, 179–80, 224
Smiling, in movies, 1, 7
Smiling Lieutenant, The, 143–44, 224
Smilin' Through, 91–94, 224
"Social Conduct and Attitudes of Movie Fans, The", 210
Socially conscious films, 199–206
Son-Daughter, The, 26
"Sonny Boy", 19
Son of India, 137, 224

Son of the Gods, 37–39, 41, 224
Son of the Sheik, The, 7, 224
So This Is College, 141, 224
Sound, 1, 17–18, 25, 35
Sparks, Ned (in Gold Diggers of 1933), 190
Speed of Sound, The, 21
Sporting Blood, 68–70, 73, 132, 224
Stage actors, 27
Stanwyck, Barbara, 68, 130, 183
Starrett, Charles (in Fast and Loose), 185
Stevenson, Robert Louis, 4, 84–85
Stewart, James, 30, 108
Stolen Heaven, 192–93, 224
Stone, George E. (in Little Caesar), 56
Stone, Lewis (in Grand Hotel), 170
Story of Temple Drake, The, 133, 224
Strand Theater (New York City), 44
Strange Interlude, 133, 224
Strange Love of Molly Louvain, The, 113–15, 124, 224
Strangers May Kiss, 142, 224
Street of Chance, 45, 224
Stuart, Gloria (in The Kiss Before the Mirror), 177
Stubbs, Harry (in Alibi), 49
Student Prince in Old Heidelberg, The, 8
Studio Relations Committee (SRC), 145, 198, 228–30
Success at Any Price, 165–66, 224
Success Story, 165
Sun Also Rises, The, 100
Susan Lenox: Her Fall and Rise, 136, 224
Sutherland, Donald, 66
Svengali, 169, 224
Swanson, Gloria, 12
Swope, Herbert, 32
Syracuse Herald, 194

Taming of the Shrew, The, 24, 225

Taylor, William Desmond, 227

Teasdale, Verree (in *Skyscraper Souls*), 150

Thalberg, Irving, 52–53, 126, 169–70

"Thank Heaven for Little Girls", 213

Their Own Desire, 141, 225

Thief of Bagdad, The, 5, 225

Thin Man series, 139

Thin Man, The, 130, 225

Thirer, Irene, 131

Thomas, Norman, 52

Three Musketeers, The, 5, 225

Three on a Match, 159, 189, 225

Thunderbolt, 50, 225

Tiger Shark, 71, 176–77, 225

Tobin, Genevieve
  in *Dark Hazard*, 177
  in *I Loved a Woman*, 165
  in *One Hour with You*, 144
  Smarty and, 179
  in *Success at Any Price*, 166

Tol'able David, 33–34, 43, 225

Tolstoy, Leo, 9, 22

Tonight Is Ours, 180, 225

Toomey, Regis (in *Under 18*), 185

Topaze, 163, 225

Torrence, Ernest (in *Tol'able David*), 33

Tracy, Lee, xi, xiii, 45, 111, 113–22, 215
  in *Advice to the Lovelorn*, 119
  in *Best Man, The*, 215
  in *Blessed Event*, 115, 117, 119
  in *Bombshell*, 118
  in *Broadway*, 114
  in *Dinner at Eight*, 117
  in *Doctor X*, 115
  in *Front Page, The*, 114
  in *Half-Naked Truth, The*, 116–17
  in *Love Is a Racket*, 115

  in *Nuisance, The*, 117
  in *Strange Love of Molly Louvain, The*, 113–14
  in *Turn Back the Clock*, 118–19, 165
  in *Viva Villa*, 119
  in *Washington Merry-Go-Round*, 109, 116

Tracy, Spencer, xiii, 45, 215
  in *Goldie*, 179
  Last Mile, The and, 67
  in *Man's Castle*, 179, 211
  in *Me and My Gal*, 179
  in *Power and the Glory, The*, 179
  in *Quick Millions*, 58
  in *20,000 Years in Sing Sing*, 179

Treasure of the Sierra Madre, The, 214

Turn Back the Clock, 118–19, 165, 225

Turner Classic Movies, 128

Turner Library, 217

Tweed, Thomas, 196

Twelve Miles Out, 151

Twelvetrees, Helen (in *Bad Company*), 75

"Twentieth Century Blues", 184

Twentieth Century-Fox, 58, 119, 183, 199, 217

Two Seconds, 71, 175–77, 189, 225

Under 18, 152, 185, 225

Unholy Three, The, 12, 77–78, 225

Union Depot, 25

Universal, 12, 14, 79, 218

Unknown, The, 15–16, 225

Untamed, 141, 225

Upperworld, 225

Valentino, Rudolph, 4, 6–8, 9, 132, 137
  in *Blood and Sand*, 7
  in *Four Horsemen of the Apocalypse, The*, 8

in *Sheik, The*, 7
in *Son of the Sheik, The*, 7
Vanity Fair, 32, 47, 97, 143
Variety, 3, 22, 36, 41, 54, 61, 152, 160
Velez, Lupe (in *Laughing Boy*), 138
Victor, Henry (in *Freaks*), 83
Vidal, Gore, 215
Vidor, King, 10, 97
Vinson, Helen
  in *Little Giant, The*, 178
  in *Power and the Glory, The*, 179
Virginian, The, 25, 225
Viva Villa, 119, 225
Von Sternberg, Josef, 134

Wadsworth, James, 47
Walker, Stuart, 103
Wallace, Morgan (in *Smart Money*), 72
Wallis, Hal, 56
Walsh, Raoul, 179
Walters, Polly (in *Blonde Crazy*), 74
Wanger, Walter, 196
War, xii, 39–41, 93–107
  Ace of Aces and, 102–3, 105
  All Quiet on the Western Front and,
    95–96
  Big Parade, The and, 97
  Broken Lullaby and, 98
  Duck Soup and, 106
  Eagle and the Hawk, The and, 102–5
  Farewell to Arms, A and, 98
  Heartbreak and, 105
  Hell's Angels and, 97
  Journey's End and, 98
  Last Flight, The and, 98–101
  Men Must Fight and, 97
  pacifism, 96, 105
  Public Enemy, The and, 94–95
  Smilin' Through and, 94
  What Price Glory? and, 97

Wings and, 97
  See also World War I; World War II
War Brides, 33
Warner Bros.
  Barrymore (John) at, 169
  Barthelmess at, 31–32, 41
  Cagney at, 61–62
  film preservation, 212
  Gable at, 68
  Gilbert and, 126
  Jolson at, 20
  journalism in films and, 124
  LeRoy to MGM from, 23
  Little Caesar and, 56
  Mayor of Hell, The and, 110
  musicals and, 188–89, 191
  Powell (William) at, 139
  Robinson at, 53
  socially conscious films, 199
  style of movies, 127
  Tracy (Lee) at, 116
  Turner Library and, 217
  Wild Boys of the Road and, 201
  William (Warren) at, 152, 155, 157
Warner, Jack, 140
Warren, Harry, 190
Washington Masquerade, 107–8, 225
Washington Merry-Go-Round, 109–10,
  116, 225
Waterloo Bridge, 133, 225
Watts, Richard, Jr., 39, 199, 201, 204
Way Down East, 225
Way for a Sailor, 23, 225
Weary River, 31, 35–36, 41, 225
Weekend Marriage, 185–86, 225
Wellman, William, 115, 199,
  201–202
Wells, H. G., 81
"We're in the Money", 187, 192
West, Mae, 131, 145

West of Zanzibar, 14, 15, 225
West, Roland, 49
Whale, James, 98, 133
What Price Glory?, 97, 225
When Ladies Meet, 142, 226
While the City Sleeps, 12
White, Alice (in *Employees' Entrance*),
    158
White, Kevin, 2
Widow from Chicago, The, 51–54, 226
Wild Boys of the Road, 199–201, 226
William, Warren, xi, 8, 70, 148–60,
    167, 206, 215
    in *Under 18*, 152
    in *Beauty and the Boss*, 152–53
    in *Bedside*, 158, 159–60
    in *Dark Horse, The*, 124–25
    in *Employees' Entrance*, 157–58
    in *Expensive Women*, 152
    in *Gold Diggers of 1933, The*, 134,
        190, 212
    in *Let Us Be Gay*, 151
    in *Match King, The*, 148, 155–56
    in *Mind Reader, The*, 149–50,
        158–59
    in *Mouthpiece, The*, 153
    in *Skyscraper Souls*, 150, 154–55,
        157
    in *Smarty*, 179–80
    in *Twelve Miles Out*, 151
    in *Woman from Monte Carlo, The*,
        152
Williams, Robert (in *Platinum Blonde*),
    122–23
Wilson, Carey, 196
Wilson, Woodrow, 96

Wingate, James, 198, 230
Wings, 97, 226
Wing, Toby (in *42nd Street*), 189
Wolf Man, 11
Woman Accused, The, 134, 226
Woman from Monte Carlo, The, 152,
    226
Woman of Affairs, A, 9, 226
Woods, Edward (in *The Public Enemy*),
    212
Woollcott, Alexander, 52
Working Man, The, 28, 161, 226
World War I, x, 3–4, 96, 101–6, 135,
    183, 191, 202
    See also War
World War II, 94, 97
    See also War
Wray, Fay, 101–2
    in *King Kong*, 83
    in *Thunderbolt*, 50
Wynyard, Diana (in *Reunion in*
    Vienna), 172

Young, Loretta, 183
    in *Hatchet Man*, 177
    in *Laugh Clown Laugh*, 13
    in *Man's Castle*, 179, 211
    in *Playgirl*, 185
    in *Ruling Voice, The*, 167
    in *Weekend Marriage*, 185, 186
Young Nowheres, 36–37, 226
Young, Waldemar, 15
Youth, 3
Youth and Life, 3

Zanuck, Daryl, 99, 101